Pro OGRE 3D Programming

■ ■ ■

Gregory Junker

Apress®

Pro OGRE 3D Programming

Copyright © 2006 by Gregory Junker

ISBN-13: 978-1-59059-710-1

ISBN-10: 1-59059-710-9

Library of Congress Cataloging-in-Publication data is available upon request.

Printed and bound in the United States of America 9 8 7 6 5 4 3 2 1

Lead Editor: Matt Wade
Technical Reviewer: Steve Streeting
Editorial Board: Steve Anglin, Ewan Buckingham, Gary Cornell, Jason Gilmore, Jonathan Gennick, Jonathan Hassell, James Huddleston, Chris Mills, Matthew Moodie, Dominic Shakeshaft, Jim Sumser, Keir Thomas, Matt Wade
Project Manager: Kylie Johnston
Copy Edit Manager: Nicole LeClerc
Copy Editor: Ami Knox
Assistant Production Director: Kari Brooks-Copony
Production Editor: Laura Esterman
Compositor/Artist: Kinetic Publishing Services, LLC
Proofreader: Lori Bring
Indexer: Broccoli Information Management
Cover Designer: Kurt Krames
Manufacturing Director: Tom Debolski

Distributed to the book trade worldwide by Springer-Verlag New York, Inc., 233 Spring Street, 6th Floor, New York, NY 10013. Phone 1-800-SPRINGER, fax 201-348-4505, e-mail orders-ny@springer-sbm.com, or visit http://www.springeronline.com.

For information on translations, please contact Apress directly at 2560 Ninth Street, Suite 219, Berkeley, CA 94710. Phone 510-549-5930, fax 510-549-5939, e-mail info@apress.com, or visit http://www.apress.com.

The source code for this book is available to readers at http://www.apress.com in the Source Code/Download section.

To Mom and Dad

Contents at a Glance

Contents

Foreword

Real-time 3D graphics—everyone loves them these days. Computing power has finally evolved to the point where it's feasible to render something as complex as the human face interactively, with enough structural and surface detail that it doesn't look like it belongs to the victim of a freak yachting accident. Every year the bar is raised further, with graphics card manufacturers, game console companies, and even mobile-phone manufacturers shoehorning ever more raw power into our unsuspecting devices, until they're almost ready to burst at the seams, showering us with a dazzling array of gloriously shaded pixels. The result has been something of a renaissance in real-time graphics in the last few years, our eyes having been treated to the kind of visuals that would have been unthinkable in real time even five years ago. All of a sudden the level of detail that used to go only into movie effects is being layered into our interactively rendered scenes— the only downside of course being that your artist may now spend an hour or two creating a character's eyes, rather than placing a pixel or two and moving on.

This sophistication has led to a tidal wave of popular interest in the field—where once the fascination with real-time 3D was relatively limited, since the results were fairly primitive and limited to mostly games and scientific fields of study, these days everyone wants to be in on the action. Operating system interfaces, mobile phones, set-top boxes, architectural systems— all of them are finding a use for the technology. And of course we all know how 3D games have exploded into mainstream culture in recent years, and remain at the vanguard of the real-time 3D movement.

So, it's all very exciting—but the question is, how do **you** get in on the action? I'm going to assume for a second that you're a programmer—a coder/hacker/software engineer/demigod of the electron universe, whatever you wish to be called; if you're not, perhaps you'd like to pick up a book on 3D modeling/texturing instead; there's bound to be one nearby.

Still here? Good—as a programmer, what you obviously need most is the fastest and most robust way to leverage this wonderful world of 3D graphics in your applications, whatever they might be. One thing many people discover is that the level of sophistication that perhaps attracted them to the subject initially also presents itself as a near-vertical learning curve— getting all those nice graphical effects into your application is hard. Sure, you can use libraries like OpenGL and Direct3D, for which there are plenty of tech demos and books, but after you've played with these for a while, it doesn't take long before you realize just how much additional work there is to do before you have a practical framework to really start being productive on—beyond simple demos, there is a *lot* that a modern 3D engine needs to do, be it support for multiple platforms, efficient resource management, shadows, fancy shaders, you name it.

Wait—don't give up! The thing is, you don't have to do all this work yourself. There are libraries out there to help you, and this book is all about one of them.

Back in 2000, with very little fanfare, I started a project called OGRE (Object-oriented Graphics Rendering Engine) with the intention of solving all these problems in an elegant and extensible software library aimed at busy developers. I released it under an open source license, mostly because I'd made a habit of openly releasing my graphics code over the preceding decade, since it had been a hobby of mine for a long time. I'd also read up on, and been impressed by, the concept of open source, which, though far from new, was only really just starting to gain traction in the business software world where I spent most of my days. I saw open source as a way to formalize the habit of cooperating with other developers over the Internet, something I'd been doing informally since the days of bulletin board systems. There really weren't any open source libraries around that I liked for dealing with real-time 3D, so I figured I'd write one. I had no illusions about the importance of this project or delusions of grandeur; at the time I just wanted to write something useful. And so it began . . .

Over the years, Ogre evolved and expanded, other developers joined the project, and a community started to accumulate around it. Ogre today is a true collaboration, the result of many man-years of work of people testing it, extending it, making content for it, or just plain talking about it and thrashing out ideas. Open source is often regarded as a true meritocracy in that good software tends to rise to the surface naturally, so it's fairly satisfying to look back over Ogre's growing popularity and take it as an indication that we're doing something right. These days, it's all got rather out of hand—as of July 2006, our site at http://www.ogre3d.org logs about 95,000 unique visitors each month (about 400,000 hits a day) and about 35,000 downloads each month. Our community forums consist of thousands of registered users having made over 150,000 posts, and it's growing by about 200 posts every day. That's a whole lotta community spirit going on right there.

The great thing is that people new to real-time 3D coding are no longer alone—they can just plug right into this rich environment, so that as well as getting a software library that solves a great many of the problems they need to get past to really exploit this exciting medium, they also get to talk to lots of people who are trying to do the same thing—and you might find it surprising how many people are happy to help out. Heck, you'll even find the author of this book in there, helping people day after day in the forums. It's people like him who help make Ogre what it is today, and after reading this book, perhaps you'll join us.

From here on in, I'll leave you in Greg's capable hands. I'm honored to have been asked to write the foreword to what is the first dedicated book on using Ogre, and wish you the best of luck in whatever you choose to do with it. Drop by the forums sometime and tell us how it went—we'd love to see what you come up with.

Steve "sinbad" Streeting
Founder and Lead Developer
Ogre Project

About the Author

GREGORY JUNKER has over a decade of large-system software engineering experience in a wide range of industries, including nationwide retail, call center and telecommunications, automotive information technology, and online information services. Five years ago, he began teaching himself 3D graphics and video game design and architecture, which ultimately led him to the Ogre 3D project, where he is a very active member of the Ogre community. He currently works as a Senior Engineer at Mind Control Software in San Rafael, CA. He currently also is lead engineer for a community-developed game project. When he finds some spare time, he spends it hiking in the mountains of beautiful Marin County.

About the Technical Reviewer

STEVE STREETING has been a professional software engineer for well over ten years, working on a wide range of projects from custom business applications to graphics rendering systems. Steve initiated the Ogre project in late 2000 and remains the lead developer to this day, running the project from his home in Guernsey, Channel Islands.

Acknowledgments

This book simply would not have been possible without the able and willing assistance of many people. First and foremost, there would be no reason for this book were it not for the efforts of Steve "sinbad" Streeting, the Ogre 3D project founder. Steve also served as technical reviewer for this book, as well as advisor, sometime editor, and all-around mojo, and without Steve straightening out the technical kinks, the book would have been a disaster.

This book specifically would not have happened without the foresight of Matt Wade, my editor. Matt recognized the void in the literary infospace made apparent by the absence of this book, and initiated a process to fill that void. He put up with my mood swings and outbursts and general dilatoriness during the production of this book, knowing that the end product would be worth it all.

Kylie Johnston, my project manager on this book, exhibited throughout the patience of Job, and the optimism and creative scheduling skills needed to bully this book (and me) into keeping the project on track and as close to on schedule as possible; to this day, I am fairly certain that the original publication date never slipped, and that feat was entirely Kylie's accomplishment, despite my best (unintentional) efforts to derail the deadlines. Kylie also had the insight or the luck to bring Apress' senior copy editor, Ami Knox, onto the project, knowing either that the book would need her experience to whip it into shape, or that the book deserved her loving yet firm touch . . . or both.

Last but not least, the management and staff at Mind Control Software: Andrew Leker, Marc LeBlanc, Ed Baraf, and my coworkers, who all were understanding enough about publishing deadlines when I was writing chapters at work—I get more "work-work" done late at night anyway, right?

Introduction

If you are reading this introduction, chances are that you have probably heard of Ogre and are wondering what the buzz is all about. Simply put, Ogre is the most powerful open source real-time 3D rendering library currently available. The rest of this book goes on to explain not only why that is, but also how you can leverage all of that power, regardless of whether you are just tinkering on the side or developing an AAA game title.

Who This Book Is For

This book is intended for experienced software engineers interested in leveraging modern 3D hardware-accelerated graphics in their games or applications.

How This Book Is Structured

This book is loosely divided into three topical areas: About Ogre (Chapters 1 and 3), Getting Started with Ogre (Chapters 2 and 4), and Ogre in Detail (Chapters 5 through 12 and Appendixes). Following is a brief outline of what each chapter covers:

Chapter 1, "What Is This Ogre?": Who the book is for, and what they should know before starting with Ogre.

Chapter 2, "Capturing the Beast": Obtaining, building, and installing Ogre, and verifying the installation is ready for use.

Chapter 3, "Ogre Design Overview": A look at the Ogre design, covering the major elements and design decision in the Ogre library. This chapter is intended to put the material covered by the rest of the book in perspective, necessary for a system as complex as Ogre.

Chapter 4, "Ogre First Steps": You begin to see actual code in this chapter, which introduces a skeleton Ogre application and explains the various actions performed by all typical Ogre applications.

Chapter 5, "Ogre Scene Management": This chapter begins the "Ogre in Detail" topics, starting with a discussion of scene management and scene graph usage in Ogre.

Chapter 6, "Ogre Materials": This chapter introduces Ogre's incredibly powerful and flexible material system, including examples of leveraging GPU programs (*shaders*) in an Ogre material.

Chapter 7, "Resource Management": Here you learn all about Ogre's resource management philosophy and implementation.

Chapter 8, "Ogre Render Targets": We discuss the difference between and purpose of the various types of render target available to the Ogre application, as well as the technique of *render to texture*, a common practice in the modern graphics pipeline. We also analyze and discuss the Ogre *Demo_Fresnel* sample application.

Chapter 9, "Animation": This chapter introduces the design and capabilities of Ogre's animation features, including skeletal, pose, and morph animations, as well as how and when to use each. We also analyze and discuss the *Demo_SkeletalAnimation* sample application.

Chapter 10, "Billboards and Particles": Here we take a look at the related topics of billboards and particle systems in Ogre, which includes an analysis and discussion of the *Demo_Smoke* particle system sample application and particle system script.

Chapter 11, "Dynamic Shadows": One of the most interesting topics in 3D graphics—dynamic shadows—is the topic of Chapter 11. We discuss all of the shadowing capabilities in Ogre, using the *Demo_Shadows* sample application as a basis throughout the chapter.

Chapter 12, "Ogre 2D and Compositing": The last area of Ogre functionality explored by this book is the 2D features of Ogre: overlays and the Compositor framework. We fully explore the Compositor, breaking down the *Demo_Compositor* sample application at the code, script, and processing-flow levels for the HDR Compositor effect provided with Ogre.

Appendix A, "Ogre Tools and Add-Ons": This appendix briefly discusses the tools and add-ons for Ogre, as well as related projects.

Appendix B, "Script Attribute Reference": This appendix provides a handy quick-reference for all scripting directives and parameters, for all scriptable systems within Ogre.

Prerequisites

You should be familiar with ISO Standard C++ and the C++ Standard Template Library. You should possess a copy of, and be familiar with, any of the following development platforms:

- On Windows, Microsoft Visual C++ .NET 2003 or 2005, Microsoft Visual C++ 2005 Express, or the Code::Blocks/MinGW IDE/compiler combination

- On Linux (2.6.*x* kernel, any distribution), GCC 3.4.*x* or above or 4.0.2 or above

- On Mac OS X (Tiger or Panther), a configured and working XCode development environment

In all cases, you should have the latest drivers for your graphics hardware from the hardware vendor.

Downloading the Code

You can find any code written for this book, as well as a ZIP file containing the version of Ogre 3D covered by this book, in the Source Code/Download section of the Apress web site.

Contacting the Author

The author may be contacted at gjunker@mind-control.com or gjunker@dayark.com, and can be found frequenting the forums at http://www.ogre3d.org, under the name "Xavier".

## CHAPTER 1

What Is This Ogre?

Ogre 3D is a mature, stable, reliable, flexible, cross-platform, and full-featured library for use in developing real-time 3D graphics applications. If you are familiar with the terms *API* and *SDK*, you can skip this discussion and move on to the next chapter. Otherwise, it will benefit both of us to go over some basic vocabulary first.

The Ogre 3D SDK

A *software development kit*, or *SDK*, provides a coherent application programming interface (API) to a system's services or functionality. For example, let's say that you want to write a program for the Microsoft Windows XP operating system. The API you would use is the Win32 (Windows, 32-bit) API, and its functionality is exposed via dozens of system-level libraries, with cryptic names such as user32.dll, kernel32.dll, and so on. Theoretically, you could access the functionality of these system DLLs directly using some low-level programming techniques, but you would find your way much easier by using the SDK provided by Microsoft for the purpose of accessing the system functionality and services: the Microsoft Platform SDK (now just called the Microsoft SDK). This SDK provides for you the header files and import libraries you need to be able to link your program to these system libraries.

■**Caution** If you do not understand what I just said about "header files" and "import libraries," you should put down this book and do some basic research on their usage and intent. These are extremely common and fundamental concepts when programming with any SDK, including Ogre. Before you read another word, I suggest you get comfy with Microsoft's MSDN Library web site (which is an online and always current version of the MSDN Library that came on three CDs or a DVD with your copy of Visual Studio—check it out at http:// msdn.microsoft.com/library). And you Linux users, you can stop snickering. If you don't understand what a -devel RPM package is, or why you would want one, I suggest spending some quality time at Red Hat's web site (http://www.redhat.com/docs/) to find out.

For system-level services such as those provided by operating systems like Windows or Linux, the SDK consists of header files and (on Windows) import libraries for the system DLLs. For nonsystem services or functionality (such as NVIDIA Corporation's Cg Toolkit), the SDK will also include the actual DLLs (or .so—*shared object*—files on Linux). Ogre is an example of nonsystem functionality, and the Ogre SDK (whether you download a prebuilt version or build one yourself from source code) will provide you with header files, import libraries where applicable, and the actual dynamically linked code modules, in both Debug and Release builds. (*Debug builds* are nonoptimized builds that contain memory checks and initialization, whereas *Release builds* are builds optimized for speed of execution—usually an important feature in a real-time 3D application.)

Why is Windows different? The job of a *linker* is to link object files (the product of compiling a source code file) to a library containing symbols—exported function names, class names, etc.—to the unresolved symbol references in your object files. On Windows, applications do not link directly to a DLL at link time. Instead, they link to what is known as an *import library*, which is a file containing information used by the linker (LINK.EXE in the Visual Studio family of products) to insert into the final executable information about how the runtime library loader can find, or *resolve*, the external references in your code. On Linux, however, the dynamic libraries are referenced directly at link time, and the Linux shared-object loader can resolve the external references directly. This is just one of those differences you accept when dealing with cross-platform projects; typically you do not have to deal with it specifically, except when trying to understand what files in an SDK are used where and why. Oh, before I forget, on Windows .lib can be either an import library or a statically linked library. Go figure. The linker doesn't care which. And on Linux, static libraries typically have a .a extension. If you don't know the difference between a static and dynamic library, or when or why you should use one, Google will gladly help you research the topic.

Ogre 3D (or just Ogre—I'll use both names interchangeably throughout the book) enables you to deal with the three-dimensional graphical presentation of your particular application in a very object-oriented manner. Ogre in fact stands for *Object-Oriented Graphics Rendering Engine*, and it is exactly this very thing.

The term *Engine* implies that Ogre 3D "powers" your 3D graphics application, allowing you to focus more on the details of your application and less on the details of rendering a 3D scene, and this is an accurate description of the role Ogre 3D plays within the larger context of a complete application. With relatively few inputs, Ogre will invoke a staggering amount of processing on your behalf that enables your 3D scene actually to appear on a computer graphics display (or even in other places; we'll get to that later). If you are familiar with programming directly against Direct3D or OpenGL, you know precisely how much processing that is, and chances are you are extremely happy that an engine like Ogre exists.

Object oriented is a somewhat nebulous term, often abused and mangled into whatever the speaker wants it to mean. The canonical definition, however, of object oriented is the definition understood by the Ogre designers and by me: simply put, a way of viewing a problem domain as a collection of collaborating objects, rather than as a sequence of discrete tasks. In other words, as the Wikipedia entry (http://en.wikipedia.org/wiki/Object-oriented_programming) puts it, a computer program is "composed of a collection of individual units, or objects, that act on each other, as opposed to a traditional view in which a program is a list of instructions to the computer. Each object is capable of receiving messages, processing data, and sending messages to other objects." Object-oriented design (OOD) and programming (OOP) provide a more intuitive, "human" feel to programming and design, because its basis is in how humans perceive the real world. If you are not familiar with OOD or OOP techniques and practices, you will probably want to become familiar before diving too deep into Ogre, because (a) I am not going to teach you OOD or OOP in this book, and (b) understanding how to use some of the more advanced or esoteric features of Ogre requires at least a fundamental understanding of object-oriented design and programming. Of course, if you are one of the chosen few who enjoy the challenge of learning to swim by diving headfirst into the deep end of the pool, then Ogre is the perfect challenge for you. If you're not, the shallow end can be found at your library, at Amazon.com, or on any of hundreds of web sites accessible most easily via Google.

Where Does It Fit?

Figure 1-1 shows a high-level simulation architecture typical of many real-time games and other interactive simulations. The actual computer system (hardware) is abstracted by the *application layer*, and the game/simulation logic deals with things like the system timer, HID (Human Interface Device) input, and the file system through this layer. The logic layer contains the rules of the simulation and maintains simulation state, acting on inputs obtained from the application layer as well as events transmitted over the network. All of this state is periodically presented to the user in terms of both visual and audio "views" of the state.

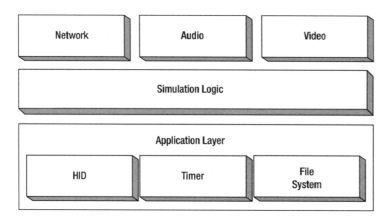

Figure 1-1. *Typical high-level simulation/game architecture*

The video view of the state is the subject of this book: specifically, rendering the video view using the Ogre 3D rendering library middleware. It is no coincidence that Ogre includes "3D" in its name, because that is all it does. It does not handle user input, it does not manage your game state, it does not communicate with the network for you, nor does it play audio cues. By design, it is only a 3D graphics rendering library, and includes only the functionality needed to support that mission. As a result, it performs that mission astoundingly well.

Features

Ogre features match, and in some cases surpass, nearly every capability offered by a commercial 3D rendering package:

- Full and equal support for both OpenGL and Direct3D

- Full support for Windows, Linux, and Mac OS X platforms

- Simple and extensible object framework, easily integrated into an existing application

- Automatic handling of render state management and hierarchical culling

- Powerful and sophisticated material management and scripting system, allowing maintenance of materials and fallback techniques without touching a single line of code

- Support for all fixed-function texture and blending techniques, as well as programmable GPU techniques and all high-level and assembled shading languages, such as Cg, HLSL, and GLSL

- Support for a wide variety of image and texture formats including PNG, TGA, DDS, TIF, GIF, JPG, as well as odd formats such as 1D, volumetric textures, cubemaps, and compressed textures such as DXTC

- Full support for render-to-texture techniques and projective texturing (decals)

- Full support for material LoD (level of detail, mipmapping) techniques

- Optimized binary mesh format with both manual and automatic LoD generation

- Official and community support and development of exporters from all major commercial and open source 3D modeling packages to the Ogre mesh and animation format

- Full access to vertex and index buffers, vertex declarations, and buffer mappings

- Full support for skeletal and pose (vertex) animations, as well as sophisticated blending of any number of each and multiple bone weights per vertex

- Support for both software- and hardware-accelerated skinning

- Support for static geometry batching

- Support for biquadric Bezier patches

- Plug in–based hierarchical scene structure interface, allowing you to use the scene graph that best suits your application (basic octree scene manager included as an example plug-in)

- Advanced maskable scene-querying system

- Full support for several shadowing techniques, including stencil, texture, additive, and modulative, all with full support for hardware acceleration

- Advanced plug in–based particle system with support for extensible emitters, affectors, and renderers (sample ParticleFX plug-in included)

- Full support for easy-to-use skyboxes, skyplanes, and skydomes

- Billboarding for sprite-based graphics and rendering optimization techniques

- Unique queue-based rendering management allowing full control over the order of the rendering process

- Automatic management of object transparency

- Sophisticated and extensible resource management and loading system with included support for file system, ZIP, and PK3 archive types

This list only touches on the capabilities incorporated into the Ogre 3D rendering engine over the past 4 years of its development, but it should serve to demonstrate the breadth and depth of the power of the Ogre 3D engine.

Origins

Ogre is an open source software project. This means you are free to use the software as you wish—mostly. This little thing called the *Lesser GNU Public License* prevents you from using it truly as you wish; Richard Stallman and the Free Software Foundation would be delighted to enlighten you on the nuances of the LGPL. However, with a tiny bit of restraint and by following a few rules, you are free to use the software produced by the Ogre project in your project, no matter what it may be. School project or graduate research aid, go for it. Personal learning or game project, code on. Full-featured community game project, Ogre is there for you. Even commercial game or other 3D applications can use Ogre, and many in fact do, including some award-winning titles.

The version of Ogre covered in this book does not carry the dual-licensing scheme of many open source applications such as MySQL; it is strictly LGPL. A few highlights of the LPGL licensing scheme:

- You may distribute only the binary builds of an LGPL project so long as the they are not built from modified versions of the publicly available source (which in effect makes them "closed source"), and providing that the source to the library is readily available (you don't need to worry about that last part, since the source is always available via the Ogre project itself).

- Where the GPL requires that software using GPL software in any way also be open source itself, the LGPL does not have this requirement (hence the "Lesser" in the name).

- You may not statically link LGPL software into your application unless your application is also open source under the LGPL (static linking also "links the license," so to speak).

Ogre got its start in 2001 when the project founder, Steve "Sinbad" Streeting, a mild-mannered business-software programmer by day, got this wild notion that what the world needed was another 3D rendering engine (John Carmack must have had the year off), but that this one should be scene-structure independent. Coupling his 10 years or so of graphics coding experience (some might instead call that "torture") with his copious experience in more "traditional" software engineering (read: "real job"), he designed the first architecture of what we now affectionately call Ogre. When asked why he thought that Yet Another Rendering Engine was worthwhile, Steve explains:

Many other engines, whilst technically impressive, lack the cohesive design and the consistent documentation to allow them to be used effectively. Many of them have long features lists, but have the feel of a bunch of tech demos lashed together with twine, with no clear vision to hold them together. Like any other software system this becomes their downfall as they become larger. Most other engines are also designed for one particular style of game or demo (e.g. first-person shooters, terrain roamers).

OGRE is different. OGRE is design-led rather than feature-led. Every feature that goes into OGRE is considered thoroughly and slotted into the overall design as elegantly as possible and is always fully documented, meaning that the features which are there always feel part of a cohesive whole. Quality is favoured over quantity, because quantity can come later—quality can never be added in retrospect. OGRE uses sound design principles learned, tried and tested many times in commercial-grade software—the object-orientation mentioned in its moniker is just one of those approaches—frequent use of design patterns is another. The core development team is kept deliberately small, and all of its members are veteran software engineers with many years of real-world experience. Patches are welcomed from community, but they undergo a strict review for both quality and cohesion with the Ogre philosophy before being accepted.

This small team of dedicated and motivated engineers hails from a wide range of backgrounds, from commercial software engineers to game developers to academic researchers to heavy-machinery simulator/trainer developers. When they are not working toward "real-life" goals, they are evolving Ogre, and when they are not evolving Ogre, they are usually available to answer questions both in the Ogre community forums as well as the official Ogre 3D IRC channel on the Freenode network. And when they are not available to answer questions, a very active and vibrant community is always eager to help those new to Ogre, or those old to Ogre with the memory loss that typically accompanies age. A few of that community are hand-picked as *Ogre MVPs*, individuals identified as those especially active and willing to help out the most with accurate and timely advice in the community support venues.

Prerequisite Knowledge

Yes, you can use Ogre without knowing a scrap of C++. Several community efforts exist to support language "ports" of or "wrappers" around the Ogre API to C#, Java, Python, Ruby, etc. However, these efforts are **not** part of the Ogre core, and themselves are in various states of stability and completeness. Ogre is developed and maintained using ISO standard C++, and compatibility with any one particular external language "binding" is not considered by the core Ogre development team.

For the most part, you will need to know C++ in order to use Ogre to its fullest. And I don't mean that you know it when you see some: you have to be able to understand object-oriented design patterns and think in C++ to understand what various constructs do. This book is based on the native Ogre C++ API, and code examples and algorithm will be implemented in C++. For example, if you do not understand this:

```
for (std::vector<int>::iterator it = m_myVec.begin();
        it != m_myVec.end(); it++) {

    // your code here

}
```

then you will need to revisit your C++ basics, because iterating through an STL container is an extremely common task in modern C++ programs, and, put simply, you will get along easier in Ogre once you understand the basics.

A commonly asked question in the support forums is, "How do I run Ogre?" Well, you don't. Ogre is not a program. There is no "Ogre executable" that you run. You write programs that use Ogre. As I explained earlier, it is a software development kit, which means that you use it to develop software. In the next chapter, you will learn how to obtain Ogre in all its forms, as well as build it from source on many common platforms.

You also need to know how to build software using an SDK such as Ogre. While I will provide some figures detailing specific Visual Studio 2003 project settings as they relate to Ogre, this book is not a "how-to" for setting up your specific development environment; you are expected to know something of how to operate your "power tools" before you try to use them.

And finally, you **will** need to understand something of basic 3D graphics and lighting in order to use Ogre (indeed, to use any 3D graphics API or library) before attempting to incorporate Ogre into your application. It would be like trying to speak or comprehend a foreign language without understanding any of the rules or semantics of the language. I will provide a light overview of basic 3D computer graphics with references to both print and online material, but for anything you don't understand after that brief primer, I highly recommend pursuing those references.

So, that said, let's get started!

CHAPTER 2

■■■

Capturing the Beast

This chapter will cover how to obtain Ogre, how to install it or build it from source, as well as how your needs best match with one or the other distribution method. No one method is inherently better than another, and in all cases the Ogre Team has gone to great lengths to ensure that the software installs (or builds) and runs reliably on the widest variety of common platforms.

Platform Support

Ogre's original development was done on the Windows 32-bit platform. This platform is still the main development platform for Ogre, but that does not mean that other common platforms are an afterthought: one of the Ogre Team's core members is responsible for the maintenance of the Mac OS X platform, and another is responsible for the Linux platform, and all three of these platforms are supported equally well and from the same source-code base. Since Ogre has native OpenGL support, it is possible to build and use Ogre on any platform for which OpenGL hardware-accelerated support exists, such as Sun Solaris. However, the core team does not directly support non-Linux UNIX platforms, and support for any porting efforts is entirely community based via forums and IRC. One enthusiastic user has even ported Ogre to Pocket PC–based PDAs under OpenGL ES. Even gaming consoles are not immune; if you look hard enough, you can find evidence of a port to Microsoft's Xbox console (not a huge stretch since the OS is Windows and the 3D API is Direct3D). For legal reasons, the Ogre Team can neither confirm nor deny the existence of any unofficial console ports by members of the Ogre user community.

The point is that Ogre's design decouples the logic from the platform and makes adding support for various hardware and software platforms as modular and straightforward as possible. The use of C++ language constructs follows modern ISO C++ standards, which means that it should port with as little effort as possible to a nonsupported platform, and also that it builds effortlessly—right out of the box, so to speak—on all supported platforms.

Dependencies

Most software systems depend on other software or SDKs for external functionality. This allows the system to leverage existing, common functionality without having to duplicate effort, and also allows the project team to focus on the specialized details of its software, resulting in a better overall product.

Ogre does not have many prerequisite dependencies, and the ones it does have are minimal, well planned, and furthermore, available for download from the same place you'll obtain Ogre during the course of this chapter. Ogre uses the following freely available libraries for various pieces of functionality:

- **FreeType**: Patent-unencumbered TrueType font management and rendering library (`http://www.freetype.org`)

- **OpenIL (DevIL)**: Image manipulation library supporting nearly every imaginable 2D graphics file format (in turn requires libjpeg, libpng, libtiff, and libmng for support for these formats when building DevIL from source) (`http://openil.sourceforge.net`)

- **zziplib (and zlib)**: ZIP file management and compression (`http://www.zlib.net`)

On Windows, the Ogre Direct3D rendering subsystem requires that at least Microsoft's DirectX Runtime be installed, and for building Ogre from source on Windows, you will need the DirectX SDK as well. The DirectX home can be found at `http://msdn.microsoft.com/directx`. And even though Ogre provides direct HLSL and GLSL GPU shader language support, Ogre (and definitely the Ogre demo applications) use the Cg API–independent hardware shader language provided by NVIDIA Corporation (`http://developer.nvidia.com/page/cg_main.html`). Cg is available for all platforms supported by the Ogre Team, and despite the fact that it comes from NVIDIA, it is not limited to NVIDIA hardware. Cg headers and libraries are also included in the Ogre Dependencies download, if you don't want to install the Cg Toolkit separately.

3D graphics acceleration support on all platforms typically comes from the graphics hardware vendor as part of its driver installation for that platform—true of both Direct3D and OpenGL. While the Direct3D SDK is provided as part of the DirectX SDK installation, OpenGL SDK files are installed when the graphics hardware drivers are installed, since Direct3D is only available on the Windows platform, and OpenGL is available on all platforms that support graphics acceleration.

Ogre Binary SDK

Ogre is supported extremely well on Windows, and is available in both source and SDK form. If you are a casual user or part of a development team satisfied with using current stable versions without having to build from source, the SDK is probably your best choice. However, should you need to build Ogre in a different way (say, for profiling), it is a simple matter to build the Ogre SDK from the same source code that was used to build the downloadable binaries, as you'll see later. SDK downloads are made available for all recently released versions, and also for particular versions of Microsoft Visual C++: for versions prior to 1.2 (Dagon), SDK downloads are available for Visual C++ 6.0, 7.0, 7.1, and 8.0. Starting with 1.2 (Dagon), SDK downloads are available only for Visual C++ 7.1 and 8.0, as well as the fully open source MingW/Code::Blocks combination.

Ogre Source Distribution

Ogre source distribution comes in two flavors: *tarball*, which refers to a packed and compressed version of the source tree for a particular version, and *CVS*, which refers to the source- and revision-control system used by the project. CVS usually will have the very latest version of the source; I say "usually" because the project host, SourceForge, manages two independent CVS systems—one for project developers (the core Ogre Team), and one for "anonymous" users (you and me), and "anonymous" CVS often lags behind developer CVS by some number of hours. For this reason, it is possible that an SDK build or source tarball **might** have a more recent version of the source, but that is rare, and infrequent at best. Use CVS whenever feasible (and you'll see in a moment when it might not be feasible).

Source tarballs are available for Windows, Linux, and Mac OS X. Additionally, dependency downloads are available for Windows, for all supported versions of Visual C++ (7.1 and 8.0) as well as MinGW/MSYS. Dependency packages for Linux and Mac OS X do not exist because those operating system distributions typically come with the dependencies already installed. We'll go over installing dependencies on Linux for the cases when they are not present.

Mac OS X users do not get shafted entirely; the Ogre source download includes the necessary Xcode frameworks needed to build Ogre on the Mac.

Installing an SDK

Let's go ahead and take a look at the simplest method of obtaining Ogre: SDK download. I'll show you how to set up Microsoft Visual C++ .NET 2003 (7.1) to work with Ogre's SDK download.

The basic steps involved in installing any SDK for any IDE are

1. Download the proper SDK.

2. Set up your IDE with the proper paths to the SDK.

3. Build the Ogre Samples to ensure a proper configuration of your development environment and correct installation of all dependent tools and libraries.

The last step is important to verify a working "baseline" installation. If (or when) you encounter issues building or running your Ogre-based application, the first thing any of the Ogre MVPs or Team members will ask is, "Do the demos (Samples) run OK?" This is to determine whether the problem is in Ogre or your code, and you can save yourself and the support staff a lot of time and "wild-goose chases" by verifying this first for yourself.

Microsoft Visual C++ .NET 2003 (VC 7.1)

Since we are using Visual C++ .NET 2003 (VC 7.1) in this example, we want the SDK for VC 7.1. Point your browser to http://www.ogre3d.org, click Downloads, and then SDKs. You will see a list of SDKs available for download, as in Figure 2-1.

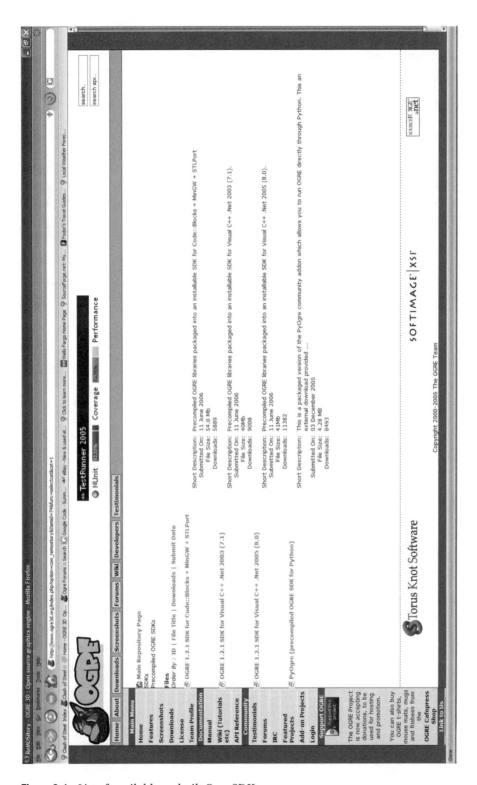

Figure 2-1. *List of available prebuilt Ogre SDKs*

Grab the SDK for Visual C++ .NET 2003, and save it to disk. You will see that it is an executable program; in fact, it is a self-extracting installer.

After starting up the installer, you can click Next at the first screen, and after reviewing the LGPL license on the next screen, check the box to indicate acceptance of the license and click Next. This takes you to the Install Location screen, as shown in Figure 2-2. Here you can set the install directory as you please. I'll use `C:\projects\ogre\OgreSDK` as the installation location for this example.

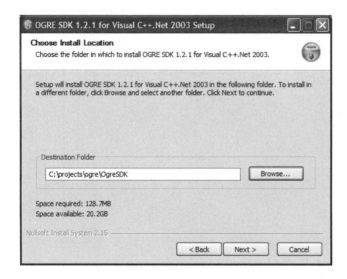

Figure 2-2. *Set the Ogre SDK installation location.*

Click Next, and on the next screen (Start Menu Folder, shown in Figure 2-3) click Install.

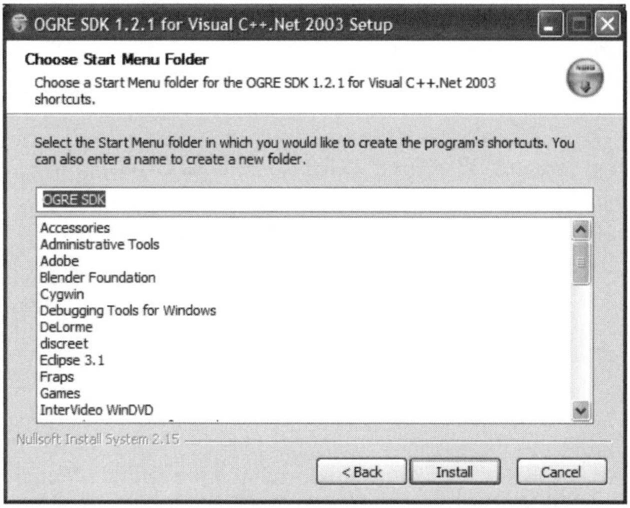

Figure 2-3. *Set Ogre SDK Start Menu information and launch the installer.*

After the installation completes successfully, your installation directory will look like Figure 2-4.

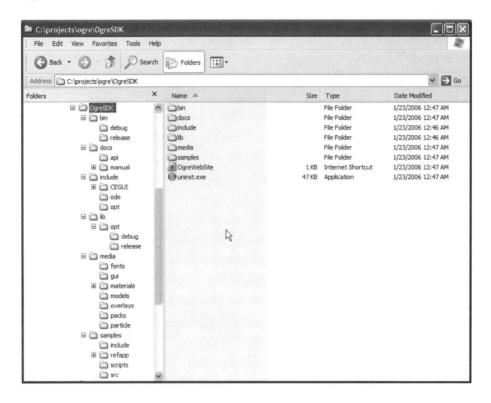

Figure 2-4. *Ogre SDK installation location contents*

Let's go over the contents of this folder. I've set the left side of the Windows Explorer view to Folders so that we can see the entire structure at a glance.

bin

This folder contains the DLLs provided by the SDK—Ogre, CEGUI (the official GUI layer for use with Ogre, even though it's a separate project), IL (the DevIL image library we discussed earlier), and zlib DLLs. These exist in the `release` and `debug` folders under `bin/` and each of those contains the respective types of DLL builds: `debug` contains nonoptimized builds incorporating debug information useful in debugging your Ogre applications, and `release` contains optimized and "stripped" (lacking debug information) builds, which are used for the builds of your application that you actually will release.

docs

This folder contains the API Reference in CHM (Compiled Help) form, and the online Manual in HTML format. The API Reference is generated from the actual code, using a tool called *doxygen* that parses the Ogre headers and creates a hyperlinked reference from their contents and specially marked comments. It is useful for finding out which classes and methods are available in the API, and also contains a light description of the use of each class. It is most useful if you are already familiar with the API and just need a quick reference.

The Manual is a condensed, concise summary of the features and usage of some of the major subsystems within Ogre, as well as a discussion of the usage of some of the more advanced features. It is written and maintained by the project team, and serves as a nice companion to the API Reference when you need a quick source for information about a particular feature in Ogre.

include

This folder contains the Ogre header files that you will reference in your code, as well as the headers for the CEGUI library and the ODE (Open Dynamics Engine) physics library (this library is used in one of the demo applications we discuss later in this chapter). You will also find in include/opt a set of headers that mostly are internal in nature, yet still can be used if you wish to extend the functionality of Ogre via plug-ins.

lib

This folder contains the Ogre import libraries you will need in order to link to the DLLs in the bin/ folder. Each DLL has a corresponding .lib: debug .lib for debug .dll and release .lib for release .dll. You will also find PDB files (.pdb, Program Database) that go with the debug .lib/.dll files; these .pdb files provide line number and source-code file information to your debugger (preventing you from having to have the entire source code to debug Ogre-based applications).

samples

This folder contains the Ogre Samples (demos), each of which highlights a particular capability or feature of Ogre. These are provided with source code as well as a Visual Studio .sln solution file so that you can easily build them. If you load up this solution and select the menu command Build Solution all of the Samples will end up in the bin/ directory, in either debug or release, depending on which solution configuration you built.

The *Demo_ReferenceApplication* in this set of demos was intended to demonstrate how to integrate Ogre with another library in the same application. As you'll find out later, this example has blossomed into several different add-on projects that "glue" together Ogre with various different types of libraries, such as physics and audio.

media

This folder was taken out of order because it contains all of the materials, textures, meshes, etc., that the Ogre Samples require for execution. This set of directories is a wonderful reference for learning the operation of various Ogre systems (especially the material scripting and particle effects systems).

Finally, in the installation root, the Ogre Team provides a convenient link to the Ogre web site as well as a handy uninstaller launcher in case you want to remove the Ogre SDK (which you will want to do, for example, if you change to a different version of Visual C++).

The OgreSDK installer also added an environment variable on your system. If you open the Properties dialog for My Computer and click Environment Variables on the Advanced tab, you will find that OGRE_HOME has been set for you, as in Figure 2-5.

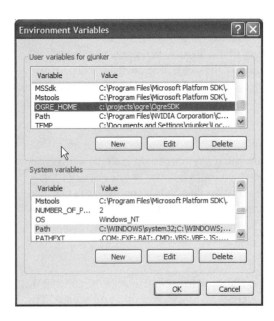

Figure 2-5. *The* OGRE_HOME *environment variable has been set to the installation location.*

This variable is used extensively in the OgreSDK sample project files to locate and properly set up the include and library search directories for each sample project, in a manner that does not require the SDK to exist in a particular location. You may also elect to use this variable if you wish in your own projects to reference the SDK headers and libraries.

With the SDK installed, you need to tell Visual Studio where to find its files. Open up Visual Studio, and select Tools ➤ Options, and then the Projects folder, as in Figure 2-6.

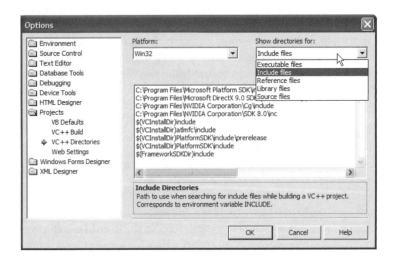

Figure 2-6. *Visual Studio directories setup*

■**Tip** Additionally, you can add the path to the `bin/` directory to the executable files path here, but it is simpler overall to add that path to your system path in the dialog shown in Figure 2-5. That way, your programs can find the Ogre SDK DLLs from anywhere, not just from within Visual Studio.

Add the paths to the SDK `include/` and `lib/` directories as demonstrated in Figure 2-7. You can either type a path out manually and Visual Studio will help with path completion (as shown in the figure) or click the button at the right end of the row and use the standard Windows File Explorer to set the path.

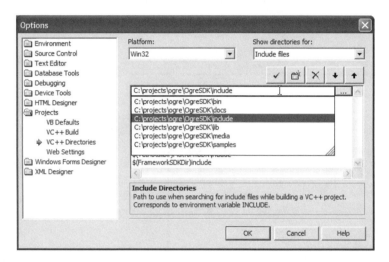

Figure 2-7. *Add paths to the Ogre SDK* `include` *and* `lib` *directories.*

That's it! Optionally, at this point you can go ahead and build the Samples that come with the Ogre SDK. Navigate to the `Samples/` folder in the SDK installation and double-click `Samples.sln` as in Figure 2-8, and build them all by right-clicking the Solution node in the Solution Explorer and selecting Build Solution (see Figure 2-9).

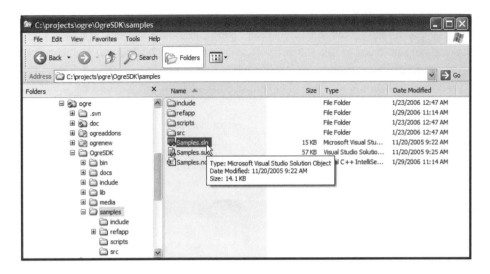

Figure 2-8. *The Samples solution file in the Ogre SDK installation*

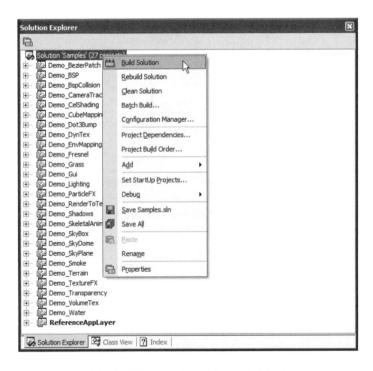

Figure 2-9. *Build all of the Samples with Build Solution.*

The Samples all will build to `bin/debug` or `bin/release` in the `OgreSDK/` installation directory, depending on which solution configuration you built (Visual Studio defaults to `debug`). I suggest building the Release configuration the first time.

■**Note** Debug builds are nonoptimized builds that are full of extra checks and variable initializations, as well as extra debugging info that allows the Visual Studio debugger to find source code from compiled object code. Debug builds are useful only to the developer for the purpose of debugging. Additionally, benchmarking or profiling your code in Debug is a pointless metric, as the extra processing present makes the results useless.

Release builds are optimized builds with no extra checks or variable initializations, and are what you send to your users. Release builds often run at least an order of magnitude faster than Debug builds, and often many times faster even than that. If you are interested in how fast your application or any of the Ogre Sample applications run, do a Release build and benchmark or profile there. That is an accurate representation of how your code actually will run.

Run one of the Samples to do a final test. *Demo_Terrain* is a simple, non-GPU-program-dependent Sample that should run on any hardware. You can select any Sample you wish to run, of course. When you start up the first Sample, you will see a configuration dialog box as shown in Figure 2-10.

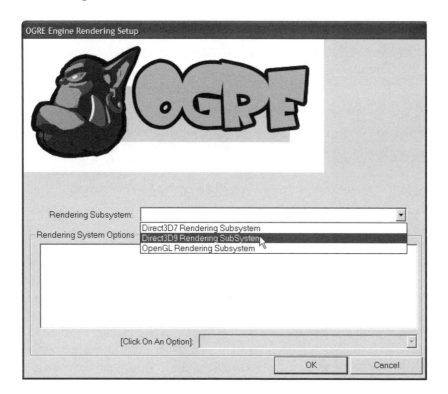

Figure 2-10. *Ogre standard configuration dialog*

Select the render system you prefer, and adjust settings further to your liking. I strongly suggest running the demos in windowed mode (Fullscreen = false, as shown in Figure 2-11) until you are sure everything is running properly. In fact, you should keep with this practice for any 3D rendering application code you write; when running in full screen, it is very easy to lose control of your display and have to reboot in the event of the slightest hang-up. There is always time to run in full screen once you have determined that the application does not crash in windowed mode.

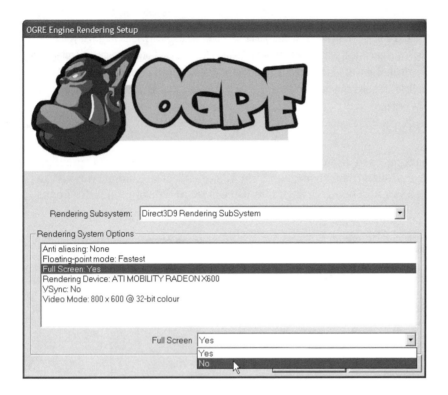

Figure 2-11. *Turn off full-screen mode until you are sure that everything is operational.*

■**Note** You will get varying performance on different systems with different graphics hardware as a result both of the capabilities of your CPU and GPU and the quality of the graphics-vendor-supplied drivers for your system configuration. This is one of the reasons that professional-quality rendering APIs, including Ogre, offer equal support for multiple render system types. End users should have the choice of using the render system that offers the best performance for them, not the API. In Figure 2-11, you see that the graphics hardware in the laptop I used to compose this book is the ATI RADEON Mobility X600. ATI has notoriously less support for OpenGL than for DirectX, which is why I chose Direct3D 9 here. Typically my framerates on this PC for OpenGL are 1/3 that of Direct3D 9, with the latest drivers. If you have an NVIDIA card, chances are your OpenGL performance might be better than Direct3D 9. This is something you would have to test for yourself on a case-by-case basis, but you will always want to allow your users to select the render system that works best for them.

Running the Samples involves a very simple set of controls where applicable (the standard FPS "WASD" controls move the camera around a scene, in demos that allow the camera to move), and the Esc key to exit the app. Play with all the demos; some of them demonstrate some quite advanced features. The Print Screen key on your keyboard works as expected in all demos; look for a file named `screenshot.png` (or similar) in the directory containing the demo for your "screenie."

At this point, you are ready to start writing Ogre-based applications. More correctly, you now have a software development environment that enables you to create Ogre-based applications. The rest of this book is devoted to making you ready to exploit all of the power that Ogre provides you.

Visual C++ 2005

The Ogre Team directly supports the Microsoft Visual C++ 2005 (Visual C++ 8.*x*) IDE as well. Setup and configuration of the Visual C++ 2005 IDE is virtually identical to the process outlined earlier for Visual C++ .NET 2003, with the exception that you want to obtain the VC 8 SDK download, and use the solution and project files marked with "VC8" in the name instead of the base versions (for example, `Ogre_VC8.sln` instead of `Ogre.sln`). The VC 8 project and solution file versions all exist in the same places as the VC 7.1 versions, and the build outputs are identical in name and location to the outputs for VC 7.1.

This also applies to the free Visual C++ 2005 Express version of the IDE. While this IDE is limited somewhat relative to the full retail version, it is not limited in any ways meaningful to using it with Ogre. You will be able to use the Ogre SDK with the Express version just as easily as you will with the full, retail versions.

Other Free IDE/Compiler Combinations on Windows

If you are reading this section, chances are you have said something like, "Wait, I can't afford Visual Studio" or "I want support for an IDE that works on multiple platforms." Luckily, you have freely available options. The leading contender at this point is the free and robust open source IDE called *Code::Blocks* (`http://www.codeblocks.org`).

Code::Blocks

Code::Blocks is an open source C++ IDE that is rapidly gaining traction, maturity, and features as time goes by. It is widely used and well supported and documented, and is a viable alternative to developing with the Visual Studio IDE. It has native support for many different compilers, including open source options such as MinGW and GCC. However, it does not come with any compiler of its own. (The Code::Blocks web site offers a bundled convenience download of Code::Blocks and MinGW for those who want to stay 100% open source, even while developing Windows applications. I will not argue that dichotomy here; suffice to say its absurdity should be self-evident.)

Eclipse

Eclipse (`http://www.eclipse.org`) is an open source, plug in–based Java development IDE, written in Java, for which many language plug-ins have been developed, including one for C/C++ (CDT, the C/C++ Development Toolkit, available at `http://www.eclipse.org/cdt`).

Eclipse is not directly supported by the Ogre Team, but a Google web search will turn up a few "how-to's" on getting Ogre to build as an Eclipse project. Eclipse/CDT knows about GCC natively, so directions on getting Code::Blocks to work with GCC should apply to Eclipse as well.

Microsoft Platform SDK

You also will need to download and install the Microsoft Platform SDK (known as just the Microsoft SDK now) in order to have the various system import libraries and headers required to build applications for the Microsoft platforms. These are included with the Visual C++ IDE retail installations (but not with the Visual C++ 2005 Express, which also requires the Platform SDK for building Windows applications). This is a hefty download, and comes in the form of either a web-based installation or a single ISO CD-ROM image that you can burn to disk, so if your bandwidth availability is rather low, you might choose to install only the Core SDK from the web-based installer.

■**Tip** The Platform SDK actually is useful even with retail installations of Visual C++, in that it always contains the latest versions of libraries and headers for the Windows platforms. The versions of the SDK contents that come bundled with Visual Studio and Visual C++ installations are static and grow more out of date with each passing month, so even retail users benefit from referencing the Platform SDK instead of relying on the bundled versions.

WHY IS MICROSOFT GIVING AWAY ALL OF THIS SOFTWARE?

Opinions and speculation vary, and Microsoft has not stated directly why it is giving away some of its best software, but smart money is on the market share gained by open source alternatives such as GCC, and the Linux build environment in general. Add to that the existence of open source alternatives on the Windows platform, such as Cygwin/GCC and MinGW/MSYS, and the success and maturity of Novell's Mono implementation of the .NET Framework, and the legitimate productivity advantages of purchasing Microsoft development tools licenses were being outweighed by the maturity and cost savings of open source alternatives. On top of all of that, the development tools revenue is not the main source of revenue for Microsoft. And Microsoft needs applications developed for Microsoft platforms, and the best way to ensure that continues is to provide the tools for free.

In other words, Microsoft needed to regain market- and mindshare, and the only way to compete with a no-cost alternative is to provide a no-cost option to you. Again, this is just speculation, but the logic is obvious from a marketing standpoint. The winner in the end is definitely the developer, who has that many more quality choices for development tools.

Code::Blocks and the MinGW Compiler

With the release of Ogre 1.2 (Dagon), the Ogre Project Team now supports the MinGW/Code::Blocks combination directly with SDK downloads for the IDE and compiler. If you are interested in this combination, I refer you to Jeff Doyle's excellent article on setting up Code::Blocks and MinGW to work with Ogre and the Code::Blocks/MinGW SDK, available at `http://www.ogre3d.org/wiki/index.php/CodeBlocks_MingW_STLPort`.

Building from Source

Here we depart from the comfort, convenience, and safety of a prebuilt set of binary files and headers, and enter the world of Ogre source builds. Despite what you may have heard, it really is not that big a deal to build Ogre from source. It builds right out of the box on all of its supported platforms, and the source distribution contains an even larger selection of IDE project and workspace/solution files than does the SDK. Building from source is also a fantastic way to learn how Ogre itself is designed and built, as you can debug through the entire code base to see what functions call other functions, and what each function does, and how the various bits all work together. It also is an excellent way of staying up-to-date with the constant Ogre code changes, bug fixes, and enhancements, and in fact is the only way to contribute patches to the project or to ride the most bleeding edge of upcoming versions.

Note If you could not tell, I am a huge fan of source code builds. This goes back to my days as a consultant in the computer labs at university, where I spent an inordinate amount of time building and rebuilding large packages such as GCC and X11R6 for use on the Engineering College network. I have always preferred to run not only the latest code, but also code built specifically for the platform I am on. Binary builds always will pander to the lowest common denominator for the widest reach in compatibility, and usually the only way to obtain a software build specifically for your platform is to build it from source yourself.

Linux

Linux provides simply an absolute wealth of development tools and options (as W. C. Fields would have called it, "an eloquent sufficiency"). A plethora, if you will. In fact, the number of different ways you can develop software on Linux is astounding, and none of it costs a dime.

We will go through two of those ways here relative to building Ogre on Linux. The first is the very basic but very powerful and elegant command-line process, and the other will be through the provided Code::Blocks IDE workspace and project files. As you'll find out, none of the hassles of Code::Blocks on Windows crop up with Code::Blocks on Linux, since all of the needed libraries and debuggers are present and available, and in fact the standard debugger on Linux, GDB, is integrated into Code::Blocks.

Linux comes in many different distributions, but regardless of distribution, Linux is Linux. Linux is not "Red Hat" or "Fedora" or "SuSE" or "Gentoo" or "Debian" or any number of countless different efforts to package Linux in subtly different ways. Linux is the Linux kernel and the various device drivers and device support that come with the kernel, as found at http://www.kernel.org. As a result, anything that runs on one distribution will run on another, given the presence of the same libraries and headers.

Usually this is one of the three main deciding factors in the choice between distributions. The others are ease of installation and ease of maintenance. I have always found Red Hat Linux (and now their developmental project, Fedora Core) to be the winner for my needs on all three of those metrics. Obtaining it is as simple as downloading the installation ISOs and burning them to CD-ROM (or DVD-ROM), and installing it is every bit as simple as installing Windows XP. Furthermore, everything you need to develop software (and then ten times more than that) is available for your use. Keeping it up-to-date is a snap with the *YUM* installation maintenance system, which will also install any necessary dependencies when you install or update software packages on your system.

Others may have their own preference in distribution, and I'm sure you do as well, if you are interested in Linux development. At the end of the day, it's all just Linux, and the following build instructions will run on every single Linux out there.

We will be building Ogre on Linux in this chapter the "standard" way. I advise you not to depend on various distributions' sometimes exotic package maintenance processing, as it may not always create what you expect and almost certainly will not be as up-to-date as getting source directly from the Ogre repository will be. If you do choose to use an alternate method of building the Ogre source (such as emerge on Gentoo, for example), then be prepared for some potentially excruciating sessions figuring out why it did not work. However, if you follow the steps I outline in this chapter, then **it will work**, without a hitch.

The only distribution-specific commands I will be using in this chapter are those regarding RPM, the leading package-management tool for Linux. RPM-based distributions include Red Hat, Fedora Core, SuSE, and others. If you have decided to try another distribution, you undoubtedly will know how to identify and install any packages your system may need to build Ogre (as you will discover, it's a startlingly small number of packages you may need to obtain). I also will use YUM, which is the command-line package maintenance system for Fedora Core. If you are not on a YUM- or RPM-based system, follow the instructions for your particular distribution to obtain whatever software or package you may need.

Graphics Drivers

The last thing to know about before we start is the graphics drivers. Linux itself does not have a GUI or windowing system; that is provided by a system known as *X Windows*, and all GUI-based applications (including your game) will run on top of X Windows. X Windows is similar in many ways to Microsoft Windows (and better in many more) and uses the same notion of modular graphics device driver as does Microsoft Windows. Just as you have to get graphics drivers for your ATI or NVIDIA card for Windows, you have to get them for Linux too (for the sake of convenience and understanding, they are always referred to, albeit incorrectly, as "Linux drivers" instead of "X Windows drivers").

Since the video hardware vendor is responsible for providing OpenGL API implementations and headers, the graphics driver download will include these items, and therefore we want to install the latest drivers before starting to build Ogre.

All X Windows (X.Org, to be accurate) installations come with a default OpenGL-compatible software rasterizer known as *MesaGL*. The easiest way to identify if your driver installation has worked is to run, either via GUI menu or at the Linux command line, the GLX (Extensions for OpenGL) diagnostic app *glxinfo*. It will produce an enormous amount of information about your graphics environment, including the name of the OpenGL vendor and the OpenGL version. You are looking for the following lines in the output of glxinfo:

```
OpenGL vendor string: Mesa project: www.mesa3d.org
OpenGL renderer string: Mesa GLX Indirect
OpenGL version string: 1.2 (1.5 Mesa 6.2.1)
```

If you see this information (or similar) in your glxinfo output, instead of information referring to NVIDIA Corporation or ATI, your X Windows configuration is not set up correctly (and if you have an NVIDIA card and see ATI information or vice versa, you have some real problems you will need to sort out before going any further). Put simply, far too many different things could be wrong to detail them here, so you will have to consult the available online and offline references for your distribution and hardware. For driver installation on Fedora Core, you should start at http://rpm.livna.org, which is the official home of the Fedora Core Extras (including the NVIDIA and ATI driver installation RPMs, which take all the guesswork and hassle out of video drivers on Fedora Core).

Once you have the video drivers sorted, you will need to confirm that you have the required dependencies installed on your system. Luckily, most of them already will exist and it will just be a matter of making sure you have the proper -devel packages installed. -devel packages are usually just the header files for a given dynamic library, although for libraries that also provide statically linkable archives, these would be provided in the -devel package as well.

Dependencies

The Linux build depends on the same software that the Windows builds depend on: FreeType, DevIL (and its dependencies), zziplib, and zlib. The optional (but highly recommended) Cg Toolkit is another dependency, but one that almost surely will not exist on your system after installation of the distribution. If you have an NVIDIA card, you may have had to go to the NVIDIA site to get the Linux drivers; might as well pick up the Cg Toolkit for Linux while you are there. Don't let the source confuse you; Cg works just fine with ATI cards as well.

Here are the RPM query commands and the output on my Fedora Core 4 system for the Ogre dependencies. We especially are looking for the –devel packages. Don't sweat the version numbers, except that Ogre expects at least 2.1.9 of FreeType, and that your –devel package version numbers should match the installed main package versions.

```
[gjunker@localhost ~]$ rpm -qa freetype* zziplib* zlib* libpng* \
libmng* libtiff* libjpeg*
```

```
freetype-demos-2.1.9-2
freetype-2.1.9-2
freetype-devel-2.1.9-2
freetype-utils-2.1.9-2
zziplib-0.13.38-2
zziplib-devel-0.13.38-2
zlib-1.2.2.2-3
zlib-devel-1.2.2.2-3
libjpeg-devel-6b-34
libmng-devel-1.0.9-1
libmng-static-1.0.9-1
libjpeg-6b-34
libtiff-devel-3.7.1-6
libtiff-3.7.1-6
libpng10-1.0.18-2
libmng-1.0.9-1
libpng10-devel-1.0.18-2
[gjunker@localhost ~]$
```

Notice that we did not look for DevIL (OpenIL) or Cg. For DevIL, I can almost guarantee that it does not exist on your system, and if it does, it probably is a version too old to use with Ogre. We will be building DevIL from source as part of the Ogre source build, and the image format libraries we are checking for at the end of the listing are for the benefit of DevIL; Ogre has no direct dependence at all on any image formats. As for Cg, you will have to have obtained that from NVIDIA Corporation already and installed it per its instructions, so you know whether it is there or not.

If you need to obtain a -devel package, the simplest way on YUM-based distributions is, well, with **yum**. You will need to be **root** to run **yum** commands; one common method of executing as **root** is with the **sudo** command, but for the sake of clarity, we will simply execute **yum** as **root**. Notice in the preceding list that you do not see any libpng packages installed. We will install them now before proceeding.

```
[root@localhost ~]# yum install libpng-devel
```

This will check with the configured YUM package repositories and will install the -devel package, as well as any packages it depends on. For example, if libpng did not show up at all (as is the case here), installing libpng-devel will grab both libpng and libpng-devel and install both.

DevIL (Developers' Image Library, Formerly Open Image Library)

The simplest way to obtain the DevIL source is via CVS (Concurrent Version System). This is one of the standard networked source-control management (SCM) systems used for open source projects (however, a newer SCM, Subversion, is rapidly replacing it, even at Source-Forge, traditionally the primary location for open source projects and the home of DevIL and Ogre and a cast of thousands). Change to the directory where you would like to put the DevIL source code, and run the following commands:

```
cvs -d:pserver:anonymous@cvs.sourceforge.net:/cvsroot/openil login
```

and then

```
cvs -d:pserver:anonymous@cvs.sourceforge.net:/cvsroot/openil co DevIL
```

This will create a directory called DevIL in the current directory and fill it with the source code and build scripts for DevIL.

■**Tip** If you are having issues getting source from SourceForge anonymous CVS, feel free to grab the tarball. At the time of this writing, the DevIL library has been at version 1.6.7 for many months (possibly years); it is a very mature and stable library and not subject to a constant stream of changes, so this is one of those cases where the tarball works just as well as the CVS source.

Change to the DevIL directory and run the following:

```
[gjunker@localhost DevIL]$ sh autogen.sh
```

Now you are ready to run **configure**:

```
[gjunker@localhost DevIL]$ ./configure
```

```
.
.
.
+----------------------------------------+
|     IL library  Supported formats      |
+----------------------------------------+-------+
BMP DCX DDS WAD GIF HDR ICO JPG LIF MDL MNG PCD PCX PIC PIX PNG PNM
PSD PSP PXR RAW SGI TGA TIF WAL XPM

+----------------------------------------+
|      ILUT library  Supported APIs      |
+----------------------------------------+-------+
OpenGL SDL
.
.
.
[gjunker@localhost DevIL]$
```

The main thing you are looking for (apart from the absence of any error messages, which usually are informative enough for you to correct whatever went wrong during the **configure** step) is the information I have just highlighted: supported image formats and supported platform APIs.

■Note autotools is the standard cross-platform mechanism for building software on Linux and various UNIXes. It has the job of checking the system for various platform-dependent values and settings, and creating a build script tailored to whatever platform it runs on. For the end user, who just wants to build some software, it is a veritable godsend, in that it really is as simple as the steps I've outlined previously to configure a software system to build on arbitrary hardware and operating systems. Trust me, it wasn't always this simple.

The next two steps are a snap: build and install the DevIL libraries. It is as simple as **make** and **make install**.

```
[gjunker@localhost DevIL]$ make
```

```
Making all in src-IL
make[1]: Entering directory '/home/gjunker/src/DevIL/src-IL'
Making all in src
make[2]: Entering directory '/home/gjunker/src/DevIL/src-IL/src'
if /bin/sh ../../libtool --tag=CC --mode=compile gcc -DHAVE_CONFIG_H
  -I. -I. -I../../include/IL -I../../include -I../../src-IL/include
  -I/usr/X11R6/include -Wall -g -O2 -msse -msse2 -Wall -g -O2 -msse
  -msse2 -MT il_alloc.lo -MD -MP -MF ".deps/il_alloc.Tpo" -c -o il_alloc.lo
  il_alloc.c; \
```

```
then mv -f ".deps/il_alloc.Tpo" ".deps/il_alloc.Plo"; else rm -f
  ".deps/il_alloc.Tpo"; exit 1; fi
mkdir .libs
 gcc -DHAVE_CONFIG_H -I. -I. -I../../include/IL -I../../include
-I../../src-IL/include -I/usr/X11R6/include -Wall -g -O2 -msse -msse2 -Wall -g
-O2 -msse -msse2 -MT il_alloc.lo -MD -MP -MF .deps/il_alloc.Tpo
-c il_alloc.c -fPIC -DPIC -o .libs/il_alloc.o
.

.

.
make[1]: Entering directory '/home/gjunker/src/DevIL'
make[1]: Nothing to be done for 'all-am'.
make[1]: Leaving directory '/home/gjunker/src/DevIL'
[gjunker@localhost DevIL]$
```

Don't worry if none of this makes any sense to you; what you are looking for are errors, and make and gcc will be sure to let you know if there are any. In fact, make will stop and tell you there was an error if any occurred. If you get to the point listed in the preceding output, your build succeeded. Now run **make install** (as **root**) to install the DevIL library on your system.

```
[root@localhost DevIL]$ make install
```

```
Making install in src-IL
make[1]: Entering directory '/home/gjunker/src/DevIL/src-IL'
Making install in src
make[2]: Entering directory '/home/gjunker/src/DevIL/src-IL/src'
make[3]: Entering directory '/home/gjunker/src/DevIL/src-IL/src'
.

.

.
make[2]: Nothing to be done for 'install-data-am'.
make[2]: Leaving directory '/home/gjunker/src/DevIL'
make[1]: Leaving directory '/home/gjunker/src/DevIL'
[root@localhost DevIL]$
```

Now you are ready to get and build the Ogre source code. Change to the directory you plan to use to store the Ogre source. For this example, I will be using the src directory in my home directory, but you can put the Ogre source anywhere you want, it does not matter to Ogre. By the way, expect this checkout to take a bit longer than did DevIL, as there is much more source in Ogre than in DevIL . . . Ogre . . . DevIL . . . there must be a punchline in there somewhere.

```
[gjunker@localhost src]$ cvs -d:pserver:anonymous@cvs.sourceforge.net:/cvsroot/ogre
 login
```

```
Logging in to :pserver:anonymous@cvs.sourceforge.net:2401/cvsroot/ogre
CVS password:
[gjunker@localhost src]$ cvs -d:pserver:anonymous@cvs.sourceforge.net:/cvsroot/ogre
 co ogrenew
cvs checkout: Updating ogrenew
U ogrenew/AUTHORS
U ogrenew/BUGS
U ogrenew/COPYING
.
.
.
cvs checkout: Updating ogrenew/Tools/dotXSIConverter/src
U ogrenew/Tools/dotXSIConverter/src/Exporter.cpp
[gjunker@localhost src]$
```

You need to do the same four-step salsa you did for DevIL (you will find that this is a very common sequence of commands for building from source for any autotools-based build scripts . . . which means most projects). For the sake of brevity, we will concatenate all four commands on the same command line here.

```
[gjunker@localhost ogrenew]$ sh bootstrap && ./configure \
--with-platform=GLX && make
[gjunker@localhost ogrenew]$ sudo make install
```

Depending on your system specs, you might have time to go grab lunch before this build finishes. On my Pentium 4 3.0GHz with a substantial amount of memory and a fast hard drive, the total build time is about 14 minutes. On my Pentium 3 866MHz with 512MB RAM, however, building Ogre takes about 45 minutes. The **sudo** step installs the libraries and headers as **root** to the standard system locations.

The --with-platform=GLX in the preceding **configure** step directs the build process to use the GLX platform manager classes instead of the SDL-based platform manager, which was dropped to "optional" status as a redundant dependency. You can still force Ogre to build against the SDL platform by supplying --with-platform=SDL to **configure**, and can even use the GTK (Gnome Toolkit) platform if you wish, with --with-platform=GTK. You can also disable building the Cg plug-in if you choose not to use it, by supplying the --without-cg option to **configure**.

When this process completes, you are ready to use Ogre. The best thing to do at this point is to change to the Samples/Common/bin directory and run one or more of the demo applications to test the installation. Upon startup, you will see a lot of debugging text and then a configuration dialog that looks like Figure 2-12.

Figure 2-12. *Ogre GLX configuration dialog*

Select the OpenGL rendering system, and you should see a dialog like Figure 2-13.

Figure 2-13. *Ogre GLX options*

Set the options to your liking, and when you click Accept, the demo will begin. This configuration dialog saves its settings so that subsequent execution of other demos will preset this dialog with your settings.

Windows and Visual C++

While Ogre is equally supported on both Windows and Linux platforms, Windows users have the added advantage that Windows and Visual C++ is the main development environment for Ogre. Building Ogre from source on Windows is actually easier than building it on Linux.

First, install a CVS Windows client; I highly recommend the *TortoiseCVS* Windows Explorer shell extension found at `http://tortoisecvs.tigris.org`. I'll be using TortoiseCVS in the following example, but the basic CVS concepts apply to all CVS clients.

After the required reboot upon installing TortoiseCVS, you can check out the source similar to how it was done for Linux. Change to, or create, a directory to hold your source (I used `C:\projects\ogre`) and right-click in the folder to bring up the TortoiseCVS context menu, as in Figure 2-14.

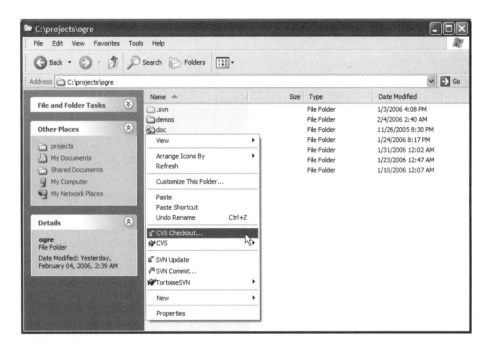

Figure 2-14. *TortoiseCVS context menu in Windows Explorer*

You will then see a dialog like Figure 2-15. Set the CVSROOT field to `:pserver:anonymous@cvs.sourceforge.net:/cvsroot/ogre` and the rest of the form will fill itself out automatically. Set the Module Name to ogrenew. Since Dagon (the version of Ogre on which this book is based) is version 1.2, you will want to change to the Revision tab and enter `v1-2` in the Choose Branch or Tag field, as in Figure 2-16.

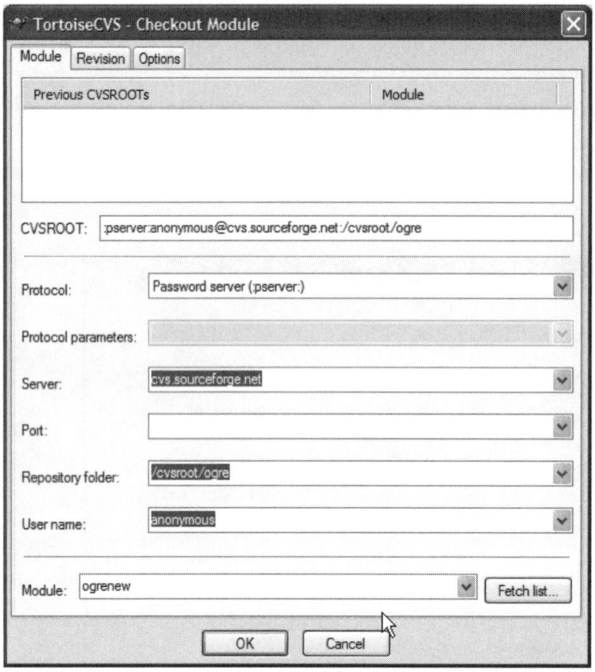

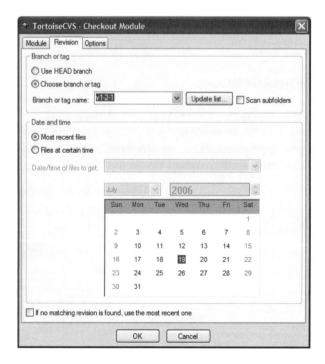

Figure 2-15. *Setting up a CVSROOT for code checkout*

Figure 2-16. *Selecting a particular code branch to check out*

Click OK. If you are lucky (or not doing this on a weekend), you will see the checkout begin as in Figure 2-17.

Figure 2-17. *TortoiseCVS status window during Ogre code checkout*

If you are unlucky, you may have to repeat this step several times before SourceForge CVS lets you connect (it is enormously congested on weekends). You can safely ignore anything you see about "try a real password" or "could not read file: 0", and simply try again. And again. And again. Or, do this checkout on a weekday or during the United States overnight hours, when the load is greatly reduced. Seriously, SourceForge CVS can be a real pain to access during weekend hours when everyone else in the world has the same idea as you; SourceForge hosts thousands of different open source projects across the entire spectrum of software classifications, and sometimes you may have to retry 20 or more times to get connected.

Once you have the Ogre source, obtain the precompiled Ogre Dependencies for source builds; these can be found on the Ogre site in the Downloads section, shown in Figure 2-18.

Figure 2-18. *Ogre Precompiled Dependencies download page*

Unpack them so that they create a Dependencies folder in your freshly minted ogrenew folder, as in Figure 2-19.

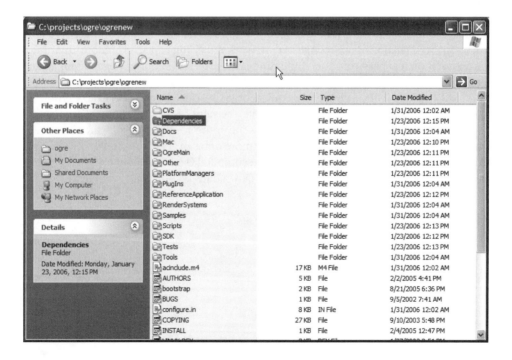

Figure 2-19. *Ogre source root folder after checkout*

As mentioned earlier, you will need to download and install the Microsoft DirectX SDK if you plan to build the Direct3D render system in Ogre. Yes, it is huge, and no, there is no way around it (other than to build only the OpenGL render system, which I do not recommend: give your users a choice). If you do this after installing Visual Studio, the DirectX installer will set up Visual Studio's directories for you; if you do this **before** installing Visual Studio (or are using Code::Blocks), then you need to point the IDE to where the DirectX libraries and headers live on your system.

Also, you should have the Cg Toolkit installed if you plan to build the **CgProgramManager** plug-in; if you do not plan to use this plug-in, then you should remove it from the solution or expect it to fail during build. Same for the **Direct3D9** plug-in; if you do not plan to use it, remove it from the solution prior to building.

Assuming you have all of the prerequisite SDKs installed, you are ready to build Ogre. In the ogrenew folder, look for the solution or workspace file for your IDE and version (.workspace for Code::Blocks, .sln for Visual C++, with the Visual C++ 2005 version marked with a _vc8 qualifier in the name). Double-click that file, and build the entire workspace or solution (see Figure 2-20), which should run to completion without errors. Any errors you encounter during building from source are, 99.995% of the time, the result of an incorrect configuration or missed step before the build, so retrace these instructions to make sure you didn't miss anything before asking for help in the online support venues. Try to run one of the Sample applications (demos) to make sure everything is in order; I suggest running the *Terrain* demo first before venturing into more complex demos. If you did not build the Cg plug-in, expect only the *Terrain* demo to work (the others likely will throw exceptions trying to access the missing plug-in). This is another reason you should just go ahead and install the Cg Toolkit; it will not give you cooties.

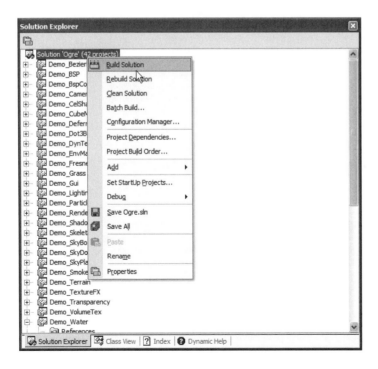

Figure 2-20. *Building the Ogre solution*

Conclusion

At this point, you are ready to use Ogre. "But," you are asking, "I don't know the first thing about it! Those demos look sweet, but I don't have a clue how Ogre does that."

In the next chapter, you will learn about the design and structure of Ogre itself, and how it both fits into and deals with the 3D rendering pipeline on your behalf, which will make writing Ogre-based applications a great deal easier.

CHAPTER 3

∎∎∎

Ogre Design Overview

A quick glance at the list of classes and methods provided by Ogre can quickly make your eyes cross. Luckily, you do not have to deal with Ogre on that basis. Ogre is an object-oriented class library, and its sophisticated hierarchical design allows you to deal with it on as simple or involved a basis as you need. It is possible to create a running Ogre-based application in a dozen lines of code or less, but you don't get to see much along the way, and you are restricted by several assumptions made on your behalf.

Design Philosophy

Ogre provides an object-oriented method of access to what inherently is procedural data processing: rendering simple geometric primitives to a render target (usually a screen buffer displayed on a CRT or LCD device). Traditionally, when using OpenGL or Direct3D to render your scenes and objects, you would follow a series of steps—procedural processing flow, in other words: set up render state with various API calls, send geometry information with various API calls, and tell the API and GPU to render your geometry with another API call. Lather, rinse, repeat until a frame is fully rendered, then start it all over for the next frame.

With an object-oriented approach to rendering geometry, the need to deal with geometry is removed entirely, and you can instead deal with your scene in terms of the objects that make up the scene: movable objects in the scene, static objects that make up the world geometry, lights, cameras, and so on. No 3D API calls needed; just place the objects in the scene, and Ogre takes care of the messy details. Furthermore, you get to manipulate the objects in your scene using far more intuitive methods than managing transformation matrices: it is simpler to instruct an object to rotate and translate in terms of degrees (or radians) and world units (with local-, world-, or parent-space qualifiers) than it is to try to work up the proper transformation matrix that makes all the rotations and translations happen. In short, you can deal with objects, their properties, and intuitive methods of manipulation instead of trying to manage them in terms of vertex lists and triangle lists and rotation matrices and so on.

Ogre provides an object-oriented framework that involves all parts of the rendering process in the object model. Render systems abstract the complexities of the underlying 3D APIs (OpenGL and Direct3D, for example) into a common interface to their functionality; scene graph functionality is abstracted into another interface that allows simple plug-and-play usage of different scene graph management algorithms; all renderable objects in a scene, whether movable or static, are abstracted by a common interface that encapsulates the actual rendering operations such as techniques and their contained passes; movable objects are represented in the scene by a common interface that allows robust methods of manipulation.

Design Highlights

For the experienced developer, the architecture of Ogre might be self-evident. For those new to object-oriented design, or new to software engineering in general, design decisions in Ogre might make a bit less sense. Let's go over some of the design features at a high level.

Intelligent Use of Common Design Patterns

Ogre makes good use of many useful and common design patterns. *Design pattern* simply refers to a common and well-tested solution for a particular type of software problem, and the name "design pattern" more or less was immortalized in the popular "Gang of Four" book, *Design Patterns: Elements of Reusable Object-Oriented Software*, by Gamma, Helm, Johnson, and Vlissides (Addison-Wesley, 1995).

Design patterns in Ogre are employed to enhance the usability and flexibility of the library. For example, Ogre is rather eager to inform the application of everything it does via the *Observer* pattern, in which client code registers to receive notifications of events or state changes within various parts of Ogre (such as the ubiquitous *FrameListener* in the Ogre demo applications, which is how the application is notified of frame-started and frame-ended events). The *Singleton* pattern is used to enforce the notion of a "single" instance of a class, and the *Iterator* pattern is used to walk the contents of a data structure. The *Visitor* pattern is used to enable operations to be performed on an object, without having to alter the object (for instance, all nodes in a scene graph). The *Façade* pattern is used to consolidate access to commonly used operations, implemented in many different subsystems, within a single class interface. And finally, the *Factory* (and cousin, *Abstract Factory*) are widely used for creation of concrete instances of abstract interfaces.

Scene Graph Decoupled from Scene Contents

The decision to decouple the scene graph from the scene contents was probably one of the most brilliant, yet underappreciated, design features in the entire Ogre project. This is such a simple design to understand, yet one of the hardest to comprehend for those used to more "traditional" scene graph designs.

Traditional designs (as used in many commercial and open source 3D engines) typically couple the scene contents and the scene graph in an inheritance hierarchy that forces the subclassing of content classes as types of scene nodes. This turns out to be an incredibly poor design decision in the long run, as it makes it virtually impossible to change graph algorithms later, without forcing a lot of code changes at the leaf-node level if the base node interfaces change at all (and they usually do). Furthermore, this "all nodes derive from a common node type" design is, in the long run, inherently inflexible and nonextensible (at least from a maintenance standpoint): functionality invariably is forced up the inheritance hierarchy to the root nodes, and myriad subclasses are required, and typically end up as minor adjustments to base functionality. This is, at the very least, a poor object-oriented design practice, and those who adopt this design philosophy almost always end up wishing they had done it a different way in the beginning.

Ogre did. First of all, Ogre operates on its scene graph(s) at an interface level; Ogre makes no assumption as to what sort of graph algorithm is implemented. Instead, Ogre operates on the scene graph only through its signature (its methods, in other words) and is completely ignorant of the underlying graph algorithm implementation. Second, Ogre's scene graph interface is concerned only with the graph structure. Nodes do not contain any inherent content access or management functionality. Instead, Ogre pushes that down into what it calls *renderable*, from which all bits of geometry in your scene (movable or otherwise) are derived. The rendering properties (also known as *materials*) for these renderables are contained in **Entity** objects, which in turn contain one or more **SubEntity** objects. These subentities are the actual renderable objects. See Figure 3-1 for a visual description of the relationship between the scene graph structure and contents. Note that even the scene nodes are attached to the scene graph; the scene graph does not manipulate the nodes' state directly.

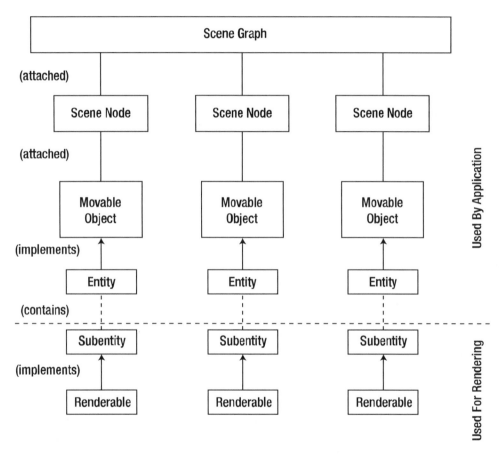

Figure 3-1. *Relationship between the scene graph structure and content management objects in Ogre*

All of this geometry and these rendering properties are made available to the scene graph via **MovableObject**. Instead of subclassing the movable object from a scene node, it is attached to the scene node. This means that scene nodes can exist without anything renderable actually attached to them, if your application has a need for that. It also means that extending, changing, refactoring, or otherwise altering the scene graph implementation has no impact on the design and implementation of the implementation and interface of the content objects; they are entirely independent of the scene graph. The scene graph interface can even change completely and the content classes would not be affected in the least.

The reverse is also true: the scene graph has no need to know about any changes to your content classes, so long as they implement a simple interface that the scene graph **does** know about. Ogre even allows you to attach arbitrary "user-defined" content to scene nodes, so if you want to carry around, say, audio cue information in your scene graph, you can do that as well. You do not need to subclass anything, you simply need to implement a very simple interface on your custom data object in order to attach it to the scene graph nodes.

This decoupling has turned out to be one of the best, yet sometimes most often misunderstood, design decisions in the history of the library.

Plug-In Architecture

Ogre is designed to be extensible. Contrary to many other rendering API designs, Ogre does not force any particular implementations on the user. Ogre accomplishes this through a *contract-based design*, which is a fancy way of saying that Ogre is designed as a set of cooperating components that communicate with each other through a known interface.

This allows incredible freedom in creating new or different implementations of various bits of functionality. For example, Ogre itself deals with its scene graph at an interface level, which means that the user is not limited to one or two choices of scene graph algorithm, choices made by the Ogre developers. Instead, scene graph implementations can be "plugged into" the Ogre library as needed, as discussed in the previous section. If a kd-tree implementation is required for a particular application, then it is simply a matter of creating a kd-tree scene graph that conforms to the interface defined by Ogre and making that scene graph plug-in available to Ogre (and therefore your application).

The same is true for all pluggable functionality: file archives and render systems are the most common forms of plug-in, but alternate functionalities such as the Ogre Particle system are also implemented as plug-ins.

One of the most attractive aspects of plug-ins is the fact that they do not require rebuilding of the Ogre library in order to be incorporated. Ogre provides a simple means of loading plug-in libraries at runtime and initializing them in order to expose their contained classes and functionality. Pluggable functionality supports a registration mechanism that allows an entirely code-free plug-in incorporation process. Each pluggable mechanism defines its own particular syntax or protocol for loading plug-ins at runtime, but typically it is simply a matter of telling Ogre "this is what I am called" or "this is what sort of resource I am here to handle" and providing a reference or pointer to the main class within the plug-in.

Hardware-Accelerated Renderer Support

Ogre is designed, on purpose, to support only hardware-accelerated graphics rendering. This means that Ogre requires a graphics coprocessor (such as those made by NVIDIA and ATI); direct software rendering is not an option. This design decision allows Ogre the freedom to work, in an optimized fashion, with *hardware buffers*, which are areas of memory shared between the graphics hardware and the application (Ogre).

This decision has a great impact on Ogre's capabilities. Since it is a hardware-based rendering API, it can take full advantage of all hardware acceleration capabilities, including programmable shaders. The integration between the programmable graphics pipeline and Ogre puts Ogre on the same level of capability as most commercial 3D rendering engines: since much of the "fancy" graphics processing in modern 3D applications and games is done via the programmable GPU pipeline, anything that, say, the Unreal Engine or CryENGINE can do, Ogre can do. The bits of additional functionality not present in Ogre (for example, direct engine support for advanced global illumination solutions such as Ambient Occlusion or Precomputed Radiance Transfer) still have to be done by the application. However, since computation of many advanced algorithms is still done "offline" at this time (not in real time, in other words), this is hardly a limiting factor.

Currently, Ogre offers two choices for render system support: Direct3D 9 and OpenGL. Given that there are no other hardware acceleration APIs of any consequence (on the platforms currently supported by Ogre), it is likely that for the foreseeable future, Direct3D and OpenGL will remain the only two render system options supported within Ogre.

Flexible Render Queue Architecture

Ogre's design takes a somewhat novel approach to the problem of ordering the rendering of various parts of a scene. The standard process (at a coarse, high level) typically works as follows: render terrain and/or world geometry, render movable objects, render effects, render overlays, then render backgrounds and/or skyboxes. However, as typically implemented (meaning, as a monolithic procedural block), this process is difficult to change if needed. For example, your application might need to render static world geometry in multiple "layers," interleaved with 3D scene objects, perhaps in a "fighting" game like Mortal Kombat or Street Fighter. Or perhaps you need to render various bits of geometry "out of order," so to speak, to create certain effects (such as with real-time shadowing algorithms). It is difficult in many cases to alter the order of rendering, or to effect "conditional rendering" directly in the main loop; the result is often a ton of hard-to-maintain special-case code and an inflexible design.

Ogre overcomes this inflexibility with the use of *render queues*. The concept is not hard to grasp: Ogre will render the contents of several ordered queues, one at a time, and will render the queues in order as well.

Figure 3-2 visually describes the render queue organization in Ogre. Queues themselves have an order, or *priority*, and objects within a queue have their own priority as well. For example, Ogre will render the set of queues in Figure 3-2 from back to front (from lower to higher priority, or order). Within each queue, Ogre will render in order as well. For example, in the Overlays queue in Figure 3-2, Ogre will render the HUD objects, and then the reticle objects, and then the UI menu objects, in that order.

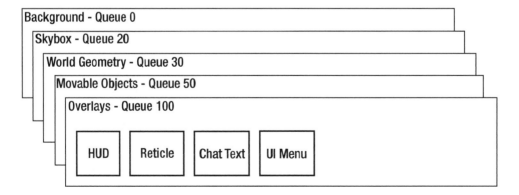

Figure 3-2. *Conceptual render queue organization in Ogre*

The flexibility of this design is in the fact that reorganizing rendering order is as simple as reassigning queue priorities. Render queues can be created at custom priorities, and the objects within any queue can be ordered at will as well. Entire queues can be turned on and off, and objects within a queue likewise can be turned on and off.

Finally, each queue provides notifications of events within the queue (such as prerender and postrender), so that the application has the opportunity to alter the rendering of the objects within the queue if needed. In terms of code development and maintenance, this is invaluable for the encapsulation of render queue management into small, easily understood chunks of code, as opposed to trying to figure out what bits of a huge monolithic procedural block are responsible for rendering which bits of the scene.

In other words, Ogre's render queue design provides an elegant object-oriented solution to what, in many complex applications, typically fast becomes an intractable and unmanageable problem.

Robust Material System

It is possible to create and render objects in a scene without ever touching a single line of code (beyond the obvious work involved in actually loading the objects in the first place). Ogre's material scripting system is one of the most flexible and powerful available in its class of software.

Ogre materials are composed of one or more *techniques*, which are simply collections of *passes*. *Pass* refers to a rendering pass, and is the unit of rendering at the material level within Ogre. In other words, a single pass on an object will result in exactly one *draw call* to the graphics hardware for the geometry being rendered. You can have as many passes in a technique as you like, but understand that in most cases, each pass will cause a completely new rendering operation (complete with full render state changes on the hardware for each pass). This has what should be obvious implications on performance, but in some cases there simply is no other way to create a particular rendering effect.

The most impressive feature of Ogre's material system is its *automatic fallback* design; Ogre can automatically apply the "best" technique available in a material, and will search "downwards" through the list of techniques until it finds one that is compatible with the graphics hardware being used. Ogre will also do its best to reorganize passes within a technique if the hardware cannot support even the least technically demanding technique in a material. For example, if a particular set of graphics hardware supports only a single texture unit in its fixed-function pipeline, and your least-complex technique requires a minimum of two texture units, then Ogre will break up the pass into two separate passes and blend the two renderings to achieve the same effect.

Ogre materials also support the notion of *schemes*. A material scheme can best be understood as support for the common "Ultra High, High, Medium, Low" graphics settings. In this case, you would define four schemes and assign material techniques to each as you see fit (each technique obviously would be developed to fit the particular scheme). Then you can limit Ogre's technique fallback search to stay within the techniques that belong to a particular scheme, making material management for your application that much easier.

You are not limited only to scripting for material management. All classes and methods that Ogre uses to create a material from the script are fully available to the application; you can create a material completely in code, procedurally, and in fact this is commonly done. The same material scheme feature and technique fallback processing are just as available to procedurally created materials as they are to scripted materials. Of course, with material scripting, no code changes are required (and in fact, material creation can be placed entirely in the hands of your artists, since material scripts typically are exported from 3D modeling packages along with mesh and animation data).

Native Optimized Geometry and Skeleton Format

Ogre utilizes a single format for its mesh and skeleton data. As a result, it does not have the ability to load third-party mesh formats, such as those used for character data in commercial games. Community-developed converters may exist for such items, but they are not part of the Ogre library.

Ogre uses this format to allow for fast, efficient loading of its mesh and skeleton data. This efficiency is enabled by the ability for Ogre to preoptimize the layout of the binary mesh and skeleton files in an exporter or offline tool (the command-line *OgreXMLConverter* tool, discussed in Appendix A). Of course, the classes used in the *OgreXMLConverter* tool are available for use in your application if you wish to employ them (for example, if you wish to export binary mesh data files directly from a 3D modeling package). One method of creating binary mesh and skeleton files is first to export your scene or character data from your 3D tool into an intermediate, human-readable XML format (Ogre XML), and then convert this data to binary format with the command-line tool. Exporters exist for most current modeling tools (both commercial and open source), such as Softimage|XSI, Autodesk 3D Studio Max and Maya, and Blender (as well as many others).

Along similar lines, the notion of loading raw XML at runtime is a performance nightmare. XML is an incredible format for exchanging data between disparate systems (which is exactly how it is used in Ogre: exchanging data between an arbitrary 3D modeling tool and the Ogre binary mesh and skeleton serializer), but it is a horrible format for any sort of performance-oriented application . . . which describes precisely the requirements of runtime asset loading. An additional bonus of the intermediate XML format is the ability to inspect or change the exported data. The inspection ability makes it much simpler to debug an exporter, as well as verify the structure and composition of an exported scene or object. Plus, you can easily insert additional tools into your asset pipeline if you wish; it often is easier to deal with the textual XML format for minor systematic tweaking than it is to work with a serialized binary file.

The optimization of the binary format is primarily in the ordering of vertex, geometry, and skeleton data, but the offline process also has other features, such as available automatic LoD (level of detail) and object tangent generation for the meshes. Performing these processes offline removes the need to perform them at runtime, enabling reduced load times.

Multiple Types of Animation

Ogre supports three types of animation: skeletal, morph, and pose.

Skeletal animation refers to the binding of vertices to bones in a skeleton (also known as *palette matrix skinning*, or just *skinning* for short). Each vertex in an object can have up to four independent bone influences. Each influence is assigned a weight along with its bone, so that when that bone moves, its influence on the position of the vertex is weighted by that amount. This is useful for realistic deformation of vertices, approximating, say, the effect that moving your arm might have on the shape of your shoulders (that is, how the muscles bunch up over your shoulder socket when you raise your arm). Skeletal animation is performed in keyframed *forward kinematic* mode only; Ogre does not support inverse kinematics (IK) at this time; if you modeled your animation using IK in a 3D tool, you must sample the positions of the bones at arbitrary intervals (a process known as *keyframing*). Typically, the Ogre exporter for your modeling tool does this for you.

Morph animation is a vertex animation technique that stores absolute vertex locations each keyframe, and interpolates between those positions at runtime. It differs from *pose animation* in that pose animation stores vertex offsets instead of absolute positions, and therefore multiple pose tracks in an animation can be blended to create complex vertex-based animations. Morph animation is far more limited than pose animation, as it cannot be blended with other morph animations due to the use of absolute vertex positions. Both types can be blended with skeletal animation.

All animation types can be performed in software or on the GPU hardware using a vertex program. For straight skeletal animation, the positions of the bones are passed to the vertex program in a separate block of program constants, along with the positions of the vertices and the blend weights and indices. Morph animations do not have overbearing data requirements when performed on the hardware; only a second vertex buffer is required to be passed to the vertex shader. For pose animations, the amount of data passed can be considerable, especially since each additional pose requires an additional vertex buffer be passed to the shader.

For the same reason that morph animations cannot be blended together, morph animation cannot be blended with pose animation, and vice versa. Both types of vertex animation can be blended with skeletal animation, however.

Ogre's animation system operates on the principle of *controllers*; that is, objects that manage a changing value as a function of another value (in the case of animations, that "other" value is time). As mentioned, Ogre's animation system is keyframed; it will interpolate between keys in an animation track on two selectable bases: linear or cubic spline. You should match the type of interpolation used in your application to the type used in the modeling/animation package, or compensate by using a higher sampling frequency in your exporter.

Compositor Postprocessing

A relatively new addition to the Ogre feature package is the *Compositor framework*, which allows the user the ability to create sophisticated two-dimensional, full-screen postprocessing effects on a viewport. For example, a viewport can be enhanced with a full-screen glow or bloom effect, or the viewport can be postprocessed into a black-and-white or sepia-toned rendering, or the viewport can be transformed into a line-art drawing with hard edges, and so on. Anything you can think of to do to a viewport can be done with the Compositor framework.

The framework operates on much the same principles as the material scripting system. Compositor *techniques* are, like with materials, different ways of achieving a particular effect. Compositor *passes* are similar to material passes in that multiple calculations and/or refinements can be done to a viewport before the final output is created. And like material fallbacks, the Compositor framework provides fallback handling for cases where a desired output pixel format is not available.

The easiest way to think of the Compositor framework in Ogre is as an extension of the fragment program (pixel shader) pipeline. In fact, the Compositor framework utilizes the fragment processing features of the graphics hardware to perform its processing; Compositor passes are defined in terms of fragment programs defined in material scripts. The difference is that while the conventional graphics pipeline only allows one fragment program per material pass, the Compositor framework will "ping-pong" pixel buffers back and forth as many times as needed to perform all of the passes required of the particular Compositor script. Granted, you could do this processing yourself and handle the management of the multiple pixel buffers needed to accomplish complex postprocessing effects, but with the introduction of the Compositor framework, there is no need.

Compositor scripts operate on viewports. As a result, they can target any render target, whether render textures or the main or secondary render windows. The final result is always drawn into a full-viewport quad overlay, whether or not geometry is rendered underneath the quad. As a result, you find yourself often rendering your geometry to offscreen buffers and displaying it in what essentially is a rendered texture applied to a quad.

As with the material system, you are not limited to scripting for Compositor effects: you can certainly create the effects entirely in code, using the same classes and methods that the Compositor parser uses. Also like materials, the Compositor supports material schemes the same way that materials do directly; in fact, schemes in the Compositor framework refer to material schemes.

Extensible Resource Management

Resources in Ogre are defined as "anything that is needed to render geometry to a render target." This obviously includes meshes, skeletons, and materials, but also includes overlay scripts and fonts, as well as ancillary material items such as Compositor scripts, GPU programs, and textures.

All of these types of resources have their own manager in Ogre. This manager is responsible primarily for controlling the amount of memory that a particular type of resource occupies in memory; that is, the resource manager controls a resource instance's lifetime. Actually, the resource manager controls this lifetime only to a point: first, it can only store as many instances of a particular resource type as there is memory allocated to that resource type (defined when the resource manager for that type starts up); second, Ogre will never remove from memory resources that are actively referenced by part of your application.

Resources themselves are actually responsible for loading themselves. This is to support a design feature of the resource system: manual resource loading. "Manual" refers to the fact that a resource is loaded, procedurally or otherwise, as a result of a method call on a class interface rather than an implicit load from the file system. Fonts and meshes are examples of manually loaded resources, as they typically require a bit of extra processing during load and initialization (compared to, say, a texture file that is already in its needed form when loaded from the file system).

A resource in Ogre can exist in one of four states at any given time. It can be *undefined* (which means Ogre knows nothing about it); it can be *declared*, which means the resource has been indexed in its archive, but that's about it; it can be *unloaded*, which means that the resource has been initialized (if it is a script, then the script was parsed) and a reference to it was created; or it can be *loaded*, which means that it actually occupies space in its resource manager's memory pool.

Ogre organizes its resources, at the highest level of management, into named *groups*. This is to facilitate the loading, unloading, creation, and initialization of resources in terms of a logically related collection. The relationship between the resources in a group is entirely up to you: they can be resources used in a particular game level; they can be all resources that are used to create your application's GUI; they can be all resources that begin with the letter *A*. A group's name and purposes really is completely arbitrary, entirely up to you and not in any way meaningful to Ogre (other than the name of the default "catch-all" resource group: General). When your application goes searching for a resource, Ogre can find it (if a reference to it has been created) regardless of the group in which it exists (if you tell Ogre to search all resource groups). This demarcation between groups is another useful feature of resource groups: you can use resource group names as a sort of "namespace" for same-named resources (if your application design needs this sort of thing).

Non–manually loaded resources in Ogre exist solely in *archives*. The archive in Ogre is simply an abstraction of a generic file container. The archive can be searched (using file name wildcards), both recursively and nonrecursively; it can return a reference to a file within itself; it can be opened and closed. Sounds a lot like a file system, doesn't it? As you might expect, the file system is just another type of archive to Ogre. The two types of archive that Ogre understands are the FileSystem and the Zip archive (the latter is a simple file in PKZIP format, compressed or otherwise). You can implement any type of archive you like. For instance, if your application uses a custom archive format for its assets, you can create an implementation of an Ogre archive that reads and manipulates this file format, to provide Ogre with access to the assets within it.

Ogre will index archives based on known file extensions, such as .material, .mesh, .overlay, and so on. Unknown file types are ignored, so you can mix Ogre- and non-Ogre-related resources in the same file if you like.

Subsystem Overview

The design highlights and philosophy outlined previously are implemented in numerous classes within the Ogre API. Luckily, you do not need to be familiar with all of them in order to be productive with Ogre. With basic knowledge of just a few bits of Ogre (and of course some available art assets), you can have a 3D application running in no time at all.

Let's briefly tour the most basic and common systems with which you will interact in a typical Ogre application. These systems and classes will be covered in more detail later in this book, but in the interests of fostering familiarity early in your experience with Ogre, I will introduce them here. You may see some things in this section that do not make immediate sense; that's OK, more specific coverage occurs in later chapters.

Root Object

The main point of access to an Ogre application is through the **Root** object. As pointed out earlier, this is a façade class, and it provides a convenient point of access to every subsystem in an Ogre application.

The **Root** object is the simplest way to fire up and shut down Ogre; constructing an instance of **Root** starts Ogre, and destructing it (either by letting it go out of scope or executing the delete operator on it) shuts down Ogre cleanly. For all objects whose lifetime Ogre is responsible, it will clean them up in an orderly fashion.

Resource Management

Anything that Ogre needs in order to render a scene is known as a *resource*, and all resources ultimately are managed by a single object: **ResourceGroupManager**. This object is responsible for locating resources (within search paths defined by the application to the manager) and initializing (but not necessarily loading) the known types of resources that it finds.

By default, Ogre recognizes the following types of resources:

- **Mesh**: Ogre supports a single binary mesh format, one that is optimized for fast loading and is generated typically by the **OgreXMLConverter** command-line tool provided with Ogre. While you can create your own geometry on the fly (or provide a manual mesh loader if you have reason to do so), typically these resources will exist on the file system, and must be named with a .mesh extension for Ogre to recognize them as mesh data. Mesh files also contain animation data for morph and pose animations.

- **Skeleton**: Skeleton resources typically are referenced within a .mesh file (but can be used by themselves if you need) and define the bone hierarchy and keyframe data used with skeletal animation. These files use a .skeleton extension and also are created typically by the **OgreXMLConverter** command-line tool.

- **Material**: Material script files define the render state used when rendering a batch of geometry. Material scripts are referenced by mesh data either in a .mesh file or manually using the Ogre renderable object methods. These scripts are output by a 3D modeling tool exporter, and Ogre recognizes them by their .material extension.

- **GPU program**: High-level GPU programs (HLSL, GLSL, Cg) are recognized by their .program extension. Low-level ASM programs are recognized by an .asm extension. Ogre will parse (but not compile) these files prior to parsing any .material files, so that the programs defined within the .program files are available before being referenced in a material.

- **Texture**: 2D texture data can exist in any format supported by Ogre (actually, by the OpenIL image library, which means an extremely wide variety of image formats). These files are recognized by their particular extensions.

- **Compositor**: Ogre's Compositor framework uses Compositor scripts the same way that the material system uses .material files; the difference is that Compositor scripts use the .compositor extension.

- **Font**: Ogre uses font definition files to define the fonts it uses in overlays. These files use a .fontdef extension.

Each of these types of resources has its own particular **ResourceManager** (for example, **MaterialManager**, **FontManager**, and so on), but unless you are writing new plug-ins or adding new types of resources to Ogre's resource management system, you will not need to deal with **ResourceManager** at all.

The **ResourceGroupManager** is responsible for finding your resources when you ask for them by name. It does not perform the actual memory management tasks required of an actual resource manager (such as unloading old resources to make room for new ones when needed); that is handled by the **ResourceManager** base class. The **ResourceGroupManager** instead allows you to load and unload groups of resources by their group name (such as unloading all **Font** resources to free up some memory).

By default, Ogre expects its resources to exist as disk files. However, certain types of resources can be manually managed; currently only the mesh and font resource types have manual resource loader implementations in Ogre, but if you have a need to create manual resource loaders for a particular type of resource, the framework is there to do so.

Scene Management

The scene graph design discussed earlier is part of a larger concept in Ogre known as the *scene manager*. All scene graph implementations are derivations of the **SceneManager** class. You will interact quite often with the active **SceneManager** in your application. Actually, you might interact with the active "scene managers," since Ogre supports multiple simultaneous active scene managers. However, the vast majority of applications will create and use only a single scene manager at a time.

Your scene manager is the source for your **SceneNode** objects. *Scene nodes* are the structural element in the Ogre scene graph design; they are what you actually move around in the scene. They can also be related hierarchically (you can have parent and child nodes, in other words); therefore you can translate them, scale them, and rotate them in world, parent, or local (object) space. Scene nodes can exist independent of the scene graph; one simple means of preventing the rendering of content in your scene is simply to detach a part of the scene graph hierarchy: the contents are unaffected, and you can reattach it at will.

Your content is, in turn, attached to these scene nodes. Almost all of your content will exist in the form of **Entity** instances, which are implementations of **MovableObject**, and also created by the scene manager. Once you have a valid entity, you can attach it to an existing scene node. An entity most often is loaded from disk, where it exists as a binary .mesh file. However, it is possible to create "manual" content objects, as well as procedural objects such as a movable plane (the only intrinsic procedural object supported currently in Ogre). Since your content is attached to a scene node, it is the node that is moved around the scene, and not the content.

You can also attach other noncontent objects to scene nodes. For example, you might have a reason to want to attach a camera to a scene node. You can also attach lights to scene nodes if you wish.

Render Systems and Render Targets

You typically will not need to interact directly with a render system. **RenderSystem** is a generalization of the interface between Ogre and the underlying hardware API (OpenGL or Direct3D). You will, however, likely interact, at least somewhat, with an object created by the render system: the **RenderTarget**. **RenderTarget** is a generalization of two important objects in Ogre: the render window and the render texture. The former is what nearly every Ogre application will use; render textures are a more specialized (yet still commonly used) object for performing more advanced rendering magic.

The render window in Ogre is your application's main window (among others; multiple render windows are supported). In some cases, the render window can be embedded within another window (useful for creating Ogre-based 3D tools), but in nearly all cases, if you want to see your scene rendered to the screen, you will need at least one render window. Exceptions to this rule would be applications that render to offscreen render targets and then display the results via another mechanism; this could be useful for a 3D tool that wanted a non–real time render preview using the 3D accelerated graphic pipeline.

The render window can be created automatically (the easy way) through the **Root** object façade, or more manually through **Root** or via **RenderSystem**. Manual creation obviously allows more customization of the render window properties, but not all applications need a great deal of customization; for those applications, automatic render window creation is more than enough.

Ogre Managers

A *manager* in Ogre is simply a class that manages access to or lifetimes of other related types of objects, hence the name. For example, the **ArchiveManager** in Ogre manages the creation and registry of **Archive** implementations, as well as access to registered **Archive** implementation instances. Each of the managers, including **Root** (which can be said to be a manager itself, the "Ogre Operations Center" if you will), exists as stand-alone "singleton" objects. One of the side-effects of the creation of **Root** is the initial instancing of all of Ogre's manager objects.

■**Note** The Singleton design pattern is commonly used for classes designed to have only a single existence throughout an application. For this reason, **Manager** classes are commonly implemented as singletons, since they typically are responsible for managing access to specific types of application data and resources. The Singleton pattern allows access to the **Manager** classes' single instance from anywhere in the global namespace of an application, a property often used to avoid having to pass around pointers to their instances, but mostly the Singleton pattern allows control over the lifetime of the class instance. Singletons are widely subclassed by Ogre managers.

I will give a brief description here of what each of those managers is responsible for managing. The more detailed discussion of each of these managers is what the rest of this book contains.

- **LogManager**: Sends logging messages to output streams for Ogre as well as for any code that wishes to use it.

- **ControllerManager**: Manages *controllers*, which are classes that produce state values for other classes based on various inputs; most commonly used for animating textures or materials.

- **DynLibManager**: Manages dynamic link libraries (DLLs on Windows, shared objects on Linux), which makes this class central to the plug in–based design of Ogre. Will also cleanly unload loaded libraries at shutdown.

- **PlatformManager**: Provides abstract access to details of the underlying hardware and operating system, such as timers and windowing system specifics (such as the Ogre configuration and error dialogs).

- **CompositorManager**: Provides access to, and management of, the Compositor framework, which in turn supports typical 2D composition and postprocessing tasks in screen space.

- **ArchiveManager**: Provides to the resource management system the correct type of class to handle file "containers" such as ZIP files or file system directories.

- **ParticleSystemManager**: Manages the details and implementations of various particle systems, emitters, and affectors.

- **MaterialManager**: Maintains all loaded **Material** instances in the application, allowing reuse of **Material** objects of the same name.

- **SkeletonManager**: Maintains all loaded **Skeleton** instances in the application, allowing reuse of **Skeleton** objects of the same name.

- **MeshManager**: Maintains all loaded **Mesh** instances in the application, allowing reuse of **Mesh** objects of the same name.

- **HighLevelGpuProgramManager**: Maintains, loads, and compiles all high-level GPU shader and vertex programs used in the application (i.e., GPU programs written in HLSL, GLSL, or Cg).

- **GpuProgramManager**: Maintains and loads low-level GPU programs (i.e., those written in assembler), as well as high-level GPU programs previously compiled down to assembler.

- **ExternalTextureSourceManager**: Manages external texture source class instances, such as those that implement video streaming.

- **FontManager**: Manages and loads defined and available fonts for use in Overlay text rendering.

- **ResourceGroupManager**: Serves as the main "point of contact" for loading and lifetime management of all registered application resources, such as mesh and material.

- **OverlayManager**: Manages loading and creation of 2D Overlay class instances, used typically for HUD, GUI, or other 2D content that is rendered on top of a scene.

- **HardwareBufferManager**: Manages lifetime of and access to shared hardware buffers (pixel buffers, vertex buffers, index buffers, and so on).

- **TextureManager**: Manages lifetime of and access to all textures referenced, loaded, and used in the application.

As you can see, there are few stones left unturned in the Ogre class design, and this is just the top-level class list. Each of these manager classes allows access to (or provides access to, in the case of custom implementations) dozens more classes that do the actual work in Ogre.

Conclusion

This chapter was not intended to cover everything about Ogre. At this point, you should be familiar with the most common Ogre objects, as well as have a passing familiarity with some of the less common ones as well. The rest of the book will cover each major area of Ogre functionality in much greater detail, but at least now you have a working base of knowledge about Ogre on which you can build as you work through the book.

If you just want to dive in and make graphics on the screen, you should carry straight on to the next chapter. However, if you are less reckless and want to get to know Ogre a bit better before becoming so intimate, you can skip Chapter 4 and come back to it when you are ready. Either way, it will be a fun ride!

CHAPTER 4

∎∎∎

Ogre First Steps

Now that you understand more about how Ogre 3D is designed and how the various parts work together, you are ready to begin writing actual programs that use the Ogre API. I will start you off easy, with a very basic bare-bones Ogre application, and work in more complicated topics as we go.

One of Ogre's best "selling points," if you will, is its flexibility. You have as much or as little control over the execution of your Ogre application as you care to exert. Ogre is rather adept at providing acceptable default behavior, and just as accommodating when you want to turn off the autopilot and grab the yoke yourself.

This chapter will cover the entire spectrum of execution patterns available to the Ogre programmer, from fully automatic to fully manual. Working source code is available for download from the book's web site, and will build and run out of the box. The code snippets in this chapter are provided to highlight points made in the text, but I will not be providing any complete source code listings in this book.

Ogre Initialization: Quick Start

The first thing you do in any Ogre application is create an instance of **Root**. You must do this before calling any other Ogre operations (except for altering **LogManager** settings as you will see). Ogre's **Root** constructor takes several optional string arguments, all of them file names.

```
Root *root = new Root();
Root *root = new Root("plugins.cfg");
Root *root = new Root("plugins.cfg", "ogre.cfg");
Root *root = new Root("plugins.cfg", "ogre.cfg", "ogre.log");
Root *root = new Root("", "");
```

All of the preceding will run just fine. The second-to-last line in the example contains the default file names for the **Root** constructor (these are the names that are assumed in the first line, with no parameters).

plugins.cfg

An Ogre *plug-in* is any code module (DLL or Linux .so file) that implements one of the Ogre plug-in interfaces, such as **SceneManager** or **RenderSystem**. plugins.cfg in the examples earlier contains the list of plug-ins that Ogre will load at startup, as well as their location (see Listing 4-1).

Listing 4-1. *Contents of the "Stock"* plugins.cfg *File That Is Included in the Ogre Source and SDK Distributions*

```
# Define plugin folder
PluginFolder=.

# Define plugins
Plugin=RenderSystem_Direct3D9
Plugin=RenderSystem_GL
Plugin=Plugin_ParticleFX
Plugin=Plugin_BSPSceneManager
Plugin=Plugin_OctreeSceneManager
Plugin=Plugin_CgProgramManager
```

Listing 4-1 is the stock plugins.cfg file that ships with the Ogre samples. If you choose to use a plug-in configuration file with your application, it will probably look a lot like this one. Of course, you do not have to call your plug-in configuration file "plugins.cfg"; you can call it whatever you like, and supply that file name to the **Root** constructor. If you do not supply an argument for this parameter, **Root** will look for a file called "plugins.cfg" in the same directory as the application and try to load whatever it finds in there. If you supply an empty argument ("", as I did in the fifth **Root** constructor example line earlier), then **Root** will not look for a plug-in configuration file at all, and you will have to load your plug-ins manually (as you will see later in the section "Ogre Initialization: Manual").

The PluginFolder directive tells Ogre where to look to find the plug-ins listed in the file. How this path is interpreted is entirely up to you: if you use an absolute path, it will look only in that directory for the plug-ins. If you use a relative specifier (i.e., a path that does not begin with / or \), then it will look in that path relative to the current working directory (usually the directory containing your application, or the directory containing the .vcproj file when running in the Microsoft Visual Studio debugger, for example). The PluginFolder specified in our example file tells Ogre to look for the plug-ins in the current working directory ("."). Note that Ogre will append a / or \ (depending on the operating system) to whatever is (or is not) in this setting, so leaving it blank will cause Ogre to look for your plug-ins in "/" or "\" (the root of the current drive on Windows, or the root directory on Linux). This setting is required if you use a plug-in configuration file; commenting out this line is identical to leaving its value empty (lines beginning with a # are treated as comments in Ogre config files). Finally, on Mac OS X, this setting is ignored since OS X looks in Resources/ for the plug-ins.

The remainder of the file contains the list of plug-ins you want Ogre to load. Notice how the extensions are left off; this is on purpose, and allows you to use the same configuration file on multiple platforms without having to sweat the details of file naming conventions (even though Linux is rather accommodating and does not care one way or another what extensions you give your files).

■**Caution** Also notice that no spaces are used on either side of the = in the file. Spaces in plug-in definition lines is a syntax error and will cause the plug-in **not** to be loaded.

The top two plug-ins listed previously are render system implementations; the rest are feature and scene manager plug-ins. You do not have to include all of these in your program; at the very least you need only a render system. If you plan to do anything beyond very simple scenes (and I mean **very** simple), you will want at least the **OctreeSceneManager** plug-in as well.

Ogre.cfg

Ogre provides a simple means of setting basic video rendering options via native GUI dialogs, such as the one in Figure 4-1.

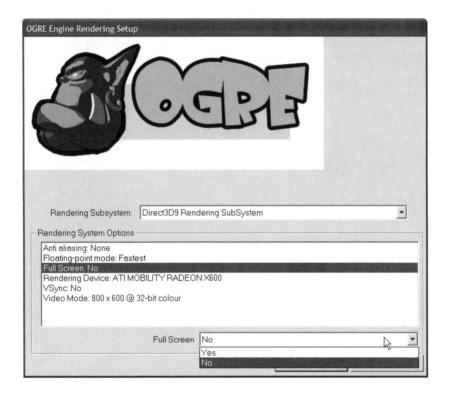

Figure 4-1. *Ogre Win32 configuration dialog*

I can hear you saying to yourself, "Neat, Ogre provides my application's setup dialog for me." Well, not quite. If you are doing only 3D graphics (for example, visualization) with no input, sound, or anything else that needs user configuration, then yes, it is probably sufficient to use Ogre's config dialog, and you can even customize it a bit (for example, if you want to use a different logo). However, you really cannot change much else about it; it is dedicated solely to managing Ogre settings, and nothing else. You should write your own configuration applet and use the manual initialization methods you will see later in this chapter.

But, let's say you want to use the Ogre configuration dialog. How to get it to show up?

```
Root *root = new Root();
bool rtn = root->showConfigDialog();
```

That's all there is to it. showConfigDialog() returns true or false depending on whether the user clicked the OK or Cancel button: true for OK, false for Cancel. You should really consider shutting down the application if the user clicks the Cancel button. Using the Ogre config dialog takes care of setting the selected render system along with all of the parameters that you can change in the dialog.

What does all of this have to do with Ogre.cfg? Well, this dialog is what generates that file. Of course, you can create one yourself by hand, and if you are using the more manual methods that you'll see later, you'll likely not even have one of these, but for now, let's look at what it contains (see Listing 4-2).

Listing 4-2. *Contents of a Sample* Ogre.cfg *File*

```
Render System=Direct3D9 Rendering Subsystem

[Direct3D9 Rendering Subsystem]
Allow NVPerfHUD=No
Anti aliasing=None
Floating-point mode=Fastest
Full Screen=No
Rendering Device=ATI MOBILITY RADEON X600
VSync=No
Video Mode=800 x 600 @ 32-bit colour

[OpenGL Rendering Subsystem]
Colour Depth=32
Display Frequency=60
FSAA=0
Full Screen=Yes
RTT Preferred Mode=FBO
VSync=No
Video Mode=1024 x 768
```

Note that these options correspond to the options available in the configuration dialog. Even though these are perfectly human-readable and intuitive, this file really is meant for machine consumption, and it's probably best, if you are using an Ogre.cfg file, to let the configuration dialog handle loading this file in case the format changes. Case is important, so it's easy to screw something up editing this file by hand, and not easily know why.

Ogre also provides a method to load an existing Ogre.cfg configuration file:

```
if (!root->restoreConfig())
    root->showConfigDialog();
```

This is a very common sequence when using the Ogre.cfg method. If the restoreConfig() call fails, then no Ogre.cfg file exists, and the application shows the Ogre configuration dialog to obtain user preferences (and save them to an Ogre.cfg file when the user clicks OK). In this way, you can avoid forcing users to see this dialog every time they run your app.

You can also save the current state of Ogre to Ogre.cfg (or whatever name you supplied when you called the **Root** constructor) at any time you wish, with the saveConfig() call:

```
root->saveConfig();
```

Ogre.log

Ogre provides diagnostic and exception logging facilities using its log management classes. This is useful for obtaining details about a crash on a client machine without having to ask users technical details about their setup. The log output that Ogre generates contains all events and system initialization, state, and capabilities information from each run of the Ogre-based program. This output is sent to a disk file; while you can change the name of this file, you cannot provide an empty value to the third **Root** constructor parameter (unless you have already created the log directly by calling LogManager::createLog(), as in Listing 4-3, prior to creating your **Root** instance). You simply are required to have an Ogre log file, regardless of its name.

Listing 4-3. *Creating a Log Manager Instance, the Custom Way*

```
// create an instance of LogManager prior to using LogManager::getSingleton()
LogManager* logMgr = new LogManager;
Log *log = LogManager::getSingleton().createLog("mylog.log", true, true, false);

// third param is not used since we already created a log in the previous step
Root *root = new Root("", "");
```

This code will direct Ogre to create a custom log file named mylog.log. This is the preferred method (only method, actually) of customizing your log output, if you need to alter more logging options than just the output file name. The second parameter tells Ogre to make this the default log file. The third tells Ogre to send messages to std::cerr as well as the log file, and the fourth tells Ogre **not** to suppress file output (write to the custom log file as normal, in other words). If you do not do any of this, and either do not supply this parameter to the **Root** constructor (which causes Ogre to default to Ogre.log) or supply an alternate file name for the log file, Ogre will send all logged data to this file as the default data logging location.

The Ogre **Log** and **LogManager** classes do not support alternate stream types. However, you can register a *log listener* with the Ogre **LogManager** class and redirect the log data any way you like. If you want no file output at all, you can direct the custom log to suppress output, but Ogre must have a log data destination.

■**Note** There is another way to suppress log files entirely, and that is by simply not calling createLog() after instancing **LogManager** prior to instancing **Root**. Since the log messages will not have anywhere to go by default, they are lost. This practice as default behavior, however, is **highly discouraged**, because if something goes wrong in your application, it becomes very difficult to figure out what happened without logging. Granted, you can walk the user through running your app with custom logging command-line options if you want, but unless you have a very good reason to suppress the log entirely, then don't.

Listing 4-4 will intercept log messages and allow you to deal with them as you see fit in the body of the write() callback method.

Listing 4-4. *Intercepting Ogre Logging*

```
class MyLogListener : public LogListener
{
public:
    void write (const String& name, const String& message,
    LogMessageLevel level, bool maskDebug)
{
    // redirect log output here as needed
};

MyLogListener *myListener = new MyLogListener;

// this is the same as calling LogManager::getSingletonPtr() after the
// LogManager has first been instanced; the same pointer value is returned
LogManager *logMgr = new LogManager;

LogMgr->addListener(myListener);
logMgr->createLog("mylog.log", true, false, true);
logMgr->setLogDetail(LL_NORMAL);

Root *root = new Root("", "", "mylog.log");
```

Notice that we changed the last parameter to the createLog() method to true; this will disable file output to the named log file, freeing you up to handle the log data as you see fit (send it to a debugging window, network stream, etc.). Since we turned off writing to std::cerr by setting the third parameter to false, the user should see no log messages anywhere, other than the messages you log in your write() method. We set the logging detail level to "normal"; other options are LL_LOW (very little detail) and LL_BOREME (probably way too much detail, but useful for particularly tricky debugging).

Render Window

At any point after a render system has been selected (in the current example, that would be when the user selects and configures a render system in the config dialog and clicks the OK button), you can call the **Root** initialise() method:

```
root->initialise(true, "My Render Window");
RenderWindow *window = root->getAutoCreatedWindow();
```

The first line will instruct **Root** to complete its initialization and create a render window with the settings the user selected in the config dialog and "My Render Window" for its title. If you do not supply a window title, it defaults to "OGRE Render Window." The first parameter, which is required, tells Ogre whether it should automatically create a render window; for the sake of this section, we take the easy road and tell Ogre to create our render window for us. The second line obtains a pointer to that **RenderWindow** instance.

The render window is only part of rendering your scene. It is the canvas, the surface onto which Ogre renders your content. Ogre needs at least one camera to "take pictures" of your scene, and one or more viewports, which are regions on a rendering surface (such as a render window) into which the camera places its contents.

You will learn more about the Ogre scene manager classes later in this chapter in the section "Scene Manager"; for now, it is sufficient to know that the scene manager API acts as a "factory" for many different types of objects that exist in your scene, including cameras. In order to obtain a new camera for rendering your scene, you call the createCamera() method on the **SceneManager** interface:

```
Camera *cam = sceneMgr->createCamera("MainCamera");
cam->setNearClipDistance(5);
cam->setFarClipDistance(1000);
cam->setAspectRatio(Real(1.333333));
```

In this example, sceneMgr is a pointer to an existing instance of **SceneManager**. **Camera** has many properties that can be adjusted and methods to adjust them.

The preceding code demonstrates the basics you will need for a minimal Ogre application. It sets the aspect ratio equivalent to a 4:3 display setup (that of most CRTs and nonwidescreen LCD displays). This value can be set or reset at any time, and usually is set to the ratio of the viewport's width to its height (as we did here, since 4/3 is nearly equal to 1.33333).

This code also sets the near and far clip plane distances. I used my standard outdoor settings of 5 and 1000 units, but you can use whatever you like, so long as the ratio between the far and near is in the neighborhood of 1000, or less.

■**Tip** A popular misconception is that clip planes are a cheap method to reduce the amount of "stuff" that a card has to render. While this certainly is a side effect of clip distance selection (and most modern cards support infinite far clip planes anyway), the primary reason for a particular set of clip plane distances is to maintain optimal depth buffer resolution. The depth buffer resolution is a direct function of the ratio between the far and near clip distances, and selecting distances that result in too coarse a resolution will invariably result in *depth fighting*. This phenomenon occurs when the depth-sorting algorithm on the GPU cannot tell which objects are "in front of" other objects. You end up with bits of objects that are at relative equivalent depths in the scene, rendering "through" each other. This occurs because the depth resolution is low enough that objects at slightly different depths were assigned the same depth value. The only solution in this case is to increase the depth precision, typically by altering the near plane distances (which give much more bang for your precision buck compared to altering the far clip distances). Google "depth fighting" for more.

Later in this chapter, you will see how to manipulate the Ogre **Camera** in more advanced ways, but for now, this is sufficient for the purposes of creating a viewport in our rendering window.

```
Viewport *vp = window->addViewport(camera);
vp->setBackgroundColour(ColourValue(0, 0, 0));
```

This code creates a new viewport in the render window we created when we called the initialise() method earlier on **Root**. It also sets the background color of the viewport to black.

Render Loop

The simplest way to set Ogre about the task of rendering your scene is to invoke the startRendering() method on **Root**:

```
root->startRendering();
```

This will cause Ogre to render endlessly whatever renderable content you have in your scene. It exits either when the render window is closed using the normal windowing system means (for example, clicking the small x button in the upper-right corner of a Windows app or closing it from the taskbar), or when a registered *frame listener* returns false. An alternate method of ending the rendering loop is to call Root::getSingleton().queueEndRendering() anywhere in your code, but typically you will just return false from your frame listener when you are using the startRendering() method.

Frame Listener

Frame listeners are the only way you can invoke your own code during the Ogre render loop when using the startRendering() method. A frame listener is simply a class that implements the **FrameListener** interface, and is just a callback that allows Ogre to invoke your code at the beginning and/or end of each frame (see Listing 4-5).

Listing 4-5. *Creating and Adding a Frame Listener to the Ogre **Root***

```
class myFrameListener : public FrameListener {
public:
    bool frameStarted (const FrameEvent &evt);
    bool frameEnded (const FrameEvent &evt);
};

bool myFrameListener::frameStarted(const FrameEvent &evt) {

    // really cool stuff to do before a frame is rendered
    return true;
}

bool myFrameListener::frameEnded(const FrameEvent &evt) {

    // really cool stuff to do after a frame is rendered
    return true;
}

Root *root = new Root();
MyFrameListener myListener;

// YOU HAVE TO ADD A FRAMELISTENER BEFORE YOU CALL startRendering()!!!
root->addFrameListener(myListener);
root->startRendering();
```

The implementation of the frameStarted() method in Listing 4-5 will be called before Ogre invokes the rendering pipeline. The frameEnded() method is less often used, and is useful if you need to clean up after your app each frame. It likewise is called after Ogre completes the rendering process each frame.

Typically during each frame, you process HID (Human Interface Device, such as keyboard, mouse, or joystick) input events. Depending on the particular event, you might cause a model in your scene to move and/or rotate, cause a camera to move or rotate, start a process for a player-character to put a sleeping hex on an NPC troll for 10 exp, or whatever. Regardless of what it is, it occurs during one or both of the **FrameListener** callback methods—usually during frameStarted(), because more than likely you will process changes to the scene **before** the scene is rendered, rather than after.

I have put together a very simple working application that implements the concepts you have learned so far; you can find it with this book's source, downloadable from the Apress web site's Source Code section; it appears in the QuickStart project in the CH04 solution. It has just about the bare minimum functionality. The frame listener I have implemented simply counts the elapsed time until 15 seconds have passed, then exits the application gracefully. Pretty boring, but a fantastic way to ensure you have your build environment set up correctly.

Ogre Initialization: Manual

In this section, I will walk you through all of the steps needed to set up an Ogre application without using any of the automatic, "behind the scenes" features at all. You will also learn how to write your own main loop that invokes Ogre's frame rendering.

I will go over, in more detail, each of the main Ogre subsystems involved in initializing and starting up Ogre, and outline by example your options for each step of the process.

Root

In the previous section, you learned that a great deal of functionality is invoked on your behalf when you supply the **Root** constructor with the names of config files that contain the plug-ins and render settings you wish to use for your application. You also saw the easy way to create a render window in Ogre, and the most basic way of running a loop to render to that window. All of this functionality is available through **Root**, and as you will find out, so is the manual way.

"Manual" simply means that you take complete control over particular aspects of the Ogre initialization process. You don't have to do everything manually; for example, you can still run an automatic render loop with an automatically created window, but with manual render system selection and setup (common in games that provide a GUI for video settings or options). In this section, you will see how to do all parts manually, and which various options exist for each part.

plugins.cfg

Loading plug-ins is probably the most straightforward part of initializing Ogre, so we will start here. **Root** provides two methods to deal manually with plug-ins:

```
void loadPlugin(const String& pluginName);
void unloadPlugin(const String& pluginName);
```

The first method, not surprisingly, loads the named plug-in. The second likewise unloads the named plug-in. The name used is the actual file name of the plug-in; for example, "Plugin_ParticleFX". Note that it is not required to provide an extension when supplying a plug-in name. Ogre will detect "missing" extensions and append the proper extension for the platform (.dll on Windows and .so on Mac OS X and Linux). You may supply an extension, of course, but then you are making your application platform-specific (Ogre will not strip extensions and append the proper one if the extension is incongruent with the platform). Moral of the story: be easy on yourself and let Ogre handle the housekeeping.

Paths to the plug-ins follow the path searching rules of the particular platform, since Ogre uses the platform-specific dynamic library loader APIs on each platform (LoadLibrary() on Windows, dlopen() on Mac OS X and Linux). Typically, the directory containing the executable is searched first, then the path defined in the system PATH environment variable, and then (on Linux) the LD_LIBRARY_PATH environment variable.

By default, Ogre does not name differently the Debug and Release builds of its plug-ins; this is a very common source of confusion, and the main culprit for the infamous "ms_singleton" assert encountered when mixing Debug and Release versions of the same DLL/.so.

■Tip The "ms_singleton" assert occurs when your application loads a Debug and Release version of the same DLL at execution time. The reason is the nature of the singleton implementation in Ogre. Ogre creates the one-and-only single instance of each of its singleton classes in the **Root** constructor and access to them is via static member methods. This is all fine and good until your app loads the "opposite" DLL type at run-time, usually because of a plug-in mismatch (Debug plug-ins into a Release app or vice versa). This plug-in will in turn have been linked against the "opposite" OgreMain library, and when they are loaded, the operating system will load that opposite OgreMain library. The next time one of the singleton classes residing in OgreMain is called, the new singleton will try to create an instance of itself, detect that an instance already exists, and BANG! . . . instant assert.

The simplest way to avoid Debug/Release clashes is to name your plug-ins accordingly; the naming standard within Ogre is to append a "_d" to the file name, as in OgreMain_d.dll. This would also require #if defined statements in your code to allow conditional builds, as in

```
Root *root = new Root;

#if defined(_DEBUG)
    root->loadPlugin("Plugin_ParticleFX_d.dll");
#else
    root->loadPlugin("Plugin_ParticleFX.dll");
#endif
```

This is a small price to pay to avoid the time (and hair loss) involved in trying to figure out which of your plug-ins is responsible for the "ms_singleton" assert. Of course, if you never use Debug builds, then you won't have this problem . . . but if you don't use the debugger, then you probably are not reading this anyway, opting instead to spend copious amounts of time staring at your code, trying to figure out (presumably using the Vulcan mind-meld) why it doesn't work. Use the debugger; that's why it's there.

You do not need to unload plug-ins. **Root** will clean up after itself rather nicely, and releasing and unloading the plug-ins is one of those cleanup activities. Of course, you may wish to unload a plug-in early in order to shut down gracefully other parts of your application, but calling `delete root` will work just fine.

Ogre comes with several plug-ins:

- **Plugin_OctreeSceneManager**: Octree-based scene graph and manager. Also contains the **TerrainSceneManager**, which is a derivative of the **OctreeSceneManager** (OSM) optimized for dealing with heightmapped terrain scenes.

- **Plugin_BSPSceneManager**: Reference implementation of a BSP scene manager for loading and dealing with Quake 3–level files. Growing more obsolete by the day, and is not regularly maintained or supported (provided as a demo reference only).

- **Plugin_CgProgramManager**: Plug-in provided for loading, parsing, compiling, and managing GPU shader programs written in Cg. As Cg falls farther and farther behind the technology curve (it supports only shader profiles less than 3.0), it becomes less useful overall; Ogre can deal with HLSL and GLSL programs internally.

- **Plugin_ParticleFX**: Particle system plug-in; provides several affectors and emitters for most common particle effects.

- **RenderSystem_Direct3D9**: Abstraction layer providing access to the native Direct3D 9 API on Windows.

- **RenderSystem_GL**: Abstraction layer providing access to the OpenGL API on all platforms.

We will go further into the **OctreeSceneManager** plug-in when we discuss Ogre scene management, and we will dive into the **ParticleFX** plug-in when we deal with the more advanced topics later in the book. As mentioned, the other two exist increasingly more for reference than actual use (though both of them work quite well), and we won't discuss them much more in this book.

You may find it odd to see the render systems included with the plug-ins. They are, however, just that: plug-ins. True to the Ogre design, they implement an abstract API and are "plugged into" Ogre using the same mechanism as all of the other plug-ins.

Render Systems

Ogre needs to have a render system loaded in order for it to be available for use. You do this with the same `loadPlugin()` API you already saw:

```
// create a new Root without config files
Root *root = new Root("", "");

root->loadPlugin("RenderSystem_Direct3D9");
root->loadPlugin("RenderSystem_GL");
```

This will load and make available both of the supported render systems (assuming the proper hardware drivers are installed and operational). **Root** provides a means to find out which render systems are loaded and available, via the `getAvailableRenderers()` method:

```
RenderSystemList* getAvailableRenderers(void);
```

Root also provides several other methods for obtaining information about and manipulating the render system list:

```
void addRenderSystem(RenderSystem* newRend);
RenderSystem* getRenderSystemByName(const String& name);
void setRenderSystem(RenderSystem* system);
RenderSystem* getRenderSystem(void);
```

Typically you will only use the setRenderSystem() method in conjunction with the getAvailableRenderers() method, to instruct Ogre to use a render system, usually as a result of a user's choice (see Listing 4-6).

Listing 4-6. *Setting the Render System to Use in an Ogre Application*

```
// RenderSystemList is a std::vector
RenderSystemList *rlist = root->getAvailableRenderers();
RenderSystemList::iterator it = rList->begin();

while (it != rList->end()) {

    // Ogre strings are typedefs of std::string
    RenderSystem *rSys = *(it++);
    if (rSys->getName().find("OpenGL")) {

        // set the OpenGL render system for use
        root->setRenderSystem(rSys);
        break;
    }
}
// note that if OpenGL wasn't found, we haven't set a render system yet! This
// will cause an exception in Ogre's startup.
```

The code in Listing 4-6 will look for the OpenGL render system in the list of available render systems, and set it if it exists. Like the warning says at the end of the listing, this code will cause an exception within the initialise() method of **Root** if no render system has been set, so treat this example as just that: an example. Most likely what you will do is populate a drop-down menu in your application's GUI with the names of the available render systems as provided by getAvailableRenderers(), and then call setRenderSystem() with the user's selection.

addRenderSystem() typically should only be called from a plug-in initialization function, unless the render system implementation comes from another source (such as a custom application logic loading system). getRenderSystemByName() is useful for quick detection of installed render systems, and returns NULL if the named render system has not been loaded. Keep in mind that spelling and case sensitivity are paramount when accessing render systems by name. As of this writing, the proper spellings and case for the two provided render systems are "Direct3D9 Rendering Subsystem" and "OpenGL Rendering Subsystem." Finally, getRenderSystem() simply returns the active render system, or NULL if no render system is active.

Render Window

The main reason you would want to create your application's render window(s) manually is closer management of both the creation parameters and the point at which the window is created. One common reason for creating your render window manually is to embed it in an alternate windowing toolkit or system (such as the Qt or wxWidgets cross-platform windowing libraries), e.g., for use in a level or map editor application. You may also wish to supply different or additional parameters to the window, even if you are using the Ogre configuration dialog to allow the user to select some of the video options.

The first thing to know is that when manually creating a render window, the method that is used is on the **RenderSystem** class selected earlier, not on **Root**. Also, you may create your render window(s) at any time once you have a pointer to a valid **RenderSystem** instance. As you can see from the code in the "Ogre Initialization: Quick Start" section, you will need to have a **RenderWindow** pointer in order to create a viewport, but when you are manually creating the render window, the call to initialise() on **Root** can be done at any time. The call to initialise() will initialize the plug-ins you have specified, so if you have special startup sequence needs pertaining to plug-ins and your application's render window(s), you can deal with the two separately (see Listing 4-7).

Listing 4-7. *Basic Manual Ogre Application Setup Steps*

```
#include "Ogre.h"

// create a new Root without config files
Root *root = new Root("", "");

// load the render system plug-ins
root->loadPlugin("RenderSystem_Direct3D9");
root->loadPlugin("RenderSystem_GL");

// pretend the user used some other mechanism to select the
// OpenGL renderer
String rName("OpenGL Rendering Subsystem");
RenderSystemList *rList = root->getAvailableRenderers();
RenderSystemList::iterator it = rList->begin();
RenderSystem *rSys = 0;

while (it != rList->end()) {

    rSys = *(it++);
    if (rSys->getName() == rName) {

        // set this renderer and break out
        root->setRenderSystem(rSys);
        break;
    }
}
```

```
// end gracelessly if the preferred renderer is not available
if (root->getRenderSystem() == NULL) {

    delete root;
    return -1;
}

// We can initialize Root here if we want. "false" tells Root NOT to create
// a render window for us.
root->initialise(false);

// set up the render window with all default params
RenderWindow *window = rSys->createRenderWindow(
    "Manual Ogre Window",  // window name
    800,                   // window width, in pixels
    600,                   // window height, in pixels
    false,                 // fullscreen or not
    0);                    // use defaults for all other values

// from here you can set up your camera and viewports as normal
```

We have not done anything very earth-shattering in Listing 4-7; we supplied the render window creation call with values that likely would be derived from some other programmatic source (such as your game's video options configuration UI). Understand that the window *name* is the same as the window *title* (as it appears in the window's title bar and windowing system widgets) if it is not overridden in the list of parameter values that is optionally provided during this call.

■**Note** The **RenderWindow** class is derived from the more general **RenderTarget** class, which implements the generalized notion of a *rendering surface*, useful when dealing with non-frame-buffer render targets such as textures. All **RenderTarget** instances are accessible via the name given them at their creation (a pattern used throughout Ogre, as you'll see), and the first parameter of the `createRenderWindow()` call is that name.

In this example, we accepted the defaults for all other parameters that the render window understands. You can see a full description of those parameters in the online API reference, or in the `OgreRenderSystem.h` header file in the SDK or the full source (in all of which I suggest looking first, as the list of options is always subject to change, and what I mention here will surely be outdated shortly after publication).

Let's say that we wanted to put the render window in the upper-left corner of the screen, and use a different string for the render window title than we used for the render window name. For this I introduce you to Ogre's **NameValuePairList** class, which is simply a typedef of the STL **map** class. The last parameter of the `createRenderWindow()` call takes a pointer to an instance of this class. This instance should be populated only with the parameters you want to change; all "missing" parameters will assume default values.

```
NameValuePairList params;
params["left"] = "0";
params["top"] = 0;
params["title"] = "Alternate Window Title";

RenderWindow *window = rSys->createRenderWindow(
    "MainWindow",    // RenderTarget name
    800,             // window width, in pixels
    600,             // window height, in pixels
    false,           // windowed mode
    &params);        // supply the param values set above
```

This code will create a render window named "MainWindow" that sets up in the upper-left corner of the screen, with the title "Alternate Window Title."

At this time, Ogre has no elegant method of reinitializing a render window or render system. For example, if your user wishes to switch from Direct3D rendering to OpenGL rendering while your application is running, obviously you would have to shut down the D3D renderer and initialize the OpenGL renderer. Less obvious is that you have to do this for the render window as well. You can adjust the size of the window (height and width) and move it around the screen, but the only way to change other settings (such as FSAA or full screen) is to destroy the existing window and create a new one.

As mentioned earlier, you may have multiple render windows open and running. This is often useful for tools such as level editors that provide multiple views of your scene. This is different from multiple viewports in that viewports are contained fully within a render window, while render windows are top-level windows.

You may also embed Ogre render windows inside windows of most window and widget systems (such as Qt and wxWidgets). The getCustomAttribute() method on **RenderWindow** enables you to obtain the system-dependent window handle for the render window. You can also supply Ogre with the parent window you would like to use for embedding the Ogre render window. For example:

```
// hWnd is a handle to an existing Win32 window
// renderSystem points to an existing, initialized instance of D3D9RenderSystem

NameValuePairList opts;
opts["parentWindowHandle"] = StringConverter::toString(hWnd);

// everything but "opts" is somewhat irrelevant in the context of an
// explicitly parented window
RenderWindow *window = renderSystem->createRenderWindow(
    "WindowName",
    800, 600,
    false, &opts);
```

This code will allow you to embed the Ogre render window in an existing windowing system window of your choice. Keep in mind that when you do this, the Ogre window message processing functionality is bypassed, and you have to take care of cleaning up the Ogre render window when the user clicks the Close button, etc., things that otherwise are done for you by Ogre.

Camera and SceneManager

I have refrained thus far from talking too much about these two classes, using just enough of their functionality to demonstrate other classes. However, these two classes actually are responsible for rendering your scene.

Scene Manager

I want to avoid getting too deep into the topic of the scene manager in Ogre, since it is covered in far greater detail in the next chapter. However, for purposes of completeness in this chapter (since I have mentioned it so many times), I figured that you should know at least the basics of creating a scene manager for use in your application.

Before you can use a scene manager instance, you must create one.

```
SceneManager* sceneMgr = root->createSceneManager(ST_GENERIC, "MySceneManager");
```

When Ogre loads its plug-ins, among those plug-ins can be various scene manager implementations, as discussed previously. Each of these implementations will register itself as a particular type of scene manager:

- ST_GENERIC: Minimal scene manager implementation, not optimized for any particular scene content or structure. Most useful for minimally complex scenes (such as the GUI phases of an application).

- ST_INTERIOR: Scene manager implementation optimized for rendering interior, close-quarter, potentially high-density scenes.

- ST_EXTERIOR_CLOSE: Scene manager implementation optimized for rendering outdoor scenes with near-to-medium visibility, such as those based on tiled single-page terrain mesh or heightfield.

- ST_EXTERIOR_FAR: Anachronism in Ogre, typically no longer used. Use ST_EXTERIOR_CLOSE or ST_EXTERIOR_REAL_FAR instead.

- ST_EXTERIOR_REAL_FAR: Scene manager implementation typically suited for paged landscape or paged scene construction. Paged landscapes often are huge, possibly entire planets.

In the preceding example we created a scene manager instance of the ST_GENERIC type. If we were loading a Quake 3 level using the **BSPSceneManager** plug-in (which registers as ST_INTERIOR), we would use the ST_INTERIOR scene type, and if we wanted to create a terrain heightfield-based scene using the **TerrainSceneManager** (TSM) plug-in, we would have created a scene manager of type ST_EXTERIOR_CLOSE (since that is what how the **TerrainSceneManager** registers itself). ST_GENERIC has no particular plug-in for its scene management, but if the **OctreeSceneManager** is loaded, it will take over ST_GENERIC duties.

Camera

A **Camera** is the same as its real-world analog: it "takes a picture" of your scene each frame, from a particular vantage point (meaning it has a position and an orientation). It is not typically a renderable object, so even if you have one camera in the field of view of another, the camera object will not render (if you're used to seeing a frustum representation of a camera in a 3D modeling tool, you know what I mean). Cameras (like lights, as you also will find out later) can either be attached to scene nodes (and therefore be "animate-able" via an animation controller) or exist in free space (which means you get to move them around manually if you want their position and/or orientation changed each frame). As mentioned, cameras have a "field of view" with near and far clip planes. This complete geometry defines what is known as a *frustum*, which is a sort of pyramid with the point chopped off, as depicted in Figure 4-2.

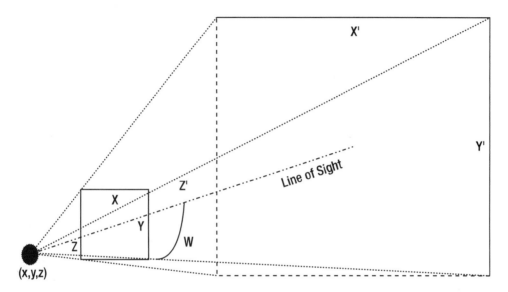

Figure 4-2. *Camera frustum*

In this figure, (x,y,z) indicates the location of the camera. X and Y are the size of the near clip plane, and are a function of the distance Z from the camera to the near clip plane. X' and Y' are the size of the far clip plane, and are a function of the distance (Z+Z') from the camera to the far clip plane. You supply the near and far clip plane distances, the aspect ratio of the camera (defined as X/Y), and the vertical angle W between the line of sight and the lower (or upper) frustum bounding plane (this is the field-of-view Y angle), and the **Camera** class calculates the horizontal angle and the size of the near and far planes.

Let's say you want to have a camera with the standard 4:3 aspect ratio, with near clip plane distance 5 units from the camera and far clip plane distance 1000 units, with a 30-degree angle between the line of sight and the lower (and upper) frustum bounding planes (W in Figure 4-2 is 30°, in other words). The following code creates a camera with these characteristics:

```
// sceneMgr is an existing instance of a SceneManager implementation. We are
// creating a camera named "MainCam" here.
Camera *camera = sceneMgr->createCamera("MainCam");

// normally you would calculate this from the size of the viewport
camera->setAspectRatio(1.33333f);

// 30 degrees will give more of a long, telescopic view
camera->setFOVy(30.0f);
```

```
camera->setNearClipDistance(5.0f);
camera->setFarClipDistance(1000.0f);
```

The view frustum defined by the camera settings defines the six clipping planes outside of which polygons are culled (discarded from the list of polygons to render for a given frame).

Rendering Modes

The **Camera** can render in one of three different modes: wireframe, solid, or "points" (only the vertices are rendered).

```
camera->setPolygonMode(PM_WIREFRAME);
camera->setPolygonMode(PM_POINTS);
camera->setPolygonMode(PM_SOLID);
PolygonMode mode = camera->getPolygonMode();
```

The mode set will continue in force until changed by a later call (in other words, this is not a one-frame-only setting). The default is PM_SOLID.

Position and Translation

A **Camera** (**Frustum**) is a **MovableObject** as well, and shares all of the methods and functionality of that class. The most common feature of a **MovableObject** is the ability to attach to a scene node and "piggyback" the camera along with renderable objects in the scene. There are reasons you might want to do this, such as various "chase" camera techniques. You will see different third-person camera techniques in later chapters; for now, we will discuss the inherent position and orientation features of the **Camera**.

```
// assume camera is a pointer to an existing, valid instance of "Camera"
camera->setPosition(200, 10, 200);

// you can also use a Vector3 to position the camera, useful for using the
// position obtained from a scene node getter
// camera->setPosition(Vector3(200, 10, 200));
```

This code will position the camera at absolute world coordinates (200,10,200). This is different from the move() and moveRelative() methods, which translate the camera from its current position in world and local space, respectively.

```
// camera is at world space 200, 10, 200 from before
camera->move(10, 0, 0); // camera moves to 210, 10, 200
camera->moveRelative(0, 0, 10); // camera moves to 210, 10, 210
```

We have to be careful with moveRelative(). Since it is carried out in local space, the translation applied is relative to the camera's current orientation. In the preceding examples, we assumed that the camera was originally aligned with the major axes, pointing in the normal +Z direction. If the camera had been rotated 90 degrees to the right, for example, the moveRelative(0,0,10) call would have moved the camera to (220,10,200).

Direction, Orientation, and "Look-At"

Ogre provides a plethora of methods to point your camera around the scene:

```
void setDirection(Real x, Real y, Real z);
void setDirection(const Vector3& vec);
Vector3 getDirection(void) const;
Vector3 getUp(void) const;
Vector3 getRight(void) const;
void lookAt( const Vector3& targetPoint );
void lookAt(Real x, Real y, Real z);
void roll(const Radian& angle);
void roll(Real degrees) { roll ( Angle(degrees) ); }
void yaw(const Radian& angle);
void yaw(Real degrees) { yaw ( Angle(degrees) ); }
void pitch(const Radian& angle);
void pitch(Real degrees) { pitch ( Angle(degrees) ); }
void rotate(const Vector3& axis, const Radian& angle);
void rotate(const Vector3& axis, Real degrees) {
rotate ( axis, Angle(degrees) ); }
void rotate(const Quaternion& q);
void setFixedYawAxis( bool useFixed, const Vector3& fixedAxis =
const Quaternion& getOrientation(void) const;
void setOrientation(const Quaternion& q);
void setAutoTracking(bool enabled, SceneNode* target = 0,
const Vector3& offset = Vector3::ZERO);
```

Most of these are self-explanatory. roll(), yaw(), and pitch() do precisely what they say: they rotate the camera around its local Z axis (roll), Y axis (yaw), or X axis (pitch) by the radial displacement specified, relative to its current orientation. setDirection() will orient the camera along the vector specified, again in local space. rotate() will cause the camera to rotate by the angular displacement around the given axis, as specified in the angle-axis versions, or by the quaternion in the quaternion version. lookAt() is a very commonly used method to orient a camera on the basis of a target point or object in world space, without having to try to do the Euclidean math to figure out the quaternion needed to get there. And finally, setFixedYawAxis() is provided to allow you to break the camera free from its own yaw (Y) axis. In first-person shooters, the camera often can look up as well as scan the X-Z plane; in this case, you want the default behavior, which is to yaw around the camera's local Y axis. However, in the case of a flight simulator, you want to be able to break the camera free of that restriction in order to implement a fully free camera.

setAutoTracking() is an interesting feature, and a useful one if you wish to have the camera always follow a certain node in the scene. Note that this is not the same as a true third-person chase camera, since that type of camera typically is not looking at a particular node, but instead is looking at whatever your character is looking at. The first parameter indicates whether to turn tracking on or off; this can be done at any time before a frame is rendered, and **must** be done (tracking turned off) prior to deleting the node that is being tracked (otherwise Ogre will throw an exception). The node to be tracked is the second parameter, and that node must exist before this method is called. The parameter can be NULL only if the first parameter is false. If the object being tracked is large and sighting on the center of it is not desirable, you can fine-tune the actual look-at point with the third (offset) parameter, which operates in local space relative to the scene node being tracked.

The following methods are available to obtain information about the camera's actual orientation, taking into account rotations and translations of attached scene nodes (and also reflection matrices in the "derived" set of methods):

```
const Quaternion& getDerivedOrientation(void) const;
const Vector3& getDerivedPosition(void) const;
Vector3 getDerivedDirection(void) const;
Vector3 getDerivedUp(void) const;
Vector3 getDerivedRight(void) const;
const Quaternion& getRealOrientation(void) const;
const Vector3& getRealPosition(void) const;
Vector3 getRealDirection(void) const;
Vector3 getRealUp(void) const;
Vector3 getRealRight(void) const;
```

The "Real" set of methods returns values in world space, while the "Derived" set returns values in "axis-aligned" local space (which means the camera is at the origin in its local space, and its local axes are aligned with the world-space axes).

Advanced Camera Features

Ogre supports stereoscopic rendering via the setFrustumOffset() and setFocalLength() methods of **Camera (Frustum)**. For example, you can adjust a second camera (frustum) horizontally to simulate the distance between the viewer's eyes. This will render from the adjusted camera at a slightly different angle, and will produce the eye-crossing output (at least, without the special red/blue glasses that blocked the opposite image) common in the "3D" movies that were the craze in the 1950s. Of course, this technique is highly specialized and "niche" but is provided in case someone needs to do such a thing (usually in research laboratories).

Ogre also allows you to manipulate the view and projection matrices directly. This is definitely a more advanced topic, and falls under the heading of "do this only if you know exactly what you are doing, and why," since these matrices are already calculated for you by your setup of the camera and the position and orientation of the camera. The following methods are available for view/projection matrix manipulation:

```
const Matrix4& getProjectionMatrixRS(void) const;
const Matrix4& getProjectionMatrixWithRSDepth(void) const;
const Matrix4& getProjectionMatrix(void) const;
const Matrix4& getViewMatrix(void) const;
void setCustomViewMatrix(bool enable,
    const Matrix4& viewMatrix = Matrix4::IDENTITY);
bool isCustomViewMatrixEnabled(void) const;
void setCustomProjectionMatrix(bool enable,
    const Matrix4& projectionMatrix = Matrix4::IDENTITY);
bool isCustomProjectionMatrixEnabled(void) const;
```

The first two listed return the render system–specific projection matrix. getProjectionMatrixRS() will return the matrix in the render system's native coordinate system (right-handed or left-handed), while getProjectionMatrixWithRSDepth() will return the matrix in Ogre's native format (right-handed). The difference is that the depth values will range from [0,1] or [–1,1] depending on the render system in use. You can avoid that and always get a depth range from [–1,1] by calling getProjectionMatrix() instead, which is essentially getProjectionMatrixWithRSDepth() with the consistent depth range.

When you set a custom view and/or projection matrix, you must be aware that Ogre will no longer update the matrix based on translation or orientation of the frustum (camera). You have to update the matrix manually every time you move its origin. You can turn the custom matrix on and off with the enable parameter in setCustomViewMatrix() and setCustomProjectionMatrix(). When the custom matrix is turned off, Ogre will resume updating the internal matrix for you as normal.

For the most part, Ogre handles LoD (level-of-detail) bias pretty well. However, there are times you may want to override its default factors, and Ogre provides **Camera** methods to do so:

```
void setLodBias(Real factor = 1.0);
Real getLodBias(void) const;
```

setLodBias() is not actually an immutable command; elements in the scene are free to ignore this directive, making it more of a hint if LoD overrides are widespread in the scene or application. The factor parameter instructs the camera to increase (or decrease) the amount of detail it renders. Higher values (>1.0) increase the detail, lower values (<1.0) decrease it. This is useful for implementing items such as rear-view cameras that do not need the full detail of the main viewport.

World Space to Screen Space

One common need, especially for mouse-picking applications, is translation of world space to screen space. The *centerline* of the camera (that is, the line in the world down which the camera is looking) intersects the screen at a particular point, namely [0.5,0.5] (in normalized coordinates). If you are moving a cursor around the screen, you probably want to determine a line from the camera origin through the screen at the location where the cursor. This line is called a *ray*, and it is returned from the getCameraToViewportRay() method:

```
// x and y are in "normalized" (0.0 to 1.0) screen coordinates
Ray getCameraToViewportRay(Real x, Real y) const;
```

With this ray, you can proceed to perform a query on the scene manager to determine what objects might intersect that ray; scene manager details are discussed later in this book.

Viewport

Referring again to Figure 4-2, consider the rectangle defined by X and Y. This rectangle is the viewport for that camera . . . or, more correctly, "a" viewport for that camera. If you recall from the example code earlier in this chapter, a **Viewport** instance is obtained from an instance of **RenderWindow**, and the method that retrieves the viewport takes an instance of **Camera** as the lone parameter. This means that a single **Camera** instance can drive zero or more **Viewport** objects.

Viewports can overlap without ill effect. By default, Ogre clears the depth and color buffers before rendering viewports that are "on top" of other viewports, to avoid depth-blending issues. You can have as many cameras and viewports as your application needs (and memory allows). One common use for multiple cameras and viewports is "picture-in-picture" zoom windows in a game.

■Tip Something to keep in mind when considering viewports and camera zoom is that it is not enough simply to narrow the field of view on the camera to create a zoomed image. This is because Ogre will still be using the camera position to calculate level of detail for the zoom, and what you will find is that the objects in your zoom window will look terrible, since they will still be at the correct level of detail for their distance from the camera. Solution: when you zoom, move the camera closer to the zoom target, or use a secondary camera (which is required for picture-in-picture zooms), or use `Camera::setLodBias()` to increase the level of detail rendered.

Viewports have a *z-order*, which determines what viewports will render "on top" of other viewports in use. Higher ordinal indicates "higher" placement in the stack (that is, a z-order of zero would indicate the viewport underneath all others). Only one viewport can occupy a given z-order for a render window. For example, you cannot have two viewports at z-order zero; this will cause an exception.

Each viewport can have an independent background color. For example, you can have a main viewport at z-order 1 that covers the entire window, with a black background, and a smaller viewport on top of that one (at z-order zero, in other words) with, say, a blue background, as in the following code:

```
// assume window is a valid pointer to an existing render window, and camera is
// a valid pointer to an existing camera instance
Viewport *vpTop, *vpBottom;

// second parameter is z-order, remaining params are position and size, respectively
vpBottom = window->addViewport(camera, 0);

// create a smaller viewport on top, in the center, 25% of main vp size
vpTop = window->addViewport(camera, 1,
        0.375f, 0.375f,
        0.25, 0.25);
// set the background of the top window to blue (the default is black so we don't
// need to set the bottom window explicitly)
vpTop->setBackgroundColour(ColourValue(0.0f, 0.0f, 1.0f));

// an alternate way to set the color is to use the manifest constant for blue
// vpTop->setBackgroundColour(ColourValue::Blue);
```

I mentioned earlier that Ogre defaults to clearing the depth and color buffers each frame; you can manage both of these settings independently, using the `setClearEveryFrame()` method on **Viewport**.

```
// As mentioned, these both default to "true". The flags are maskable; in other
// words, setClearEveryFrame(true, FBT_COLOUR|FBT_DEPTH) is valid.
vpTop->setClearEveryFrame(true, FBT_COLOUR);
vpTop->setClearEveryFrame(false);
```

Another important consideration when using picture-in-picture style viewports is the fact that overlays are rendered by default in all viewports. This is not something you would want in a zoom window (you do not want your HUD repeated in miniature in the zoom window), so you can turn off overlay rendering on a per-viewport basis. Likewise for skies (skyboxes) and shadows; these are renderable on a per-viewport basis.

```
vpTop->setOverlaysEnabled(false);
vpTop->setSkiesEnabled(false);
vpTop->setShadowsEnabled(true);
```

You can do more advanced things with viewports, such as altering the render queue sequence, and using a per-viewport material scheme, but we will cover those topics in more detail in later chapters devoted to these more advanced topics.

Main Rendering Loop

The typical Ogre application will render one frame after another, ceaselessly (at least until you tell it to stop). We saw earlier in this chapter one method of invoking this render loop: the `Root::startRendering()` method. However, this method simply starts a small loop that calls another method: `renderOneFrame()`.

The existence of `renderOneFrame()` is important for several reasons. For one, you may wish to incorporate Ogre into an existing application or framework, and if you had to rework your application's main rendering loop to accommodate Ogre's `startRendering()`/**FrameListener** *Observer* duolith, you might simply give up and choose another, less capable 3D rendering API . . . and we can't have that.

Another reason you might use `renderOneFrame()` over `startRendering()` is that it is literally otherwise impossible to integrate Ogre into a windowing system's message loop. Let's take the Windows `WM_PAINT` message, for example. When a Windows application processes this message, it goes about the task of redrawing the contents of the window's client area (at least the part that has been invalidated by whatever action another window performed, such as covering part of the current window). If you have embedded an Ogre rendering window inside the window processing the `WM_PAINT` message, you want to update the Ogre render window (by calling `renderOneFrame()`) only when the message is processed, not all the time as would be the case for `startRendering()`.

However, the primary reason for choosing a manual render loop and `renderOneFrame()` over `startRendering()` and a frame listener is that the design and architecture of many 3D game engines or applications are such that driving the application's main loop from the rendering engine turns out to be a poor choice. For example, a networked game engine design might run mostly the same loop on a dedicated server as it does on the full client, but without any rendering support. If the engine design has Ogre driving that server's main loop, and Ogre is not present on the server, then the problem is self-evident.

Luckily, Ogre does not force one method or the other on your application: you are free to choose the method that best suits your situation. For those that prefer the manual render loop, `renderOneFrame()` is for you.

Listing 4-8 is deliberately minimal; it is intended only to show you how you might implement the manual render loop in your application, and where it typically exists in the flow of your code.

Listing 4-8. *Skeleton Example of a Manual Main Rendering Loop in Action*

```
bool keepRendering = true;

// Do all of the Ogre setup we've covered so far in this chapter: loading plug-ins,
// creating render window and scene manager and camera and viewport, and putting
// some stuff in our scene.

while (keepRendering)
{
    // process some network events into engine messages

    // process some input events into engine messages

    // update scene graph (manager) based on new messages

    // render the next frame based on the new scene manager state
    root->renderOneFrame();

    // check to see if we should stop rendering
    // Note: NextMessageInQueue() is completely fictional and used here only
    // for purposes of illustration -- it does not exist in Ogre.

    if (NextMessageInQueue() == QUIT)
    {
        keepRendering = false;
    }
}

// Do whatever cleanup your application needs
// Then, shut down Ogre
delete root;
```

It is worth noting that you can still use **FrameListener** classes with renderOneFrame().
renderOneFrame() is actually the method that notifies any registered frame listeners in **Root**,
as Listing 4-9 demonstrates. (Not much to it, is there?)

Listing 4-9. *The Full Implementation of the* renderOneFrame() *Method of* **Root** *(Found in*
Root.cpp *in the Ogre Source)*

```
bool Root::renderOneFrame(void)
{
    if(!_fireFrameStarted())
        return false;

    _updateAllRenderTargets();

    return _fireFrameEnded();
}
```

Listing 4-9 contains the entire body of the renderOneFrame() method. As you can see, it fires the frame-started and frame-ended events in your **FrameListener** implementation; clearly **FrameListener** and renderOneFrame() are perfectly compatible if you prefer to use a **FrameListener** with a manual render loop.

Conclusion

In this chapter, you learned how to initialize and start up an Ogre application, and how the various visualization classes (**RenderWindow**, **Camera**, **Viewport**) work together to present your scene to the viewer. In the next chapter, we will begin putting actual content into the scene, which should make the techniques you learned in this chapter a lot more interesting.

■■■

## CHAPTER 5

Ogre Scene Management

Every 3D rendering library on the planet (and even some on other planets) uses a scene graph to organize its renderable items. This scene graph typically is optimized for fast searching and querying, providing the user with the ability to find items in the vicinity of other items, and allowing the library to find, sort, and cull polygons as needed in order to provide the most efficient rendering possible. Occasionally the scene graph is used for collision detection. Sometimes a single scene graph is used for all subsystems in an application, including audio and physics. All of these are valid uses of a scene graph.

Ogre is no different in that it uses a scene graph to organize the polygons that compose the objects in its scene. It is very different from most other scene graph implementations used by other libraries, in that it does not use *a* scene graph. Instead, Ogre relies, as it often does, on a pluggable architecture for the scene graphs it uses (or, more correctly when dealing with Ogre, "scene manager"). The Ogre **SceneManager** class is an interface that is implemented by a pair of reference scene managers (provided with Ogre) and also by many community efforts such as the Paging Scene Manager (`http://tuan.kuranes.free.fr/Ogre.html`) and commercial/free-for-noncommercial-use efforts such as oFusion (`http://ofusion.inocentric.com`).

Users familiar with full engines such as Torque, Unreal, CryENGINE, etc., as well as other rendering libraries such as Irrlicht3D, TrueVision3D, or Blitz3D, to name a few, often are greatly confused by the Ogre scene management design. Many packages go to great lengths to ensure a complex inheritance hierarchy that tries to subclass everything from a root "scene node" type. What they inevitably find out is that this design becomes very unwieldy very fast, once they try to extend their design to take into consideration other types of data (such as audio or physics data).

Ogre, as you learned during the Ogre design overview in Chapter 3, decouples the structure (the scene graph) from its content as a core design concept from the outset, flattening the inheritance structure of the scene graph and its data nodes. This provides an elegant and powerful architecture that allows for much greater accommodation for alternate scene types (for example, BSP versus octree versus kd-tree) as well as easily implementing alternate data types with a minor interface implementation. In other words, Ogre's scene graph design is one of composition, not inheritance.

Ogre takes the design one step further: you can use multiple scene managers **in the same scene at the same time**. This was an often-requested feature for years. Whether your application benefits from using more than one scene manager type in the same scene or not depends entirely on the design of your application, but many see this to be the answer to the "portalling" issue. *Portal* is the common term for the boundary between one optimization/complexity-management strategy and another, such as looking out a window into a landscape scene from inside a complex indoor level. The management headaches of this sort of scene complexity should be obvious, and if they are not to you, then consider yourself lucky not to have had to deal with the problem. Many still consider the answer to portalling to be a well-designed single scene manager; the purpose of this book is not to enter the argument, but instead simply to provide you with the knowledge you need to leverage all of Ogre's available features.

Scene Manager

Generally speaking, a scene manager in Ogre is responsible for the following:

- Creating and placing movable objects, lights, and cameras in the scene in such a way as to access them efficiently in a graph traversal

- Loading and assembling world geometry (differentiated from movable entities in that world geometry is large, sprawling, and generally not movable)

- Implementing *scene queries* to provide answers to questions such as, "Which objects are contained in a sphere centered at a particular point in world space?"

- Culling nonvisible objects and placing visible objects into render queues for rendering

- Organizing and sorting (by increasing distance) nondirectional lights from the perspective of the current renderable

- Setup and rendering of any shadows in the scene

- Setup and rendering of all other objects in the scene, such as backgrounds and sky-boxes

- Passing this organized content to the render system for rendering

Scene Manager Types

One common question asked often in the Ogre forums is, "Why do you have this thing called 'scene types'? Why not just have a scene manager and be done with it?" The reason is that scene managers in Ogre are implemented as plug-ins, and you can load multiple different scene manager plug-ins for use by your application. For example, your game might have both densely populated indoor levels as well as sparsely populated outdoor landscapes, each of which are better served by a scene manager optimized for that particular type of world geometry (as you will learn later in this chapter).

Each scene manager plug-in will register a factory class instance with Ogre along with a string identifying the type of scene manager it creates. For legacy support, it will also register itself with a type mask identifying itself as one of the older Ogre predefined scene types.

> ■**Note** If you are new to Ogre, you can skip this note. If you have used Ogre in the past, you may be wondering what's up with the scene manager stuff in the version of Ogre covered in this book (1.2, Dagon). Starting with this version, multiple scene managers can register for a given type, and the preferred means of identifying that type is a text string, such as "OctreeSceneManager" or "TerrainSceneManager". You can still iterate over the registered managers for a given type, or just take the last manager registered. You can also supply a bitwise combination of scene type masks now (i.e., ST_INTERIOR\!ST_EXTERIOR_CLOSE). This all was added to allow the scene manager developer to identify the type of scene manager instead of trying to fit it into one of the more limiting types that previously existed. If you like you can still use the old method; it still compiles and works just fine.

You can provide a name for the scene manager instance you create, or let Ogre assign a name for you. Typically, you will be storing a pointer to this manager in your code, so giving the scene manager instance a name is not that useful in most cases.

The **OctreeSceneManager** plug-in that comes with Ogre provides two scene manager types: **OctreeSceneManager** and **TerrainSceneManager**. As you will learn later in the chapter, the **OctreeSceneManager** is a general-purpose scene manager that can safely be used for any scene. The **TerrainSceneManager** is a specialized scene manager optimized for dealing with heightmapped terrain scenes.

Scene Object Creation

The most common use of the scene manager by the application developer is for creation of all manner of objects, both movable and nonmovable: lights, cameras, entities, particle systems, billboards, and so on, as well as skyboxes, static geometry, and loading world geometry. Anything that can exist in a scene (whether it is renderable or used to render) is managed by the scene manager implementation. This allows the developer of the scene manager to customize the behavior of the object creation process if needed (say, for example, that the scene manager implementation needed a specific type of custom camera to work with the scene manager's optimizations). Note that "manage" relates to the entire life cycle of objects created by the scene manager: methods for each object type are provided for creating, getting, destroying, and "destroying all" of that type. Any object obtained from the scene manager must be destroyed by the scene manager: in other words, you do not "delete" any of the pointers that the scene manager returns to your application. If you want to free scene objects or clear your scene manually (as opposed to letting Ogre do it during the normal course of **Root** shutdown), then you need to let the scene manager do it for you.

Scene Nodes

The scene manager is also the source of the nodes used to define the scene graph's structure. Scene nodes are organized within the scene manager in a hierarchy: a scene node has a single parent and can have zero or more child nodes. You can attach and detach scene nodes from the scene manager at will; the scene node is not destroyed until you tell the scene manager to destroy it. This is handy as a shortcut for turning off whole sections of your scene: simply detach the root node of the hierarchy you wish not to be rendered, and it will not be rendered.

■Caution If you destroy a scene node with live (meaning referenced) content or data still attached, Ogre will not crash, but you will need to ensure that the objects that **were** attached to the node are properly disposed of to avoid memory leaks. You can manage the lifetime of scene nodes as you see fit, but you do have to exercise caution and due diligence with your godlike powers over the helpless scene nodes.

The scene manager is guaranteed to be created with at least one node already present: the root scene node. This is the only node in the scene graph that is exempt from the single-parent rule: the root node, by definition, has no parent. You cannot destroy the root scene node. This node is most useful, obviously, for acting as the parent to all other nodes in the hierarchy, but it is also useful, less obviously, as a handy place to attach static or world geometry. While you can move the root scene node in the scene graph, there rarely (if ever) is a good reason to do so, so for all practical purposes you should consider the root node immobile.

The scene node hierarchy is created by adding children to existing nodes in the scene graph. This means that the first node you add to the scene graph will be a child of the root scene node. Figure 5-1 shows the hierarchy of the scene graph after several node additions.

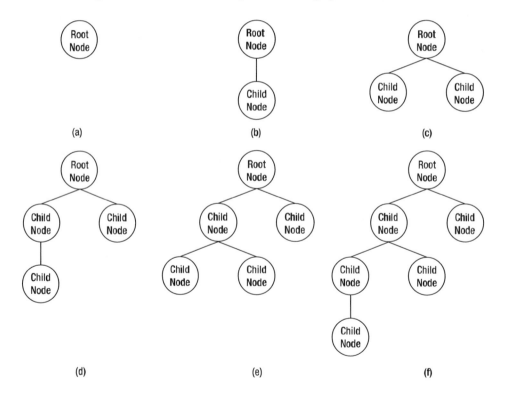

Figure 5-1. *Scene graph state over the course of six node additions, starting with an empty scene graph in (a) and progressing through the final state in (f)*

The scene manager does not put the content or data objects in the scene when you create them; you have to attach the newly created objects to a scene node. This scene node does not have to be attached to the scene graph for you to attach content to the node; you can attach content to any scene node in any state at any time you wish. You can also attach more than one content object to a scene node. There is no real limit on how many content or scene management objects can be attached to a single scene node; you could theoretically attach all of your objects to the root scene node if you like, but you would not have much luck moving any of them around independently.

You can also detach content objects from scene nodes at will; they likewise will not be destroyed or deleted, as they have no dependency on the scene manager or nodes for their existence. However, you cannot attach an instance of a content object to two scene nodes at the same time, nor can you make a scene node a child of two different parents; both of these actions will cause an exception within Ogre.

It is important to understand that the three major spatial operations (translation, rotation, scaling) are done on scene nodes, not content objects. In other words, it is the scene nodes that move, not the content; the content is just along for the ride, as you will see shortly.

Scene Queries

The second most common use of the scene manager is creation of scene queries (that is, getting information back out of the scene): ray queries, sphere queries, bounding-box queries, bounding-plane queries, and intersection queries. *Ray queries* provide information about which objects in the scene are intersected by a given ray (imaginary line drawn between two points in 3D space). *Sphere queries* provide information about objects that lie within a given sphere (described by an origin point in 3D space and a radius). *Bounding-box queries* utilize axis-aligned bounding boxes: you provide two 3-vectors that define the opposing corners in 3D space, and Ogre provides all of the objects that lie within that box. *Bounding-plane queries* provide information about all objects that lie within a volume formed by a set of given planes. *Intersection queries* provide information about all objects in the scene that are close enough that they could be intersecting.

These queries are reusable and movable, which is handy for situations such as the common terrain-clamping scenario, where the query must be executed every frame from a different location.

■**Note** *Terrain clamping* refers to the process of maintaining a constant distance (possibly zero) between an object and world geometry (usually outdoor terrain or landscapes). In order to do this, you need to know the height of the terrain directly underneath an object, and the simplest way to do that in Ogre is with a *raycast* (ray scene query) pointing straight down, to obtain a world fragment. You can then get the world height of that fragment and set your object's offset on that basis. This is a very common technique.

All of these queries are designed for optimized execution (which is one of the reasons that the axis-aligned bounding box is used instead of, say, a more tight fitting oriented bounding box, something significantly more complex to calculate). All query types are *maskable*, which means you can filter out types of objects you do not want. For instance, you might only want to obtain the list of all lights that lie in a given sphere, but do not want any terrain fragments returned. You would set a query mask before executing the query to limit the results returned.

Spatial Relationships and 3D Transforms

Those new to 3D application development often have a hard time visualizing the relationship between the nodes and content objects, and even the relationship between nodes themselves. To help alleviate that a bit, and to make sure you understand the relative terminology, let's look at some visual examples of 3D operations.

Spatial Transforms

If you recall your basic 3D mathematics, you know that the position, orientation, and scale of any object in 3D space can be expressed as a 4×4 transformation matrix in a particular relative space. This relative space is defined as "in terms of a given set of coordinate axes."

The most common transform spaces (and those used in Ogre) are *world*, *parent*, and *local*. Transforms in world space are relative to the origin of the global coordinate system: (0,0,0) in 3D space. In Ogre, this typically is the same as the location of the root scene node, so world space in Ogre can also be understood as "relative to the root scene node." World space also means coordinates are expressed in the global X, Y, and Z axes.

Transforms in parent space are relative to the parent of a scene node, and transforms in local space are relative to the node to which the object is attached. This means that translations, rotations, and scaling are calculated along the coordinate axes defined by the parent node's orientation. Most of the time, you will be doing translations in parent space and rotations and scaling in local space: these are the default transform spaces in Ogre for these operations.

However, you are probably using Ogre so that you do not have to deal with the actual transforms: you simply want to move your objects around in much "cleaner" ways. Lucky for you, as part of the basic scene node translation, rotation, and scaling methods, Ogre manages these ugly transforms for you in the spatial relationships between the nodes in the scene graph. If you ever want to obtain the transform used to put a scene node in its current position, orientation, and scale, the scene node will provide that upon request. It will even provide it to you in one of the three coordinate spaces Ogre manages.

Object Space

When you create an object, whether in a 3D modeler or procedurally or manually within Ogre, vertices of that object are defined in terms of the world space at the time of creation. For example, if you create a 1×1×1 cube centered at (0,0,0) in 3DS Max, the inherent position of its vertices are all some sign permutation of (0.5,0.5,0.5), as in Figure 5-2. When Ogre loads this object, those values never change: the vertices will always have an inherent position in *object space*.

■**Note** "Object space" and "local space" sometimes are used interchangeably in other works; in this book and in this chapter, object space is defined as "an object's inherent coordinate system."

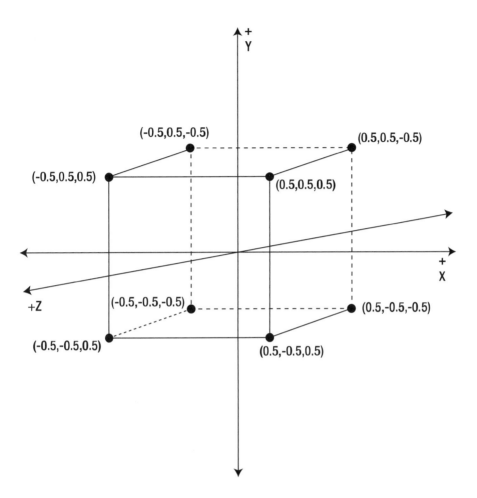

Figure 5-2. *Inherent object-space positions of the vertices of a unit cube*

When this object is attached to a scene node, the current world-space transform matrix of the scene node is applied to those positions to produce the actual vertex positions in world space; this is how your object is positioned, scaled, and oriented in the 3D world. The original vertex positions are never altered directly; the object's vertices will always be the same distance from the scene node to which the object is attached, as shown in Figure 5-3.

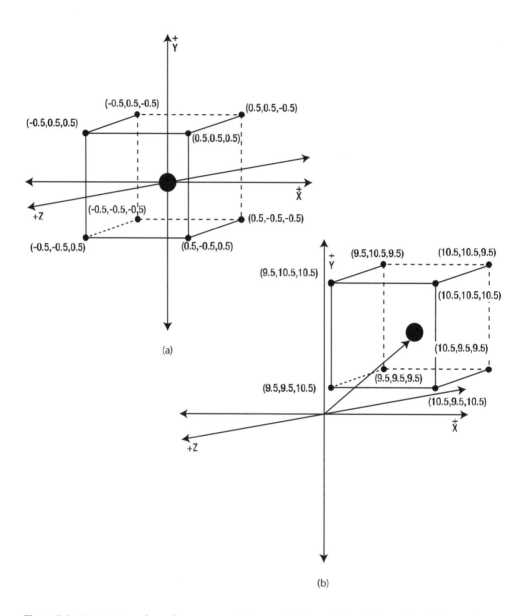

Figure 5-3. *No matter where the scene node is moved, the position of the cube relative to its scene node is unaltered.*

In (a) the scene node (black dot in the center of the cube) is at (0,0,0) in world space. In (b) it has been moved to (10,10,10) and the world-space position of the cube's vertices are shown.

This last statement causes a lot of confusion for those beginning with 3D graphics (especially integrating content created in a modeling tool such as Softimage|XSI, Maya, 3DS Max, or Blender into a 3D scene). The natural inclination is to assume that the coordinates in the tool and the coordinates in Ogre somehow are different. They are not: so long as the tool and exporter do not make any assumptions about "units of measurement" and export vertex coordinates in "world units" (unitless, in other words), then all is well with the world. A vertex at (1,1,1) in the tool will be offset from its parent scene node in Ogre by those same coordinates. The base of the head of a human model might be at (0,2,0) in Blender: it will be at (0,2,0) from the object's scene node in Ogre.

Local Space

Translation is defined as a displacement relative to "something else" (in terms of a 3D node-based scene, that "something else" is either a node's parent or the world origin). You can in fact translate a node relative to itself (in local space, in other words); for example, you can move a node in its forward-facing direction by translating it along the Z axis.

For rotation and scaling, "local space" means simply that a node is rotated around its own axes, or scaled based on its own properties. Figure 5-4 shows rotation in local space, and Figure 5-5 demonstrates scaling in local space.

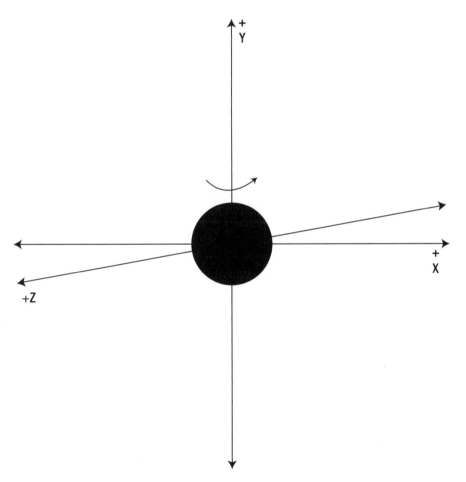

Figure 5-4. *In local space, a node rotates around its own axes. The arrow indicates a positive rotation around the local Y axis.*

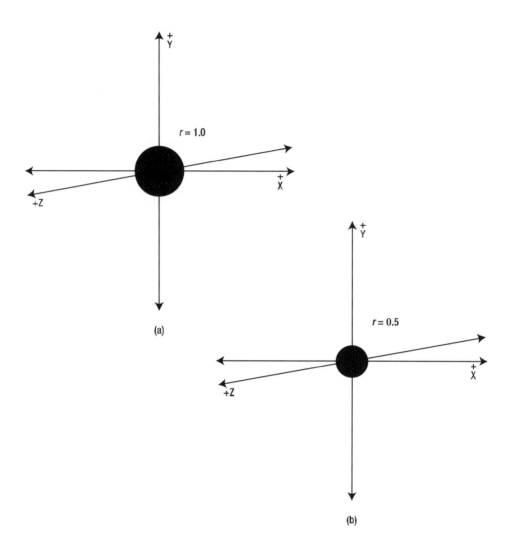

Figure 5-5. *In local space, a node is scaled based on its own properties. The sphere in (b) is reduced to 1/2 its original radius in (a) by scaling its scene node by 0.5.*

First, we should define what scaling and rotation do in terms of a scene node. In fact, they do nothing to the node itself; a scene node is not something that is visual or renderable. When applied to a scene node, scale affects how the vertices that define the objects attached to that scene node are transformed, as shown in Figure 5-5. Meshes appear to grow or shrink, and any normals defined for the mesh vertices are scaled proportionally as well. The only effect on the node is that its local transform is updated to reflect the new state. Rotation likewise simply updates the node's transform based on yaw, pitch, and roll changes (or changes in direction or orientation).

Parent Space

Parent space transforms are transforms performed relative to a node's parent. Figure 5-6 demonstrates a parent-space translation.

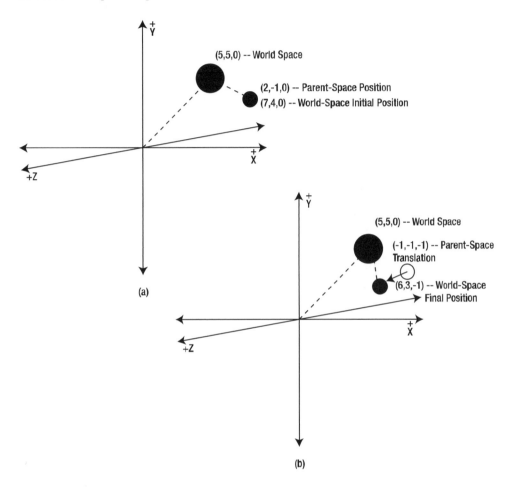

Figure 5-6. *(a) Parent and child nodes before translating the child node, and (b) parent and child nodes after translating the child node by (–1,–1,–1) in parent space*

In Figure 5-6(a), the parent node exists at (5,5,0) in world space. The parent node has not been rotated, so its axes are aligned with the world-space axes. The child node exists at (2,–1,0) in parent space; when the parent node's world-space transform is applied to the child node, it results in a world-space position of (7,4,0) for the child node (for only translation and position, it is easiest to think of the transform as simple vector addition). In Figure 5-6(b), the child node has been moved by (–1,–1,–1) in parent space, resulting in a new world-space position of (6,3,–1), since the translation was performed relative to the node's previous position.

■**Caution** Keep in mind the difference between performing a translation in Ogre and setting a position. Translations can have any frame of reference (world, local, or parent space), while setting a node's position with `setPosition()` is performed in parent-space coordinates always. Furthermore, translations are cumulative: they perform a repositioning relative to the node's last position. Setting position directly is always an absolute operation.

Figure 5-7 illustrates the effect on a node's children of rotations to the node. Notice two things in Figure 5-7. First, rotating the parent node also rotates the coordinate axes that will be used by the node's children. In Figure 5-7(b), the parent node has been rotated by 45 degrees around the Z axis, relative to the configuration in Figure 5-7(a). The effect of this on child node spatial operations is that all translations, rotations, and scaling will reference this rotated frame of reference: moving a node by (1,0,0) in this new coordinate system will move it along the parent's "tilted" X axis, not the world's "normal" X axis.

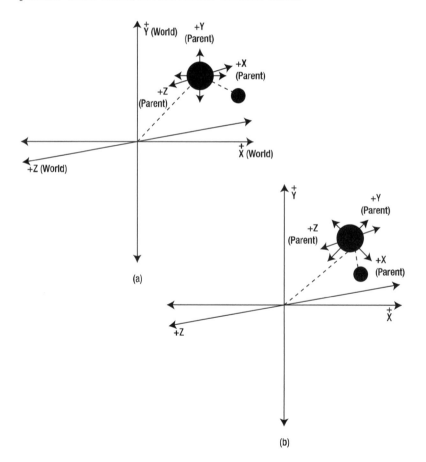

Figure 5-7. *Rotating a scene node also rotates the coordinate axes in parent space. In (b), the parent node's axes have been tilted by rotation around the parent's Z axis (local-space rotation of the parent node).*

The second thing to notice is the effect of this new transform on the position of the child node(s). The reason that the child nodes move when a parent node is moved, rotated, or scaled, is that transforms are cumulative. That is, the transform at each node in the hierarchy is applied to the child node, all the way down the tree. So when a parent node is rotated, for example, all children of that node rotate around the parent node as well to maintain the same position relative to the parent, and the child's children will do the same, and so on. Entire branches of the hierarchy will be affected by changes to the transforms higher in the hierarchy.

World Space

World space is the simplest space to work in, but world-space coordinates also involve the most work to extract from the position of a leaf node in the node hierarchy. To prevent numerous calculations when trying to obtain the world-space coordinates of a node, Ogre calculates this information when a node transform is changed and caches the data in the node. (This is done mostly for the purposes of faster organization of nodes during scene rendering.)

World space is always aligned with the global coordinate axes, and world-space coordinates will always be expressed in terms of those axes.

World space is mostly meaningful for rendering and view projection manipulation. You typically do not want to work in world space except in certain cases, such as placing objects in the world geometry. When you insert movable objects into the scene, you nearly always will work in other coordinate spaces than world.

Movable Scene Objects

Speaking of inserting movable objects into the scene . . .

Movable objects in Ogre are created by the scene manager, attached to nodes in the scene manager, and destroyed by the scene manager when you indicate you are done with them. Movable scene objects certainly can exist outside the scene graph, so you can detach and reattach them as needed, but a movable object can only be attached to one scene node at a time. As mentioned earlier, however, you can attach as many movable objects to a node as you like.

Renderable movable objects such as meshes contain only geometry and material information; they neither contain nor hold any scene graph structure information. Other movable objects (typically nonrenderable objects such as lights and camera that instead are used for rendering a scene) have no geometry or material data, other than a bare-bones knowledge of how to draw themselves if the need arises (for example, you can make a camera visible in the scene if you need to).

Resource-Based Objects

The most common resource-based (which typically also means disk-based) movable object in Ogre is the mesh (followed closely by the skeleton). Both of these types of objects are managed by the Ogre resource management system (which you will learn in Chapter 7), so the path from the disk to your scene involves an intermediate point of access to your disk-based objects. I bring this up only to point out that the scene manager is not responsible for the actual loading or your meshes and skeletons; instead, it just asks the Ogre resource manager for them.

You obtain a mesh entity by instructing the scene manager to create one for you. This process may also invoke a couple of other steps, such as obtaining from the Ogre resource system a reference to a skeleton and/or material used by the mesh. This means you do not have to load a skeleton separately; however, you can load one by itself if you wish (for example, you can attach arbitrary mesh objects to a bare skeleton if you have a need).

When you create a mesh object, it is not attached to any scene node. You need to attach each object you create to a scene node in the scene graph in order for it to be at all renderable. As mentioned earlier, the vertex positions defined in the mesh are positioned in the node's local space (that is, relative to the node to which it is attached).

■**Note** This usually goes without saying, but I will say it anyway. When your artists (or you yourself) are creating 3D models for use in your application, they typically should be created at the origin in the 3D modeling tool. Any offset from the world origin in the tool will faithfully be duplicated in your scene (relative to the node to which the object is attached) when rendered by Ogre. Likewise for rotations; Ogre uses a Y-axis-up coordinate system, something that is not shared by most 3D modeling tools (which prefer a Z-axis-up system). If your model is inserted into your scene on its face or back, this is why. Most exporters for Ogre have a "rotate 90 degrees" option to deal with this issue.

Quad-Based Objects

This is a rather broad category of movable objects that includes particle systems, billboards and ribbon trails, overlays and skyboxes (and skyplanes and skydomes). These quad-based objects typically are camera-facing and often dynamically textured. Since they are constructed from simple planar quads (quads that are generated dynamically) and not mesh-resource-based objects, their primary resource is scripts that define how they are textured, as well as their lifetime (for particle systems and ribbon trails). Skyboxes, skydomes, and skyplanes are defined directly with the scene manager. Particles, billboards, and ribbon trails will be discussed in more detail in Chapter 10, and overlays will be discussed in Chapter 12.

The differences between skyplanes, skydomes, and skyboxes are subtle but important, as are the few ways in which they are similar. The primary similarity is that they all maintain a constant distance from the camera. They all can be set to render before everything else (the default) or after all other geometry in the scene, which is an optimization that allows the skybox to conserve fillrate in scenes where the sky would be largely occluded. They all use normal Ogre materials, so animating sky textures is no different than animating any other texture (as you will see in the next chapter, which covers Ogre materials). They can all be turned on and off at will through the scene manager, and the distance from the camera to the sky can be set for all of them.

Skyplane

A *skyplane* is a single plane that represents the sky in a world. The plane is defined like any other plane in Ogre; the distance and normal of the plane define how it is positioned in the scene. Typically, the plane is just that, a plane; however, you can specify that the plane "bends" so that it can appear below the level of the camera. Additionally, you can have the scene manager tessellate the plane into multiple segments for greater control over the appearance of the curvature of the plane, and also to allow for per-vertex effects on the plane. Curved skyplanes are similar in operation to skydomes, but work better with fog. The skyplane allows tiling of the plane texture an application-defined number of times.

Skydome

Where a skyplane is made of a single plane, a *skydome* is made of five planes that define the top and sides of a box. The bottom face of the box is left off; the expectation is that world geometry will fully occlude any bottom face of a box, as well as the horizon (where some truly nasty artifacts can be seen due to the apparent curvature applied to the texture of a flat face). The texture coordinates of the skydome are created such that a curved effect is achieved. This curvature is configurable, with lower curvature creating a gentler curve (good for the "big sky country" typical of outdoor landscapes), and higher values creating a "steeper" curve (more suitable for the sky outside indoor levels, where very little of the sky can be seen at any one time and the extra curvature looks better).

The faces of the box are all kept a constant distance from the camera. This could become an issue with injudicious selection of far clip and skydome distances in your scene: your sky could potentially render in front of unclipped world geometry if you do not select a great enough distance for the skydome.

Similar to the skyplane, you can specify the tiling of the texture applied to the skydome; this can produce, for example, good, inexpensive cloud effects. For finer control over the tiling, you would need to use more advanced texture-coordinate transform methods (as you will learn in the next chapter).

Skybox

A *skybox* is not the same as a skydome with an extra side. For starters, a skybox does not "curve" the texture coordinates on its faces; each face in the skybox is UV mapped uniformly. Additionally, a skybox can use cubic textures (something you will learn more about in the next chapter), as opposed to a single texture that may be tiled. As for tiling, you cannot tile the textures on a skybox, nor would you want to.

The goal of a skybox (as opposed to a skydome or skyplane) is the ability to control the appearance of the sky in all six directions from the camera. A skybox can also potentially leverage the hardware acceleration of cubic texture mapping for more efficient rendering.

Rendering Objects

The two primary rendering-support objects that can inhabit a scene are the camera and the light. The camera "takes pictures" of your scene, and movable lights can make your scene far more realistic than simple ambient (i.e., "magic") scene lighting.

Camera

The camera's primary job is to define a *view frustum*. This is the "box" that contains everything the "eye" can see (where the "eye" is defined as "the point in space where the four sides of the view frustum converge"), as shown in Figure 5-8.

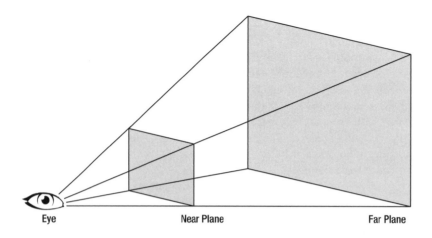

Eye   Near Plane   Far Plane

Figure 5-8. *Graphical depiction of a view frustum*

The eye in Figure 5-8 is the representation of "you," the viewer, in the scene. The near clip plane is defined by two factors: distance to the near plane from the eye, and *field of view*, which is an angular measurement of how "wide" a view you want. The size of the far clip plane is defined by these two parameters, plus the distance to the far clip plane from the camera (eye). These two planes define the front and back of a sort of "perspective box," and the top, bottom, and sides of the frustum complete the definition of this box.

These six planes are then used by Ogre to cull objects from the scene that are not visible, and by the graphics hardware to cull "out-of-bounds" geometry at a much finer granularity (at the polygon level).

The camera is also a movable object in the scene, so it can be translated, rotated, and repositioned (the frustum it defines is recalculated whenever the camera moves or is repositioned). Furthermore, the camera is one of those special objects in the scene that do not have to be attached to a scene node to be moved around: it can (and nearly always is) positioned directly in the scene. In fact, once a camera is created by the scene manager, it is ready to go right away; cameras are created at position (0,0,0) in world space so the next step you probably want to take after creating one is to move it somewhere more useful.

Tip This is not to say there is never a reason to attach a camera to a scene node. However, you must take special care when rotating the node to which the camera is attached: you will most likely need to turn off the default camera setting of "use fixed yaw axis," which tells the camera to maintain a constant "up" vector (making rolls impossible). If you try to pitch or roll the scene node containing a camera with a fixed yaw axis, undefined results can happen: more than one orientation satisfies the rotation, since you are dealing with three variables but only two degrees of freedom when you lock the third axis. Just something to keep in mind.

Light

Lights, on the other hand, can often benefit from being attached to scene nodes. Consider the following cases:

- Headlights on a car model

- A torch or flashlight in your character's hand

- A fireball shooting down a dark hallway

Each of these examples describes the need for dynamic lights in a scene that must be attached to an object in the scene (and therefore a node in the scene graph).

Anything designed to illuminate the scene in any way is a light. Lights can be movable, or they can be stationary. Regardless of the type, position, or intensity of an Ogre light in the scene, however, they contribute only to local object illumination calculations.

■**Note** *Global* illumination refers to lighting models that take into account all scene lighting (including reflected light from other objects) when shading a polygon in the scene. Examples of global illumination models are raytracing and radiosity. Neither of these models is, at the time of this writing, feasible for real-time 3D graphics due to the computational complexity of both, and Ogre does not directly support any global illumination models. Quasi-global illumination models (more accurately, *soft shadow* models) such as ambient occlusion (AO) and precomputed radiance transfer (PRT) have been "ported" somewhat to 3D hardware solutions. However, Ogre does not perform any global illumnination calculations for you either (which is to say, Ogre will not, for example, calculate a radiosity or raytracing solution for you). On the other hand, Ogre is more than happy to apply your AO shadow map to your object for you.

Local lighting calculations take into account only the lights incident on an object. The normals on the surface of an object and the material properties of the object are used to calculate how much light is reflected toward the camera, and a color value is created on that basis. Ogre can use any number of lights in the scene to calculate this color value; as you will see in the next chapter, however, there is a practical limit on how many you can use, and a common sense limit as well. The first limit is doubly defined: the 3D hardware will only use so many lights per pass, so if you want to use more than that limit (usually eight lights maximum), then you must use multiple passes, which can become potentially expensive. The second limit is defined in terms of how many lights actually contribute to the lighting of the object in question: far away (or occluded) lights that are greatly attenuated at the position of the object make no significant contribution to the lighting of the object, so do you really need to take them into account? Ogre will sort the lights near an object for you (from nearest to farthest) so typically you just use the nearest *N* lights in a single pass when calculating the color of a pixel.

Lights in Ogre come in three flavors (which corresponds to the types of lighting supported by the 3D hardware): *point*, *spot*, and *directional*. All of these types are movable, but moving makes more sense for some than others; for example, directional lights have no intensity falloff with distance, so moving them nearer to or farther from an object has no effect (indeed, they have no position, so moving them is in fact impossible). The most you would want to do with a directional light is change its orientation (its direction, in other words). Point and spot lights both have an intensity as well as a *falloff equation*, for which you can supply the coefficients (constant, linear, and quadratic). They also both have a range over which they are effective; objects beyond this range receive no illumination from the light. And of course, all lights produce light of a certain color; this color also is taken into account when calculating the light reflected toward the camera from an object in the scene.

Point Lights   Point lights are rather common in a 3D scene. They have the characteristic of radiating light in all directions from a single point in space (different apparent sizes of the light
can be simulated in the material definition for an object, as you will learn in the next chapter).
Point lights are rather useful for simulating the light radiating from, say, a lighting fixture such
as a wall sconce or table lamp, as well as any moving object that needs to radiate light on its
surroundings in the scene.

Spot Lights   Spot lights are similar to point lights, with the additional characteristic of direction.
A spot light also has a *cone effect*; you can specify an additional falloff rate as a function of the
angle of deviation from the light's *inner cone* to its *outer cone*, as shown in Figure 5-9.

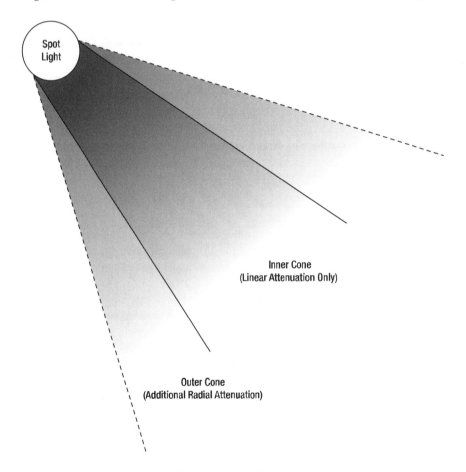

Figure 5-9. *Spot light area of effect and cone effect*

Spot lights are excellent candidates for items such as flashlights and automobile headlights.

Directional Lights   Directional lights are entirely unlike either of the other two types of lights discussed. Directional lights, as you might expect, have a characteristic direction, but as mentioned
earlier, have no need for position, since the light they produce is assumed to come from
a particular direction regardless of the position of an object in the scene. A perfect example of

a directional light is the sun; it is so far away that all of the rays of light it emits strike the earth at the same angle. Also like the sun, it has no apparent falloff with distance. Therefore, it has no need for falloff functions, and any coefficients supplied for these parameters are ignored for directional lights. As you might expect, directional lights are an excellent way to simulate sunlight in your scene.

World Geometry

World geometry is everything in your world, that **is** your world. Heightmapped terrain, mesh landscape, buildings and naturals (trees, foliage, and so forth) on those landscapes, interior levels with walls and windows and doors and monsters . . . well, not the monsters, and not the actual swinging doors either: those would both be movable objects. In other words, world geometry is the "stage" on which your actors live, the world they inhabit and in which they move around.

World geometry is typically created in an offline tool, such as a 3D modeler like Softimage|XSI, 3D Studio Max, Maya, or Blender, or in a specific heightmap generation tool such as Terragen (http://www.planetside.co.uk/terragen). World geometry can be mesh based, which is the norm for indoor levels, buildings and structures such as bridges, and foliage like trees, bushes, etc. Terrain and landscape geometry can also be mesh based, but for performance reasons should be "cut up" into smaller chunks that are then "stitched together" when loaded.

■**Note** When creating mesh-based landscapes or levels, you need to partition the mesh into smaller chunks that can be culled when nonvisible. Otherwise, Ogre will always render the entire mesh, even if only a small part is visible, and the performance detriment of this should be self-evident. Scene managers such as the Paging Scene Manager provide tools to perform this partitioning. Heightmapped terrains do not suffer from this since they are easily partitioned into separate tiles at load time.

Ogre scene managers can load world geometry in two different (but similar) ways: either directly from a file on disk or through an arbitrary data stream. This second option allows you to pack your world mesh and configuration data into a custom or proprietary format and send it to the scene manager directly. Most applications typically use the first option, as world files often live on their own and can be opened and read directly from disk.

Common Spatial Partitioning Schemes

Scene managers are designed and optimized for the assembly and management of world geometry in a way that makes sense for the type of world geometry in question. The type of partitioning scheme is chosen based on how much geometry is immobile, how much is movable, and the expected density and placement of each. This space partitioning, from the perspective of the Ogre scene manager, is intended to manage objects, not actual polygons. Since Ogre is a hardware-acceleration-based 3D rendering engine, it depends on the characteristic handling of geometry by modern 3D hardware. As a result, scene manager implementations that maximize geometry batching will work much better than those that try to partition space on the basis of actual polygons (which is how it was done in the "good old days" of software rasterization and 3D hardware without transform-and-lighting acceleration).

Quadtree and Octree

Quadtree is historically a 2D partitioning scheme, but still applies well to flatter 3D scenes such as those that are terrain or landscape based, since the vertical (altitudinal) variations of the world geometry of such scenes is kept to a limited range. *Octrees* are better suited for smaller outdoor levels and indoor levels where the space around the camera exists with arbitrary vertical extent as well (floors above and below the camera, for instance).

Figure 5-10 provides a visualization of the octree and quadtree partitioning schemes, for three levels of spatial subdivision.

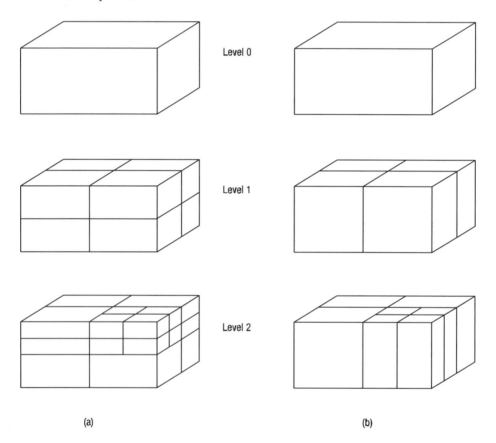

Level 0

Level 1

Level 2

(a)   (b)

Figure 5-10. *Spatial visualization of (a) octree and (b) quadtree space-partitioning schemes*

In Figure 5-10(a), you can see how each progressive step of the spatial partitioning subdivides the 3D space into eight *cells* (hence the name "octree"). Similarly, the quadtree subdivides the space in a cell into four smaller cells, as shown in Figure 5-10(b). Both are recursive schemes, treating cells of any size on an individual basis.

Both octrees and quadtrees have the characteristic of good batching of geometry when it comes to assembling polygons for rendering, something that traditional binary-space partitioning implementations (discussed in the next section) typically do not do well. For a more complete introduction to the quadtrees and octrees (as well as alternate space-partitioning schemes such as kd-tree or cell-portal), the Internet is a wealth of information on the topic.

Binary-Space Partitioning

BSP (binary-space partitioning) is a perfectly valid scene organization scheme, but its primary benefit in modern applications is for fast collision detection, not so much for geometric polygon organization. Ogre comes with a sample BSP (Quake 3 Arena format) scene manager, but the Quake 3 scene file format in particular does not play well with modern graphics hardware, as it organizes its geometry into many small chunks of data as opposed to larger batches of polygons (which is what modern hardware likes to process). For that reason, development and maintenance of this sample implementation has long since been abandoned (even though the scene manager still exists for those who want to load and use their existing Quake 3–level content and tools).

Static Geometry

The opposite of movable objects in a scene is static geometry. Well, not so much opposite: static geometry often is made up of otherwise movable objects that are no longer set to move.

The idea, again, is batching efficiency. Modern GPUs prefer to render a few large batches of geometry instead of many small batches.

■Note For this reason, raw triangle count often is a meaningless figure when measuring performance data in a 3D application: 1,000,000 triangles might render at, say, 300 frames per second in a single batch, whereas 1,000 batches of 1,000 triangles each (which is still 1,000,000 triangles) might render at 30 frames per second, if the batching is organized poorly.

The more visible geometry you can render in a single batch, the better your application's performance is likely to be (within reason, of course; other classic issues such as fillrate and overdraw can still take over if you just blindly blast polygons at the GPU, batched or not).

It might sound like static geometry is the answer to all framerate problems in complex scenes. However, as you might expect, there are a few caveats for the use of static geometry:

- Static geometry must be built in advance of its use. This is not necessarily a fast process, so it is not something you can do every frame.

- Static geometry will sort by material all of the objects put into it, and dump all of the geometry that matches on material into the same render operation (batch, in other words). This does not mean that just because you group together a bunch of geometry into a single static geometry object everything will magically render in the same operation: different materials still require a separate batch. It becomes a classic compromise scenario: you want to maximize the number of triangles rendered in a single call and minimize the number of calls (as determined by how many different materials come into play).

- You cannot move objects once they are included in static geometry. That is the definition of "static." A single world transform applies to the entire static geometry object. Think of it as dissolving sugar into water: you can no longer deal with the sugar separately.

- Memory usage for static geometry is more than would be required for the same number of instances of movable geometry; this is because instances of a mesh in movable geometry share the mesh data between them, while static geometry creates a copy of the mesh data for each instance in the static geometry. That is, at the time of this writing; with GPU geometry instancing right around the corner, this may change shortly after this book is published, at least for hardware with such support.

- Static geometry typically will render everything in the group if any of the group is in the view frustum. This can be an issue if you try to group, say, all of the trees in a scene into the same static geometry: even those that are behind the camera (out of the view) will be rendered.

Luckily, the news is not all bad for static geometry. The scene manager implementation will (should) in fact try to group static geometry on the basis of its partitioning scheme, and will therefore cull nonvisible geometry somewhat, even if it is in the same static geometry. Furthermore, all material and mesh LoD settings are observed, on a limited basis: the farthest LoD distance for a mesh in the group is used for all meshes in the group, so that all meshes change detail level at the same distance from the camera (for generated LoD distances only). In other words, like anything else in software engineering, you have to make a compromise (or many) to increase performance.

Scene Management by Example

I think I have said more than enough about the "why" of Ogre's scene management design and features. I am sure, anyway, that you are tired of hearing it and would like to see it in action (in code at least), so that is what we will do with the rest of this chapter.

Most of the code I will present in this book will be taken from the Ogre Samples. I will not be simply listing the code, as there is no need: it is readily available in the source and SDK downloads. Instead I will be focusing on snippets of the overall programs and describing what they do and why.

The Simple Things

On this list of the most common things you do with a scene manager, obtaining an instance of one to use is probably something every Ogre-based program in the world will do at least once. Next on the list is obtaining at least one camera to use, followed closely by many occurrences of "putting an object in the scene."

Creating a Scene Manager and Camera

The first two tasks are so common that the Ogre demo framework code does them for all of the demos: you will find the code that obtains a scene manager instance and creates a camera in the `chooseSceneManager()` and `createCamera()` methods of **ExampleApplication** in `ExampleApplication.h` (see Listing 5-1).

Listing 5-1. *Ogre Demo Framework Methods to Obtain a Scene Manager Instance and Create a Camera for Use in the Demos*

```
virtual void chooseSceneManager(void)
{
    // Create the SceneManager, in this case a generic one
    mSceneMgr = mRoot->createSceneManager(ST_GENERIC, "ExampleSMInstance");
}

virtual void createCamera(void)
{
    // Create the camera
    mCamera = mSceneMgr->createCamera("PlayerCam");

    // Position it at 500 in Z direction
    mCamera->setPosition(Vector3(0,0,500));
    // Look back along -Z
    mCamera->lookAt(Vector3(0,0,-300));
    mCamera->setNearClipDistance(5);
    mCamera->setFarClipDistance(1000);

}
```

The two methods listed in Listing 5-1 are fairly self-explanatory. To create a scene manager at all, you need to tell Ogre what type to create and what name the scene manager will have, since you can have multiple scene managers active at the same time, even multiple scene managers for the same type. For example, you can create two different scene managers of type ST_GENERIC, they will just need different names. If we instead had wanted to use, say, the **TerrainSceneManager** in the preceding code, we would have created a scene manager a bit differently:

```
mSceneMgr = mRoot->createSceneManager("TerrainSceneManager");
```

In this example, we create a scene manager using the type name registered by the scene manager plug-in, instead of the older ST_* constant type of identification. We also declined to provide a specific name for the instance, opting to let Ogre assign one automatically; if we are going to store the pointer to the scene manager (which we do), then we do not really need the instance name.

Cameras likewise need to be named uniquely; trying to create two cameras with the same name will cause an exception. You might wonder if that code for positioning and orienting the camera looks a bit odd. The reason the camera is pointed along the negative Z axis is that is the direction "into the screen" from your perspective at the keyboard. The camera is moved "out of the screen" 500 world units and pointed back to look at the center of the scene. This allows the objects in the scene to be placed simply around the world origin and be visible by default without having to worry about where the camera is and is pointing.

The near clip distance is set to 5 world units; as mentioned earlier in the book, the defaults for the camera at creation are 100 units for the near clip and 100,000 for the far clip. Recall also that only the ratio between the far and near distances is important: this sets up the depth buffer precision. For the sake of demonstration and in the interest of keeping the ratio on the order of 1000:1 (as discussed previously), I added a line that does not exist in Listing 4-1 to decrease the far clip distance. This step typically is performed in the demo overrides of the createCamera() method.

Creating Entities and Lights

In each demo is a method named createScene(), called by the framework to load whatever needs loading into the scene (see Listing 5-2). Typically, this includes entities, lights, billboards, particles, whatever.

Listing 5-2. *Scene Creation Method in the Environment Mapping Demo (*EnvMapping.h*)*

```
void createScene(void)
{
    // Set ambient light
    mSceneMgr->setAmbientLight(ColourValue(0.5, 0.5, 0.5));

    // Create a point light
    Light* l = mSceneMgr->createLight("MainLight");

    // Accept default settings: point light, white diffuse, just set position
    // NB I could attach the light to a SceneNode if I wanted it to move
    // automatically with other objects, but I don't
    l->setPosition(20,80,50);

    Entity *ent = mSceneMgr->createEntity("head", "ogrehead.mesh");

    // Set material loaded from Example.material
    ent->setMaterialName("Examples/EnvMappedRustySteel");

    // Add entity to the root scene node
    mSceneMgr->getRootSceneNode()->createChildSceneNode()->attachObject(ent);
}
```

Again, Listing 5-2 is straightforward, no surprises. The mSceneMgr pointer is stored in the **ExampleApplication** class, and initialized in the code in Listing 5-1. Listing 5-2 creates a single light named MainLight, and a single instance of the mascot Ogre head mesh. The code overrides the default Ogre material (encoded in the binary .mesh file referenced in the createEntity() method call) with a material that will perform environment mapping. The code also sets the ambient light color in the scene. The Ogre head mesh is left at the origin (where all objects are set when loaded into the scene). Finally, the instance of the **Entity** that contains the Ogre head mesh data is attached to an anonymous scene node created as a child of the root. There is no need to be able to find that scene node again in this demo because the Ogre head never moves; it would have been just as correct to attach it to the root scene node directly.

Moving and Rotating Scene Nodes

It is worth mentioning briefly the mechanical nuances of rotations, translations, and scaling in the context of the Ogre scene node hierarchy. We discussed earlier in the chapter the "why" of the spatial relationships and operations; here I would like to touch on the "how."

The default translation space is TS_PARENT, so you do not need to specify parent space when you perform a translation:

```
mSceneNode->translate(100.0, 10.0, 0.0);
```

If you need to perform a translation in world space, you must inform Ogre of that:

```
mSceneNode->translate(100.0, 10.0, 0.0, TS_WORLD);
```

Likewise for local space. The following will move a node "forward" 100 units in the direction it is facing:

```
mSceneNode->translate(0.0, 0.0, 100.0, TS_LOCAL);
```

For rotations, the default is TS_LOCAL; if you need a different rotation space, you must tell Ogre:

```
// rotate around object's own Y axis by 1 radian, about 57 degrees
mSceneNode->yaw(Ogre::Radian(1.0));

// rotate around parent's X axis by 1 radian, about 57 degrees
mSceneNode->pitch(Ogre::Radian(1.0), TS_PARENT);

// rotate around world Z axis by 1 radian, about 57 degrees
mSceneNode->roll(Ogre::Radian(1.0), TS_WORLD);
```

Scaling has no relative space; it performs the operation on the node itself, as well as the node's child hierarchy.

```
// scale along the X axis by a factor of two; other axes are left unscaled
mSceneNode->scale(2.0, 1.0, 1.0);
```

Caution If you scale your scene node only to find out that the object(s) attached to it suddenly have increased (or decreased) significantly in intensity when rendered, then you probably did not realize that **everything** attached to the node is scaled . . . including vertex normals. Since local lighting calculations assume that the normals they are using are normalized (unit-length vectors), those calculations will happily (and unquestioningly) use the scaled normals when shading your polygons. The fix: after you scale a scene node, call setNormaliseNormals() on the affected entities to reset their normals to a "normal" state. Understand that this operation does have a performance cost.

Scene Manager Features

Let's examine several of the broader areas of the **SceneManager** functionality from a more mechanical perspective.

Loading World Geometry

The examples used so far have loaded objects into an empty world. Most applications, however, prefer a "set" for their actors to inhabit: world geometry, in other words. Ogre provides a method in the **SceneManager** interface that scene manager implementations override to facilitate loading of world geometry into the scene.

Basic Terrain Scenes

Let's have a look at the *Terrain* demo application (see Listing 5-3).

Listing 5-3. *Loading World Geometry in the Terrain Demo Application*

```
void createScene(void)
{
    // Set ambient light
    mSceneMgr->setAmbientLight(ColourValue(0.5, 0.5, 0.5));

    // Create a light
    Light* l = mSceneMgr->createLight("MainLight");

    // Accept default settings: point light, white diffuse, just set position
    l->setPosition(20,80,50);

    ColourValue fadeColour(0.93, 0.86, 0.76);
    mSceneMgr->setFog( FOG_LINEAR, fadeColour, .001, 500, 1000);
    mWindow->getViewport(0)->setBackgroundColour(fadeColour);

    std::string terrain_cfg("terrain.cfg");
    mSceneMgr -> setWorldGeometry( terrain_cfg );

    // Infinite far plane?
    if (mRoot->getRenderSystem()->getCapabilities()->
        hasCapability(RSC_INFINITE_FAR_PLANE))
    {
        mCamera->setFarClipDistance(0);
    }

    // Define the required skyplane
    Plane plane;
    // 5000 world units from the camera
    plane.d = 5000;
    // Above the camera, facing down
    plane.normal = -Vector3::UNIT_Y;
```

```
    // Set a nice viewpoint
    mCamera->setPosition(707,2500,528);
    mCamera->lookAt(0,0,0);
}
```

If you are following along in your copy of the Ogre demo source code, you will notice that a few things look different in this code than in the actual demo code. I have removed some distracting code from Listing 5-3 and changed a couple of less-than-clear method calls (such as the last one in the listing that sets the camera's initial orientation; the code in the demo actually uses raw numbers to create a quaternion, and I did not think that would explain much).

The first part of Listing 5-3 looks an awful lot like Listing 5-2, except that no Ogre head is created. After creating the scene lighting, the code then sets up the scene fogging function: first the actual fog color, and then the fog equation parameters. Note that the background color of the viewport is set to the fog color: if you were to set the viewport background color to, say, a nice deep blue to simulate a sky (or black to simulate space or night), then you would get a nice, deep blue (or black) for the parts of the scene that are not blocked by world geometry or the skyplane.

Skyplanes, Skyboxes, Skydomes, and Fog

Notice that the code does not actually set the scene manager to use the skyplane it creates. There is a reason for this, and that reason is fog. Let's take a look at a series of screenshots of the *Terrain* demo, and I will explain why.

In Figure 5-11, I have moved the camera to one edge of the terrain heightmap to show how blending the viewport background with the fog color creates the illusion of a continuous zone of fog in all directions. You can see how the terrain in the distance ultimately blends with the fog at the *fog distance* (the point at which the fog obscures all geometry in the scene).

Figure 5-11. *The Terrain demo, at the edge of the terrain heightmap*

In Figure 5-12, I have moved the camera to an edge again, but this time I commented out the step that matches the viewport background to the fog color. As you can see, the nice blending we had in Figure 5-11 has given way to a stark black backing to our scene. Notice that the fog is still in effect on the terrain in the distance.

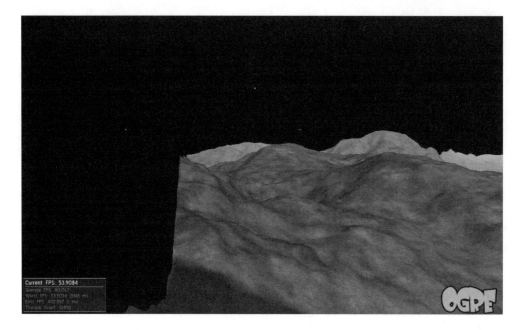

Figure 5-12. *The Terrain demo, without setting the viewport background color*

Now let's put in the skyplane that was defined in Listing 5-3. The code we will use to do this is

```
mSceneMgr->setSkyPlane(true, plane, "Examples/CloudySky");
```

Hmm, OK, we see the plane (it's above us, facing down, as shown in Figure 5-13), but now it just looks like Figure 5-11 with the lower parts missing. The reason is that the skyplane itself is far too far away (5000 world units) to be visible within the fog (which is set to kick in at 500 world units and provide full obscurity by 1000 world units). The skyplane is fogged as well because it is just another object in the scene; on modern hardware fogging is performed after all other processing is complete in the graphics pipeline, so the GPU does not make any distinction between a skyplane and any other geometry in the scene. Let's see what happens when we move the skyplane to 500 world units instead (see Figure 5-14).

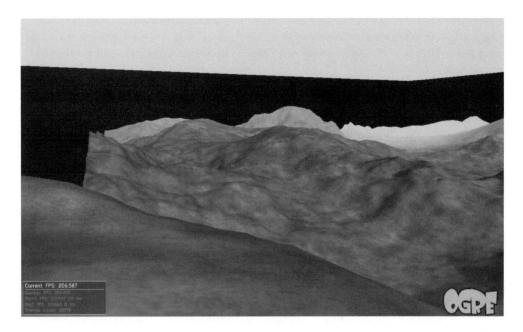

Figure 5-13. *The Terrain demo, with the skyplane*

Figure 5-14. *The Terrain demo, with the skyplane distance corrected*

This time I kept the camera in a depression in the terrain and looked up toward the sky. Not bad, is it? It looks somewhat like a foggy morning before the fog burns off. The reason we can see a bit of the sky now is that it has been moved to 500 world units, easily within the range of the fog function.

This, by the way, is one of the reasons that, with landscape scenes, you use a skybox or skydome (or curved skyplane, at least) as opposed to a flat skyplane. You can easily see the edges of the skyplane from most parts of a terrain if you do not take measures to cover the viewport background with the sky. Skyplanes are a decent optimization over skyboxes or skydomes, but only for limited viewing angles.

So why does the *Terrain* demo application not use the skyplane it creates (even though the code was left in)? The reason is that it could not be seen at the distance it is set, and that setting the viewport background color to the fog color made for an even better optimization: if it cannot be seen, do not bother rendering it.

terrain.cfg

You will notice in Listing 5-3 that the file terrain.cfg is referenced. This is just a text file containing "name=value" pairs that provide the definition of the various parameters Ogre needs to construct a terrain from a heightmap. As used in the listing, the file is simply loaded directly from disk. Listing 5-4 shows the contents of that file (which is included with the Ogre source and SDK distributions).

Listing 5-4. *Contents of the* terrain.cfg *File Provided with the Ogre Demos*

```
# The main world texture (if you wish the terrain manager to
# create a material for you)
WorldTexture=terrain_texture.jpg

# The detail texture (if you wish the terrain manager to create
# a material for you)
DetailTexture=terrain_detail.jpg

#number of times the detail texture will tile in a terrain tile
DetailTile=3

# Heightmap source
PageSource=Heightmap

# Heightmap-source specific settings
Heightmap.image=terrain.png

# If you use RAW, fill in the below too
# RAW-specific setting - size (horizontal/vertical)
#Heightmap.raw.size=513
# RAW-specific setting - bytes per pixel (1 = 8bit, 2=16bit)
#Heightmap.raw.bpp=2
```

```
# How large is a page of tiles (in vertices)? Must be (2^n)+1
PageSize=513

# How large is each tile? Must be (2^n)+1 and be smaller than PageSize
TileSize=65

# The maximum error allowed when determining which LOD to use
MaxPixelError=3

# The size of a terrain page, in world units
PageWorldX=1500
PageWorldZ=1500
# Maximum height of the terrain
MaxHeight=100

# Upper LOD limit
MaxMipMapLevel=5

#VertexNormals=yes
#VertexColors=yes
#UseTriStrips=yes

# Use vertex program to morph LODs, if available
VertexProgramMorph=yes

# The proportional distance range at which the LOD morph starts to take effect
# This is as a proportion of the distance between the current LODs effective
# range, and the effective range of the next lower LOD
LODMorphStart=0.2

# This following section is for if you want to provide your own
# terrain shading routine
# Note that since you define your textures within the material this makes the
# WorldTexture and DetailTexture settings redundant

# The name of the vertex program parameter to which you wish to bind the morph LOD
# factor. This is 0 when there is no adjustment (highest) to 1 when the morph
# takes it completely to the same position as the next lower LOD.
# USE THIS IF YOU USE HIGH-LEVEL VERTEX PROGRAMS WITH LOD MORPHING
#MorphLODFactorParamName=morphFactor

# The index of the vertex program parameter to which you wish to bind the morph
# LOD factor. This is 0 when there is no adjustment (highest) to 1 when the morph
# takes it completely to the same position as the next lower LOD.
# USE THIS IF YOU USE ASSEMBLER VERTEX PROGRAMS WITH LOD MORPHING
#MorphLODFactorParamIndex=4
```

```
# The name of the material you will define to shade the terrain
#CustomMaterialName=TestTerrainMaterial
```

As you can see, you can set a considerable number of parameters for defining a heightmapped terrain in Ogre. However, if you examine the file closely, they are broken down into two major sections: the first is used for defining parameters that Ogre will use to generate the terrain mesh and material entirely automatically from heightfield data and raw textures. The second is used for defining custom materials and GPU vertex morphing programs, so that you can override the automatic terrain shading and provide your own.

This file is well commented and fairly self-explanatory; however, a few parameters should be described:

- The **TerrainSceneManager** provided by Ogre will "cut up" the heightfield into a certain number of *pages*. Each page is composed of a number of *tiles*. These both are just names for a square grouping of vertices in the generated mesh.

- The source heightfield in WorldTexture does not have to have the same size (in world units) as the desired terrain. That is, if you want a 2000×2000 world, you do not need to supply a 2000×2000 heightmap.

- The reason for the previous note is that you will tell Ogre how to scale your heightfield with the PageWorldX and PageWorldZ parameters.

- Likewise, you will tell Ogre how to scale the heightfield texel values to world coordinates with the MaxHeight parameter.

- DetailTexture specifies only a single diffuse texture to be applied to the heightmap. If you want to "layer" other textures on top of that (perhaps for alpha masking, etc.), then you need to specify a custom material.

Creating Terrain Without a Config File It is perfectly reasonable and feasible to load terrain data without having to lug around an actual text file. For example, in one project I am working on, the terrain information is kept in a game-specific binary-level format, and extracted at load time into a form that Ogre can use to create the terrain. However, that form looks precisely like the terrain.cfg file: we extract the terrain data into an STL map (whose keys match the names of the parameters in the terrain.cfg file) and iterate the values into an Ogre **MemoryDataStream**, which is accepted by an override of the **SceneManager** setWorldGeometry() method, as shown in Listing 5-5. **SceneData** is just a typedef of std::map. Ogre::DataStreamPtr is a reference-counted smart pointer, so returning it by value from a local variable is safe.

Listing 5-5. *Loading Ogre Terrain Data Without an Actual* terrain.cfg *File*

```
Ogre::DataStreamPtr Process_Loader::getSceneDataStream(SceneData &data) {

    // create what looks like a config file for the edification of Ogre
    std::string mem;
    SceneData::iterator it;
```

```
    for (it=data.begin(); it!=data.end(); it++) {
        mem += it->first;
        mem += "=";
        mem += it->second;
        mem += "\n";
    }

    void *pMem = (void *)new unsigned char[mem.length()+1];
    memset(pMem, 0, mem.length()+1);
    memcpy(pMem, mem.c_str(), mem.length() + 1);

    // stuff this into a MemoryDataStream
    Ogre::DataStreamPtr pStr(new Ogre::MemoryDataStream(pMem, mem.length() + 1));
    return pStr;
}

// and then elsewhere in the world loader:
Ogre::DataStreamPtr pStr = getSceneDataStream(terrainDef);
m_sceneMgr->setWorldGeometry(pStr);
```

Performing Scene Queries

Scene queries are used to find the answer to the question, "What is in this particular area of space?" You can find this answer based on various spatial shapes:

- **Axis-aligned bounding box**: Defined by the two corners of the box.

- **Sphere**: Defined as a center and a radius.

- **Plane-bounded volume**: Arbitrary volume bounded by three or more planes.

- **Ray**: A line from one point in space to infinity in a particular direction; finds out if anything intersects the line.

- **Arbitrary intersections**: Any intersecting objects in the scene.

All queries can filter out objects you do not want returned, or can specify the objects that should only be returned. For example, we can create an axis-aligned bounding-box scene query that returns only the movable lights within its volume (see Listing 5-6).

Listing 5-6. *Simple Axis-Aligned Bounding-Box Query Example*

```
const unsigned int LIGHT_QUERY_MASK = 0x00000001;
Light* light1 = mSceneMgr->createLight("Light1");
Light* light2 = mSceneMgr->createLight("Light2");
light1->setPosition(12, 12, 12);
light2->setPosition(5, 5, 5);
light1->setQueryFlags(LIGHT_QUERY_MASK);
light2->setQueryFlags(LIGHT_QUERY_MASK);
```

```
AxisAlignedBoxSceneQuery* lightQuery =
    mSceneMgr->createAABBQuery(
        AxisAlignedBox(0, 0, 0, 10, 10, 10), LIGHT_QUERY_MASK);

// sometime later in the application's code, find out what lights are in the box
SceneQueryResult& results = lightQuery->execute();

// iterate through the list of items returned; there should only be one, and it
// should be light2 created above. The list iterator is MovableObject type.
SceneQueryResultMovableList::iterator it = results.movables.begin();

for (; it != results.movables.end(); it++)
{
    // act only on the lights, which should be all we have
    assert ((*it)->getQueryFlags() & LIGHT_QUERY_MASK) != 0);

    // do whatever it was we needed to do with the lights
}

// destroy the query when we are done with it
mSceneMgr->destroyQuery(lightQuery);
```

The basics of all scene queries is covered in Listing 5-6. You want to create the query during scene creation and store it for later use, as the query creation is relatively expensive but the execution is not. In other words, the query execution is lightweight enough to run every frame if you like, but the query creation is not.

The most important part of this example (indeed, of every scene query) and the part that confuses many developers the most, is the notion of a *query mask*. Without defining a query mask for your query, and without defining movable objects with the same mask flags, it can get rather bothersome trying to sort through all of the "stuff" that a query might return. The **SceneQueryResult** class defines only two public members: movables and worldFragments. That leaves a whole lot of room for interpretation: you are responsible for providing that interpretation. Since Ogre uses an abstract **MovableObject** model for its scene content, it cannot possibly enumerate the "types" of objects in your scene (beyond "movable object" and "world geometry"). This is where you come in.

In Listing 5-6, the first thing we do is set up an application-specific mask to identify our light object types. This has meaning only to the application; Ogre's part in this is solely to carry around that mask information and provide it on demand (and we demand it when the objects listed in the query result come out the other side of the query execution). The ASSERT in the code is used simply to show how to match the object returned with the query mask; it could just as easily have been an if statement.

Raycasting

Most queries return objects that exist within a volume (or, in the case of the intersection query, all objects that are intersecting at that time). The **RaySceneQuery** is kind of a hybrid of the two: it returns all objects that intersect with an arbitrary ray in space. (A *ray* is defined mathematically as an origin and a direction, as the ray has no "other end"; it carries on to infinity.)

Terrain Clamping The best way to show how to use a **RaySceneQuery** is with some example code. I will again draw from the codebase on one of my current projects to provide an implementation of *terrain clamping*, which is a commonly needed operation that "glues" a character or camera to the terrain under it (see Listing 5-7).

Listing 5-7. *Terrain Clamping*

```
void Entity::clampToTerrain() {
    static Ogre::Ray updateRay;
    updateRay.setOrigin(m_controlledNode->getPosition() + Ogre::Vector3(0, 15, 0));
    updateRay.setDirection(Ogre::Vector3::NEGATIVE_UNIT_Y);
    m_raySceneQuery->setRay(updateRay);
    Ogre::RaySceneQueryResult& qryResult = m_raySceneQuery->execute();

    if (qryResult.size() == 0) {
        // then we are under the terrain and need to pop above it
        updateRay.setOrigin(m_controlledNode->getPosition());
        updateRay.setDirection(Ogre::Vector3::UNIT_Y);
        m_raySceneQuery->setRay(updateRay);
    }

    qryResult = m_raySceneQuery->execute();
    Ogre::RaySceneQueryResult::iterator i = qryResult.begin();
    if (i != qryResult.end() && i->worldFragment)
    {
        Ogre::SceneQuery::WorldFragment* wf = i->worldFragment;
        m_controlledNode->setPosition(m_controlledNode->getPosition().x,
            i->worldFragment->singleIntersection.y,
            m_controlledNode->getPosition().z);
    }
}

void Entity::init()
{
    // lots of other irrelevant entity init stuff goes here
    m_raySceneQuery = sm->createRayQuery(
    Ogre::Ray(m_controlledNode->getPosition(),
        Ogre::Vector3::NEGATIVE_UNIT_Y));

    // move this node is such a way that it is above the terrain
    clampToTerrain();
}
```

In general, terrain clamping via raycasting operates by checking "down" from the position of the ray to look for a world fragment (there should only be one in a heightmapped terrain). The Y position (world height) of the world fragment can then be used to reposition the node's Y position each query (usually performed once per frame) so that the node "follows" the terrain as it moves. You can reposition the ray or even set the ray used in the query to an entirely different ray each time (as is done in Listing 5-7). The code in `clampToTerrain()` is called each frame by our application.

Listing 5-7 is not by any means the "only" way to do terrain clamping, but it does extend the method used in the Ogre *Terrain* demo application in one or two ways. First, this code will move the *controlled node* (the node being clamped to the terrain) above the terrain if it is below the terrain somehow. It does this by "flipping" the query ray if no world fragments are found along the `NEGATIVE_UNIT_Y` direction (directly underneath the node, in other words); it instead checks the `UNIT_Y` direction to look for world fragments, corrects the node's Y position, and then reverts back to the "normal" terrain clamp raycasting.

Conclusion

This chapter should get you more than just started with creating a dynamic world in your Ogre-based application. You should now have a very good grasp on how the Ogre scene management design fits within the broader context of your application, and with that in hand, you are ready to move on in the next chapter to the finer points of manipulating your objects' material properties.

CHAPTER 6

■■■

Ogre Materials

In the previous chapter, you learned how to put various objects in your scene. In this chapter, you will learn how to make them look like more than nonfeatured bits of white plastic. The secret is the *material*, a term that, at its most basic, means how your objects reflect light when rendered. As you will discover, in practice it actually means much more than that: so much more that I gave it its own chapter.

Materials are, as mentioned, simply a definition of how an object assigned that material will reflect incident light. As you might expect, this implies a dependency on the characteristics of the incident light. Spotlights will interact with materials differently than will point lights, and both interact differently than directional lights. These types of lighting sources are understood rather well from a physical aspect, and modeling them in a 3D renderer follows several well-defined rules.

■**Note** In Ogre, the material defines how your object reflects the light, but not how that reflected light interacts with other objects in your scene. In other words, your objects do not actually become additional lighting sources in the scene as they reflect and/or emit light. This is often referred to as *global illumination* and is the domain of raytracing, radiosity, and a host of other computationally complex lighting models that may or may not be suitable for real-time 3D rendering. While global illumination lighting models can produce some incredibly realistic scene lighting, they nearly always are unsuitable for calculation of a complex dynamic scene in a 33-millisecond time window (33 milliseconds corresponds to 30 frames per second, a typical minimum target for interactive 3D applications). For this reason, they most often are features of "offline" photo-realistic rendering applications such as Pixar's RenderMan (http://www.pixar.com), mental ray (http://www.mentalimages.com, included with many commercial 3D modeling tools such as 3D Studio Max), POV-Ray (http://www.povray.org, an open source raytracing renderer), and Aqsis (http://www.aqsis.org, a freely available open source RenderMan-compliant offline renderer).

Materials 101

Ogre is a real-time hardware-accelerated 3D rendering engine. As such, it tends to defer to hardware (the GPU) as much processing as possible. However, even the most complex object materials have one thing in common: color. Colors, in fact. Ogre is a very typical rendering engine in that it supports four different types of color descriptions for a material: ambient, diffuse, emissive, and specular.

Basic Object Shading

In Chapter 5, you learned that the dynamic lights in Ogre contribute only to an object's **local** lighting reflections. This means that the only contributing factors to how an object appears when rendered are the angle and color of incident light, the viewing angle of the camera (also referred to as the *eye*), and the material properties of the object.

- *Ambient* light typically serves as an approximation of the global illumination in the scene; it is an approximation of all of the interreflected light in the scene. Accordingly, the ambient color property of an object's material defines how it reflects this type of light.

- *Diffuse* color is the color that the object reflects when actively lit by a light source. "Diffuse" refers to the fact that the light is reflected evenly in all directions (scattered, in other words).

- *Emissive* color is the color of an object's self-illumination, if any. This can lead to an unnatural look for an object, especially in the absence of any global illumination calculations (imagine an object in your room just glowing, but not actually lighting anything around it, and you get the idea).

- *Specular* color describes the "highlights" on the object as a result of direct lighting. Imagine a red rubber ball, and imagine it is fairly shiny. Now put it under a light bulb; the small bright shiny spot is the specular highlight. It is a result of the light from the bulb reflecting directly off the surface of the ball to your eye.

The color of this highlight is adjustable because in the real world, the color of a specular highlight is not just a function of the color of the incident light and the diffuse, emissive, and ambient colors of the object. The reflected light might take on different colors because not all components are reflected equally. Altering the color of the highlight can allow more flexibility in achieving realistic results at a low cost. Finally, the "power" of the specular highlight can be controlled; the short version of this parameter is that you can control the size of the "bright spot" on that red ball, to alter the perceived shininess of the object: higher power provides a smaller highlight.

Figure 6-1 shows the part of the material editor in 3D Studio Max that adjusts the specular highlight properties, along with the resulting rendered image. The Specular Level parameter corresponds to Ogre's specular power value, and Glossiness corresponds to Ogre's shininess specular parameter. Specular power defines the amount of light reflected (represented by the height of the curve), and shininess defines how much the highlight "spreads" (glossier surfaces will have tighter highlights). Figure 6-1(a) is a basic rendering of a shiny plastic ball with the specular highlight from one light. Figure 6-1(b) has the same specular power but less shininess, and Figure 6-1(c) has the same shininess as in Figure 6-1(a) but with much less power.

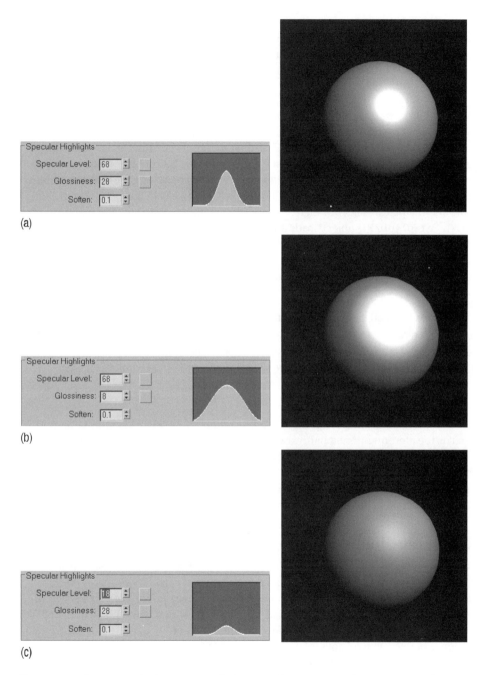

Figure 6-1. *The material editor in Autodesk 3D Studio Max provides a good visual representation of the actual mathematics of the specular highlight. The renders to the right are the classic "shiny plastic ball" used in many specular highlight demonstrations.*

These basic shading parameters are **always** available with Ogre, even for graphics hardware without hardware transform and lighting (T&L), which is commonly understood to be the absolute minimum requirement for consideration as hardware acceleration. If you define multiple techniques in your Ogre material (which you will learn a bit later in the chapter in the section "Techniques and Schemes"), then you should always provide, as an absolute fallback, at least the basic fixed-function shading described here.

Texture Mapping

Most graphics hardware still in use will support at least one or two *texture units*. These units allow your application to map your object with a separate set of coordinates that correspond to areas within a *texture*. This is more than just a fancy name for "2D image"; textures used in 3D graphics also contain data such as mip levels and can be organized as cube or volume maps, and so on. Examples of 2D images are every GIF, PNG, or JPG on a web page, the screen shots in this book, and the pictures in your digital camera or cell phone. Using texture mapping, you can effectively "wrap" your 3D objects with these 2D images, and the pixels in the image will either combine with or replace the diffuse shading parameter from the previous section.

■**Note** Texture mapping is the "application" portion of a two-step process. The first half of the process involves the art pipeline: in a 3D modeling tool, an artist assigns texture coordinates (typically known as *UV coordinates*) to the vertices of a mesh, usually based on a particular texture, although the mesh can be prepared for any texture that conforms to the UV coordinates assigned. These UV coordinates are used in the graphics hardware to map the addressed parts of the texture between the vertices: texture mapping.

This is the other half of what is known as the *fixed-function pipeline* in graphics hardware (the first half is the aforementioned hardware T&L). "Fixed" because it is nonprogrammable; you tell the hardware what vertices in your object correspond to which pixels in the image, and the hardware does the rest: it calculates the positions of those vertices in scene (world) space, and paints the areas between those vertices with the basic and textured (if applicable) shading and color/alpha blending data described in this section.

Programmable Shading

The biggest leap in the history of real-time 3D graphics acceleration (thus far) was the advent of the programmable graphics pipeline. This means simply that calculations on per-vertex (vertex shading) and per-pixel (pixel or "fragment" shading) bases can be done in a program, written either in a high-level language or in GPU assembler, which can replace the fixed-function pipeline. Note that I say "can"; this does not mean "must." You can still use a strictly fixed-function pipeline, even on an NVIDIA GeForce 7950 GTX 2 (the most hopped-up card available at the time of this writing) if you want. Such programs allow nearly unlimited flexibility in how you calculate not only colors at a vertex, but also the colors in between, as well as the positions of the vertices themselves if needed. Textures can be used as inputs to shaders, not only for use as color data, but also for any arbitrary meaning you impose on the data. The possibilities are endless, to the point that GPUs sometimes are used solely as massively parallel and incredibly fast general-purpose computation engines.

Ogre supports all manner of programmable GPU shaders, including low-level assembler and high-level languages such as Cg, GLSL, and HLSL. "Support," however, does not mean Ogre will generate anything for you; you still need to write the shaders, but Ogre provides a very flexible and robust framework for making your shaders available on the GPU. You will learn about that framework in this chapter in the section "Materials and the Programmable Pipeline."

Materials and Application Design

In Chapter 5, I described the relationship between an **Entity** object in Ogre and the geometric meshes that define the construction of the object, and touched briefly on the relationship between those and the materials that make them look like they are made of, well, various real-world materials. However, before we get too deep into the mechanics of materials in Ogre, you need to understand some high-level programming concerns.

Batching

The most important impact of the relationship between materials and meshes in Ogre is the effect on the *render state changes*. In most cases, the *unit of rendering* in Ogre is the *renderable*, from which the **SubEntity** is derived. This notion of unit of rendering is important because it is where Ogre will begin and end *draw operations* in the video drivers. A draw operation (also known as a *batch*) refers to the entire process of clearing out the "paint" (colors, textures, etc.) and "stuff" (vertex or display lists), and starting a new set of operations from scratch. It is like a painter washing off his palette every time he wants to put a new object on the canvas. With 3D hardware, this process involves sending a new list of vertices and index data to the GPU (or referencing existing vertex/index data, if it has not been flushed to make room for other data), as well as setting up the GPU with all of the texture, color, and metadata needed to rasterize the faces defined by those vertices. Therefore, it is most efficient to send the largest number of vertices at a time that can be painted with the same render state data.

Note Textures are usually sent once to the GPU and referenced by render states. However, if your application tends to use all of the memory on the GPU, it is possible that your application will experience *texture thrashing* as textures are sent to the GPU memory each frame (or near enough). Therefore, you want to manage your texture usage carefully: once a texture is on the GPU, you do not want to have to reload it unless absolutely necessary!

Ogre will do what it can to minimize the impact of render state changes, but it will defer to your decision as to what constitutes a single *renderable* (which in turn makes up an atomic batch), implemented in the structure you give your object. For example, if you have a model made of 20 pieces that all use the same material, you could potentially merge all of those into the same renderable instead of submitting them to the card as 20 separate batches: it makes no sense to keep sending the same state data when once will do. There is a definite quantifiable upper limit on the number of batches possible per frame, but the discussion is beyond the scope of this book. For a more in-depth handling of the topic, see the GDC presentation slides on batching by NVIDIA engineer Matthias Wloka at http://developer.nvidia.com/docs/ IO/8230/BatchBatchBatch.pdf and http://download.nvidia.com/developer/presentations/ 2005/GDC/Direct3D_Day/D3DTutorial03_Optimization.pdf. Later in this book, you will learn how to gain closer control over the render state changes in code. For the purposes of this chapter, you would need to reorganize the model in a 3D modeling tool.

Material Cloning

Materials in Ogre are shared by default. When you obtain a pointer to a material from the material manager, it is the same pointer possessed by all other objects using that material. This means that if you want to change a property or component of the material for a single object, you have to clone the material, or the changes will be propagated to all of the other objects as well. This holds true for even the smallest change, such as altering the intensity of the red channel in the ambient color specification: that is an entirely different material as far as the rendering pipeline is concerned. One alternative to changing and cloning materials is altering the parameters in a programmable GPU shader, possibly using a texture as the color data. This avoids the impact on batch count we just discussed.

GPU Shaders

GPUs are specifically designed to deal with the inherently parallel vector computations present in 3D computer graphics, and you would do yourself a great service by learning the how and why of programmable GPU shaders. They are designed to offload processing from the CPU to the GPU, balancing the overall workload and assigning computations to the resource most able to handle them. In addition, GPUs are increasing in power at a far greater rate than CPUs, and that trend is not likely to end anytime soon. You should plan programmable shaders into your design and asset pipeline early, especially if you plan to use real-time shadowing or more advanced techniques such as the render-to-texture technique.

Techniques and Schemes

Materials and schemes are truly two of the most powerful and robust features of Ogre. Materials in Ogre are composed of one or more *techniques*, which allow you to provide the means to tailor the material to the varying capabilities provided by different graphics and platform hardware combinations. A technique is best described as an "alternate way of rendering an object": different material levels of detail and different schemes can also choose different techniques from the same material. The reasons Ogre might automatically select a different technique are many, but in all cases you have complete control over which technique is chosen in which situation.

Schemes in Ogre are higher-level concepts that allow application of a more general description to a particular set of techniques. For instance, you might have high, medium, and low graphics settings in your application, allowing users to drive the process of selecting the "best" technique(s) for their needs.

Ogre does have a definite order in which it looks for techniques when choosing one to apply. First, it will look for the techniques that belong to a named scheme (falling back to those assigned to "Default"). Then within the selected scheme, it will look for techniques that apply to a particular active material LoD (level of detail). Finally, within that list of techniques, Ogre will select the "best" technique that fits the current runtime hardware setup. Failing everything, Ogre will simply shade your object a nice flat white, which is a dead giveaway that you need to work on your material scripting system a bit more. By default all techniques belong to detail level zero, which corresponds to the highest detail: in other words, the most complex technique is employed for all objects using that material.

Techniques and schemes perform a lot of "housekeeping" for the developer. If the materials are left fully scripted (the typical method of defining materials in Ogre), then virtually no code needs to be written to handle the vast array of hardware configurations your application might encounter. Of course, as with everything else in Ogre, anything that can be done using scripts can also be done in code as well.

Material LoD

Level of detail in computer graphics often is discussed in terms of levels of geometry complexity as a function of distance from the camera in a scene. However, the same concept applies to material definitions. Say, for example, you have a material definition that includes several layers of texture maps (with the various blending functions between them) along with both vertex and fragment GPU programs. At close distances, that "high-definition" material looks great on your mesh. However, is it really necessary to use all of those resources to shade your object when it occupies about 12 pixels on the screen (when the object is in the distance, in other words)?

The answer, obviously, is no, and the solution is material LoD management. Continuing our example, it might be sufficient simply to shade that group of pixels all the same color (perhaps not even bothering with dynamic lighting calculations). Ogre provides you the means to define which techniques are to be used at which levels of detail, so that you can optimize your use of the GPU resources. You define in the material the distances at which the detail levels will change, and then assign each technique in your material to a detail index. You are encouraged to provide more than one technique per LoD index if you intend to provide scheme support or hardware capability fallbacks.

Material Composition

Figure 6-2 provides a conceptual overview of the composition of a material. In short, a material contains one or more techniques, which in turn contain one or more passes. Only one technique is active at a time; in Figure 6-2, if Technique 0 is active, then the rest of the techniques are not used in a given rendering pass.

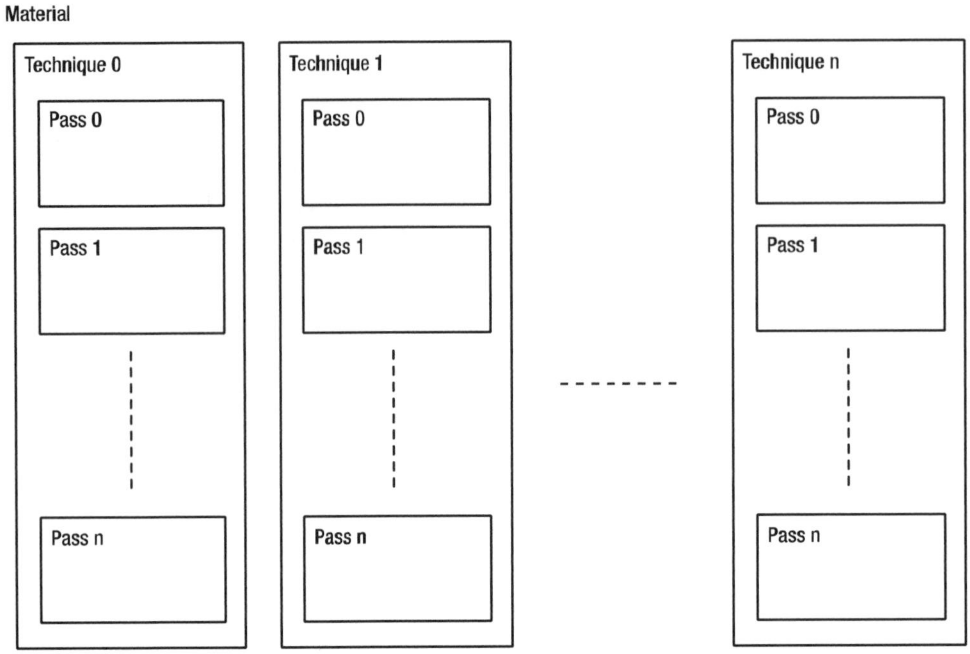

Material

Figure 6-2. *Relationship between material, technique, and pass in Ogre*

Pass

The pass, as you might suspect, is the complete atomic rendering state for a given renderable in a given draw operation on the GPU. A single renderable references a single material, and as you learned earlier, Ogre picks the technique from that material on a variety of bases. Once a technique is chosen, each pass in the technique is rendered in the order in which it appears. In other words, if Ogre selects a technique with three passes for a renderable object, it will draw that renderable three times every frame the object is drawn.

A pass also references any texture unit definitions needed for the execution of the pass. A pass does not need to include any texture unit definitions.

Texture Unit

The texture unit in an Ogre material actually refers to a *texture sampler* on the GPU. Most modern graphics hardware has more than one texture sampler (and therefore can support *multitexturing*, which allows a material to invoke more than one texture unit in a pass), but all hardware that Ogre supports will have at least one available texture sampler.

The texture unit contains the reference to a single texture, whether that texture originates from the disk, is rendered at runtime, or is streamed in from an external video source. You can specify as many texture units per pass as you like; Ogre will detect the number of available texture samplers on the GPU and automatically split up your pass into multiple passes if needed (assuming you have no fragment programs referenced in your material). For example, let's say you specify six texture units in a pass, but your hardware only has four samplers; Ogre will split the pass into two, and the passes will be blended to achieve the same end result (at the expense of a second rendering pass on the object).

Textures typically exist in video memory until they are no longer needed. Ogre does not send the texture across the bus each time it is needed unless the texture is constantly discarded from video memory (usually a symptom of texture thrashing, caused by your application using too many or too large textures for them all to remain in video memory at once).

Texture Compression

While modern graphics hardware typically supports compressed textures (such as the DXTC schemes), Ogre will simply load your textures and send them as is on their way across the bus to the graphics hardware. It will not do any compression on the textures (for example, transcoding the texture from an uncompressed RGBA TGA to a highly compressed DXT1 format). You would need to perform the conversion offline (usually to a format such as DDS) and use the precompressed textures in your application. If your hardware does not support compressed textures, Ogre will decompress the texture at runtime for you, for use on that hardware.

Streaming Video

Ogre does not natively support streaming video in texture unit definitions, but it does have a more generic mechanism that allows texture units to obtain texture data from an external source such as a video streamer. Theora (http://www.theora.org) is one such video streamer, and a freely available Theora-based plug-in exists in the Ogre Addons. With this plug-in you can stream any video you like into your Ogre application, even live streaming video from a broadcast source: your imagination is the only limit.

Entities

There is nothing particularly magical or complex about an **Entity** in Ogre. In terms of rendering, the entity is largely just a container for the subentities that define the actual units of rendering in Ogre (the renderables, in other words). In the context of materials, the subentity has a one-to-one relationship with a particular submesh, which in turn provides the original material reference (usually defined in the 3D modeling tool that created the mesh). Conceptually, the **Entity** (and **SubEntity**) provide access to an object's rendering properties (such as the material) and the **Mesh** (and **SubMesh**) provide access to the object's structural properties (its geometry data).

Materials by Example

The best way to learn about material scripting and definition in Ogre is to learn from examples, so let's examine an actual material script. We will start with the simplest possible script that actually does something.

Materials and the Fixed-Function Pipeline

Listing 6-1 defines a material with a single technique, which contains a single pass. This material, when applied to an object in a scene, will shade the object with a flat medium gray.

Listing 6-1. *The Simplest Ogre Material in the Universe*

```
material VerySimple
{
    technique
    {
        pass
        {
            diffuse 0.5 0.5 0.5
        }
    }
}
```

The material defined in Listing 6-1, while incredibly underwhelming from an aesthetic standpoint, does serve to introduce the layout and structure of an Ogre material script. As you can see, the nested structure of the material is fairly intuitive: material contains technique(s), which contains pass(es).

Now let's look at something a bit more complex. In Listing 6-2, we create a second technique in the material, with more fixed-function shading directives.

Listing 6-2. *Extending the Material of Listing 6-1 to Include a Second Technique with Additional Fixed-Function Shading Directives*

```
material NotQuiteAsSimple
{
    technique
    {
        pass
        {
            diffuse  0.5 0.5 0.5
            ambient  0.1 0.2 0.3
            specular 0.8 0.8 0.8 68

            texture_unit
            {
                texture ReallyCool.jpg
                colour_op modulate
            }
        }
    }

    technique
    {
        pass
        {
            diffuse 0.5 0.5 0.5
        }
    }
}
```

Listing 6-2 approaches what would be a more practical material definition. The first technique listed employs texture mapping with the texture_unit section of its pass, referencing a fictional ReallyCool.jpg texture file. The more interesting part of the texture unit definition is how it defines the blend of the texels with existing colors: colour_op modulate instructs Ogre to multiply the color data from the texture with the current color value of the pixel (which may have been the result of previous color operations). In our case, the "current" color is simply the result of application (within the local lighting model) of the diffuse, ambient, and specular colors defined in the same pass.

Listing 6-2 is also our first material script that has a "fallback" technique. In the highly unlikely event that you encounter graphics hardware without the ability to map texture data to geometry, the second technique will be selected and your mesh will be shaded a nice, boring but safe, flat gray. This fallback is possible because both techniques belong to the same scheme ("Default") and material LoD (level 0).

■**Note** What is more likely to happen is that your application would not get even this far. Hardware old enough not to include texture mapping features very possibly also will not allow your 3D API (DirectX or OpenGL) to initialize, and therefore neither would Ogre be able to start up. Ogre is a very capable library, but it cannot upgrade your graphics hardware for you.

Listing 6-3 shows the first material defined in the file Example.material that comes with Ogre in the Samples\Media\materials\scripts directory.

Listing 6-3. *Material Definition Containing Only Texture Mapping Directives*

```
material Examples/EnvMappedRustySteel
{
	technique
	{
		pass
		{

			texture_unit Diffuse
			{
				texture RustySteel.jpg
			}

			texture_unit Environment
			{
				texture spheremap.png
				colour_op_ex add src_texture src_current
				colour_op_multipass_fallback one one
				env_map spherical
			}
		}
	}
}
```

One of the first things you notice about Listing 6-3 is that it defines a material named Examples/EnvMappedRustySteel. Even though this looks like a file system pathname, understand that it has nothing to do with any sort of hierarchy, and that the naming convention is for convenience only: as far as Ogre is concerned, everything to the right of the material tag, on the same line, is the name of the material. **This name must be unique throughout your application**. Ogre does not implement the concept of namespaces in terms of its materials; loading same-named materials into different resource groups will not "hide" the duplicate names from each other. If you want to use the same names for materials, you should use something similar to the path-like convention used in the preceding example.

Ogre will provide default names for your material elements (techniques, passes, texture units) if you do not. The convention is for the names to match the ordinal of the item in the script. For example, in Examples/EnvMappedRustySteel, the technique would be named 0, as would the pass. The texture units would be named 0 and 1, respectively, matching their order of appearance in the script. Naming of techniques, passes, and texture units is optional, so backward compatibility with existing scripts is maintained. Contrary to the overall material naming restrictions, you are not required to use globally unique names for techniques, passes, and texture units (although they must be unique within their containers, of course).

Listing 6-3 specifies that its second texture unit is a spherical environment map (the env_map directive). Environment mapping is an inexpensive means of achieving a reflective surface on an object without raytracing. This texture is additively blended with the texture specified before it, the rusty-steel texture. What would an object look like if this material were applied to it? Let's look at the textures referenced by the material. Figure 6-3 is RustySteel.jpg, and Figure 6-4 is spheremap.png.

Figure 6-3. RustySteel.jpg, *a basic diffuse texture*

Figure 6-4. `spheremap.png`, *an environment mapping texture*

The two textures in Figures 6-3 and 6-4 are additively blended and applied to the Ogre head mesh in Figure 6-5.

Figure 6-5. *The Ogre* Demo_EnvMapping *sample application, demonstrating the blending of the environment map with the rusty-steel texture*

Material Inheritance

What if we wanted to reuse `Examples/EnvMappedRustySteel` in Listing 6-3 with different textures (perhaps a version with hardware-supported compressed textures)? We do not have to copy the entire material script; we can just inherit the existing script and redefine the texture references in the texture units.

The Ogre code and documentation calls this *material copying*, since it is not true inheritance in the object-oriented sense of the term. However, you can create new materials, using existing materials as a sort of base class. All of the attributes of a material will be copied into the new material, and you can make slight adjustments by changing only the properties that are different from the original material. This can save a considerable amount of effort in large material libraries, or with complex or lengthy material declarations.

Keep in mind that the difference between object-oriented material inheritance does not stop with the material scripting; Ogre will not track inherited material properties in code. A material definition that inherits from another is truly a copy of the original: changes to the parent material have no effect on materials that inherited from it.

Naming

If you need to add techniques, passes, or texture unit definitions to a copied material, you very possibly may come up against name clashes between elements within the parent and child (*source* and *destination* in copying parlance). You must use unique names for the new elements in the copied material; for example, you cannot add a new technique named "Primary" if the source material already has a technique named "Primary"; you will have to use a different name for the added technique.

Texture Aliases

Naming of texture units enables simplified replacing of only the textures used in a copied material. For example, you might have a complicated material involving several techniques with several textures each. Instead of rewriting the entire texture unit declaration in the copied material, you can simply replace the textures used in each by addressing the texture unit in the cloned material.

```
material Examples/EnvMappedCompressedRustySteel : Examples/EnvMappedRustySteel
{
  set_texture_alias Diffuse rustySteel.dds
  set_texture_alias Environment sphereMap.dds
}
```

That is all there is to it. Now `Examples/EnvMappedCompressedRustySteel` differs from `Examples/EnvMappedRustySteel` only in the textures used. Quite a bit easier to manage, you might say, than playing copy-and-paste with a hundred slightly different material definitions.

Let's round out this section with a couple of examples that demonstrate several different aspects of materials in the same script. First in Listing 6-4 is a material used in the *Demo_TextureFX* sample application.

Listing 6-4. *Texture Effect Material in* Samples/Media/materials/scripts/Example.material

```
material Examples/TextureEffect4
{
    technique
    {
        pass
        {
            ambient 0.3 0.3 0.3
            scene_blend colour_blend
            cull_hardware none
            cull_software none

            texture_unit
            {
                texture Water02.jpg
                scroll_anim 0.01 0.01
            }
        }
    }
}
```

It might be somewhat difficult to see on a static printed page, but the water texture in Figure 6-6 is animated. If you run the *Demo_TextureFX* sample you get a much better idea of what it looks like, but if that is not handy, imagine the waves on the water moving as a result of the texture scrolling set in motion in the texture unit block in Listing 6-4.

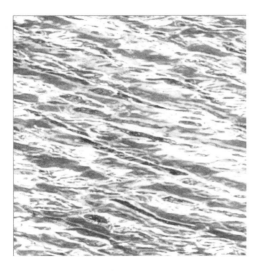

Figure 6-6. *Screenshot of the part of the* Demo_TextureFX *sample application that uses the material in Listing 6-4*

By default, Ogre will set up hardware culling in clockwise fashion (meaning that the graphics hardware will cull all triangles that are in clockwise winding order from the perspective of the camera). Some scene manager implementations may cull in software all triangles whose normal is facing away from the camera. This is the antithesis of two-sided polys, so if you need to render two-sided polygons you need to turn off culling for the objects you want rendered two-sided (such as the plane that uses this material in the *TextureFX* demo).

The quad rendered with this material is blended with the rest of the scene by adding the rendered output of the quad to the existing scene contents; however, the texture used by the material has no transparency so there is no blending performed. Alpha blending is a different directive: scene_blend alpha_blend.

Materials and the Programmable Pipeline

Scripting materials for the programmable graphics pipeline is a bit more involved than we have seen so far. Most of the directives you use for the fixed-function pipeline apply as well when referencing GPU programs; however, some are ignored because, well, when you are using the programmable pipeline, the fixed-function pipeline is ignored.

Three items are involved when including a GPU program in your material: the program itself, the program declaration, and a reference to the program in the actual material. Let's have a look at one of the simpler examples of a material with a GPU program: the hardware skinning example material that comes with Ogre and is used in the hardware skinning demo application (see Listing 6-5).

Listing 6-5. *The One-Weight Hardware Skinning Program Found in* Example.cg *in* Samples/Media/materials/programs/Example.cg *in the Ogre Distribution*

```
/*
  Single-weight-per-vertex hardware skinning, 2 lights
  The trouble with vertex programs is they're not general purpose, but
  fixed-function hardware skinning is very poorly supported
*/
void hardwareSkinningOneWeight_vp(
    float4 position : POSITION,
    float3 normal   : NORMAL,
    float2 uv       : TEXCOORD0,
    float  blendIdx : BLENDINDICES,


    out float4 oPosition : POSITION,
    out float2 oUv       : TEXCOORD0,
    out float4 colour         : COLOR,

    // Support up to 24 bones of float3x4
    // vs_1_1 only supports 96 params so more than this is not feasible
    uniform float3x4  worldMatrix3x4Array[24],
    uniform float4x4 viewProjectionMatrix,
    uniform float4   lightPos[2],
    uniform float4   lightDiffuseColour[2],
```

```
    uniform float4    ambient)
{

    // transform by indexed matrix
    float4 blendPos = float4(mul(worldMatrix3x4Array[blendIdx], position).xyz, 1.0);
    // view / projection
    oPosition = mul(viewProjectionMatrix, blendPos);
    // transform normal
    float3 norm = mul((float3x3)worldMatrix3x4Array[blendIdx], normal);
    // Lighting - support point and directional
    float3 lightDir0 = normalize(
        lightPos[0].xyz - (blendPos.xyz * lightPos[0].w));
    float3 lightDir1 = normalize(
        lightPos[1].xyz - (blendPos.xyz * lightPos[1].w));

    oUv = uv;
    colour = ambient +
        (saturate(dot(lightDir0, norm)) * lightDiffuseColour[0]) +
        (saturate(dot(lightDir1, norm)) * lightDiffuseColour[1]);

}
```

Do not be concerned if you do not understand what the program in Listing 6-5 does; for now, you can pay attention only to the bold text: the program's name. Also, you can name files containing GPU program source code whatever you want, with whatever extension you want; as you will see next, the file name is entirely arbitrary and meaningless to Ogre.

■**Note** If I have not mentioned it yet, you will not learn GPU programming in this book. Any GPU code listed will be for purposes of example only, and it is entirely up to you to do further research and education if you do not understand any of the GPU programs that appear in this book.

Once you have a program definition, you need to create a program *declaration* so that it can be included in a material. Listing 6-6 is such a declaration.

Listing 6-6. *One-Weight Hardware Skinning Program Declaration in* Samples/Media/materials/ scripts/Examples.program

```
// Basic hardware skinning using one indexed weight per vertex
vertex_program Ogre/HardwareSkinningOneWeight cg
{
    source Example_Basic.cg
    entry_point hardwareSkinningOneWeight_vp
    profiles vs_1_1 arbvp1
    includes_skeletal_animation true
}
```

Listing 6-6 declares a GPU vertex program called `Ogre/HardwareSkinningOneWeight`. It declares this program to be of type `cg`, which tells Ogre that it needs to invoke the Cg runtime to compile the program for use by the hardware. This declaration tells Ogre it can find the source in `Example_Basic.cg` (the code we listed in Listing 6-5). Since this is a Cg program, it has an *entry point*, which is the name of the Cg function to run first (Cg is a C-like language that supports a modular code structure). This entry point is the function listed in Listing 6-6 (the only function used in this program, but if you look in `Example_basic.cg`, you will find that it defines many different functions). (Side note: HLSL programs also have definable entry points, while assembler and GLSL programs do not: GLSL always uses a function named `main` as its entry point, and assembler programs simply run from top to bottom.)

The `profiles` attribute informs Ogre which Cg *profiles* the program requires in order to run. Ogre can then use this information for technique matching and fallback: if a particular set of hardware does not support the required profile, Ogre will fall back to the next technique, and so on. Cg programs use this notion of profiles; assembler programs use a similar mechanism called *syntax*, and DirectX HLSL uses a *target* to define the GPU capability requirements. All of these are different ways of saying the same thing: they all use the same values (namely, the options available for the assembler syntax). GLSL programs are compiled directly to native GPU machine code and therefore do not need anything like this.

Finally, in this example anyway, the program declaration informs Ogre that the program provides hardware skeletal animation acceleration support, and that Ogre should use this program to provide skinning instead of performing a software skinning pass (we will deal more with Ogre's animation capabilities in Chapter 9). This line obviously applies only if the program provides such support; you would not include this line in, say, a cel-shading GPU program.

Listing 6-7 is the actual material definition that uses the hardware skinning program. You can find this material in `Samples/Media/materials/scripts/Example.material`.

Listing 6-7. *Material Used by the Old "Robot" Hardware Skinning Demo*

```
material Examples/Robot
{
 // Hardware skinning technique
 technique
 {
    pass
    {
      vertex_program_ref Ogre/HardwareSkinningOneWeight
      {
          param_named_auto worldMatrix3x4Array[0] world_matrix_array_3x4
          param_named_auto viewProjectionMatrix viewproj_matrix
          param_named_auto lightPos[0] light_position 0
          param_named_auto lightPos[1] light_position 1
          param_named_auto lightDiffuseColour[0] light_diffuse_colour 0
          param_named_auto lightDiffuseColour[1] light_diffuse_colour 1
          param_named_auto ambient ambient_light_colour

      }
      // alternate shadow caster program
      shadow_caster_vertex_program_ref Ogre/HardwareSkinningOneWeightShadowCaster
```

```
        {
            param_named_auto worldMatrix3x4Array[0] world_matrix_array_3x4
            param_named_auto viewProjectionMatrix viewproj_matrix
            param_named_auto ambient ambient_light_colour
        }

        texture_unit
        {
            texture r2skin.jpg
        }
    }
}

// Software blending technique
technique
{
  pass
  {

      texture_unit
      {
          texture r2skin.jpg
      }
  }
 }
}
```

Listing 6-7 is mostly about populating the GPU program's input parameters. The first technique in this material is the hardware skinning technique; the second technique is strictly fixed-function in the event that the graphics hardware cannot support even this simple program, and Ogre must fallback to software skinning and the fixed-function pipeline.

■**Note** The robot mesh is textured with r2skin.jpg in either case. In the GPU program technique, this texture is made available to the GPU program (via the TEXCOORD0 input parameter semantic), not the fixed-function pipeline (which is idle during programmable passes).

So what exactly is going on in this material? In the first technique's first pass, we are telling Ogre that we want to use, in this pass, the GPU vertex program we declared earlier. (The second program reference, shadow_caster_vertex_program_ref, will make more sense once you have finished Chapter 9.) The next seven lines tell Ogre to populate automatically the five "uniform" parameters to the vertex program (the input and output parameters are filled automatically by the hardware, based on the semantics of the program parameters).

GPU Program Parameters

We need to pause here so I can describe for you the different types of parameters to GPU programs in Ogre. First of all, in GPU parlance parameters are called *constants*; from the perspective of the GPU program, these parameters you supply are in fact constant. This is why you see the terms *constant* and *parameter* used interchangeably in Ogre when dealing with and referring to GPU programs.

There are two types of parameters: *indexed* and *named*, and each of those can be either *auto* or *manual*. Their material directives are, as you might suspect, param_indexed, param_named, param_indexed_auto, and param_named_auto.

Indexed parameters are most often used for assembler programs (indexed is the only method of setting parameters to assembler programs), and the index in question is based on the way constants are stored on the card, namely in four-element blocks. Therefore, the first parameter index is zero, and the second and subsequent depend on the size of the parameters. For example, if the first parameter was a simple float4 (4-vector of floats), then the next index is 1. If the first parameter was a matrix4x4 (16 floats, or four 4-vectors of float4), then the second available index is 4. Figure 6-7 demonstrates the concept.

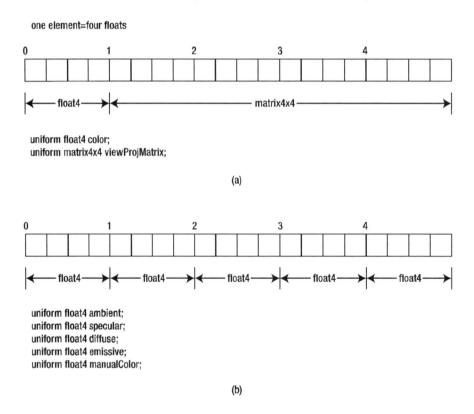

Figure 6-7. *(a) shows how two parameters of different sizes affect the indexing, and (b) shows how five parameters of the same size are indexed.*

Named parameters are much simpler to deal with; you simply use the same name in the material that you gave the parameter in the program, and Ogre sorts it out from there. However, named parameters are only supported by high-level shading languages such as Cg, HLSL, and GLSL. Assembler programs cannot use named parameters.

The difference between auto and nonauto parameters is in whether or not Ogre will take care of finding and assigning the values for you. Ogre can provide a plethora of different automatic values to your program. For a full listing of the available automatic parameters, see Appendix B.

However, you probably are most interested in getting data from your application into the GPU program: this is the `param_named` or `param_indexed` type. In order to set actual runtime values to GPU programs, you need to use the `GpuProgramParameters::setNamedConstant()` or `GpuProgramParameters::setConstant()` methods, respectively.

```
GpuProgramParametersSharedPtr params = entity->getSubEntity(0)->getMaterial()->
    getTechnique(0)->getPass(0)->getVertexProgram().createParameters();

params->setNamedConstant("ambient", ColourValue(0.5, 0.5, 0.5, 1.0));
```

Fragment programs (sometimes called *pixel shaders*) use the same mechanisms as vertex programs for declaring and populating GPU program parameters.

Custom Automatic Parameters

You can also bind CPU program data as a custom parameter to the GPU programs on a per-**Renderable** basis; this will allow you to avoid having to call `setNamedConstant()` each time your data changes. This magic involves the custom material directive (see Appendix B) and the `setCustomParameter()` method of **Renderable**.

For example, let's say we wanted to map a variable in our code to the ambient parameter to the shadow caster GPU program in Listing 6-7. We first need to change the automatic parameter data directive from `ambient_light_colour` to `custom`.

```
// alternate shadow caster program
shadow_caster_vertex_program_ref Ogre/HardwareSkinningOneWeightShadowCaster
{
    param_named_auto worldMatrix3x4Array[0] world_matrix_array_3x4
    param_named_auto viewProjectionMatrix viewproj_matrix
    param_named_auto ambient custom 12

}
```

The extra parameter supplied to the custom data directive informs Ogre which custom parameter to use, as defined next. The CPU program data variable that is supplied must be a 4-vector of float (the Ogre `Vector4` class, in other words), but what the four components mean to your CPU and GPU program is entirely up to you. In this case, we are using the components as R, G, B, and A color components.

```
Vector4 myColor;
entity->getSubEntity(0)->setCustomParameter(12, myColor);
```

Now when the GPU program is executed during a pass, Ogre will automatically provide to the program whatever is the current value of `myColor`. The index used does not have to be zero-based; it is used only for the purposes of looking up the bound data element.

A More Complex Example: Offset (Parallax) Mapping

I will close out the chapter with a more advanced, fully programmable example that involves both vertex and fragment programs. *Parallax mapping* (also known as *offset mapping*) is a means to add view-independent apparent depth (to a limit) to textured surfaces in a 3D scene. Figures 6-8 and 6-9 illustrate the effect in practice; notice that the apparent depth to the texture is independent of the viewing angle.

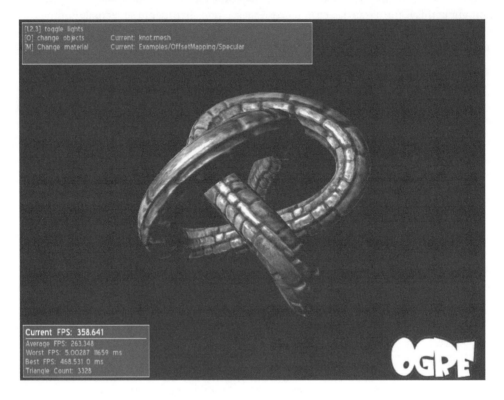

Figure 6-8. *Parallax (offset) mapping in the Demo_Dot3Bump sample*

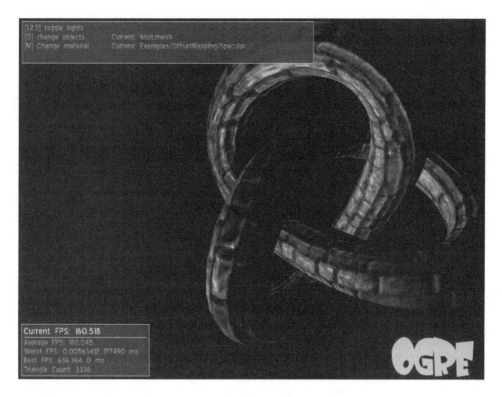

Figure 6-9. *Same scene as in Figure 6-8, but from a side view*

Listing 6-8 provides the material used for the offset-mapping portion of the *Demo_Dot3Bump* sample.

Listing 6-8. *Complete Parallax-Mapping (Offset-Mapping) Material Script (from* Samples/ Media/materials/scripts/OffsetMapping.material), *with GPU Program Declarations*

```
// Bump map with Parallax offset vertex program, support for this is required
vertex_program Examples/OffsetMappingVP cg
{
    source OffsetMapping.cg
    entry_point main_vp
    profiles vs_1_1 arbvp1
}


// Bump map with parallax fragment program
fragment_program Examples/OffsetMappingFP cg
{
    source OffsetMapping.cg
    entry_point main_fp
    profiles ps_2_0 arbfp1
}
```

```
// Bump map with parallax fragment program
fragment_program Examples/OffsetMappingPS asm
{
    source OffsetMapping_specular.asm
    // sorry, only for ps_1_4 and above:)
    syntax ps_1_4
}

material Examples/OffsetMapping/Specular
{

    // This is the preferred technique which uses both vertex and
    // fragment programs, supports coloured lights
    technique
    {
        // do the lighting  and bump mapping with parallax pass
        pass
        {

            // Vertex program reference
            vertex_program_ref Examples/OffsetMappingVP
            {
                param_named_auto lightPosition light_position_object_space 0
                param_named_auto eyePosition camera_position_object_space
                param_named_auto worldViewProj worldviewproj_matrix
            }

            // Fragment program
            fragment_program_ref Examples/OffsetMappingFP
            {
                param_named_auto lightDiffuse light_diffuse_colour 0
                param_named_auto lightSpecular light_specular_colour 0
                // Parallax Height scale and bias
                param_named scaleBias float4 0.04 -0.02 1 0
            }

            // Normal + height(alpha) map
            texture_unit
            {
                texture rockwall_NH.tga
                tex_coord_set 0
            }

            // Base diffuse texture map
            texture_unit
            {
```

```
            texture rockwall.tga
            tex_coord_set 1
        }
    }
}


// This is the preferred technique which uses both vertex and
// fragment programs, supports coloured lights
technique
{
    // do the lighting and bump mapping with parallax pass
    pass
    {

        // Vertex program reference
        vertex_program_ref Examples/OffsetMappingVP
        {
            param_named_auto lightPosition light_position_object_space 0
            param_named_auto eyePosition camera_position_object_space
            param_named_auto worldViewProj worldviewproj_matrix
        }

        // Fragment program
        fragment_program_ref Examples/OffsetMappingPS
        {
            param_indexed_auto 0 light_diffuse_colour 0
            param_indexed_auto 1 light_specular_colour 0
            // Parallax Height scale and bias
            param_indexed 2 float4 0.04 -0.02 1 0
        }

        // Normal + height(alpha) map
        texture_unit
        {
            texture rockwall_NH.tga
            tex_coord_set 0
        }

        // Base diffuse texture map
        texture_unit
        {
            texture rockwall.tga
            tex_coord_set 1
        }
    }
}
```

```
// Simple no-shader fallback
technique
{
    pass
    {
        // Base diffuse texture map
        texture_unit
        {
            texture rockwall.tga
        }
    }
}
}
```

The material in Listing 6-8 includes a vertex program declaration (Examples/ OffsetMappingVP) and two fragment program declarations (Examples/OffsetMappingFP and Examples/OffsetMappingPS). The reason for the two different fragment program declarations is that the technique that uses the Examples/OffsetMappingPS supports Pixel Shader 1.4 or above; in other words, it is a less-capable pixel shader than that referenced in Examples/OffsetMappingFP, which requires Pixel Shader 2.0 or above support. Listing 6-9 provides the Cg program definitions referenced by the program declarations in Listing 6-8, and Listing 6-10 provides the assembly program referenced by Examples/OffsetMappingPS.

Listing 6-9. *Cg-Language Offset-Mapping Vertex and Fragment Programs, Available in* Samples/ Media/materials/programs/OffsetMapping.cg

```
/* Bump mapping with Parallax offset vertex program
   In this program, we want to calculate the tangent space light-end eye vectors
   which will get passed to the fragment program to produce the per-pixel bump map
   with parallax offset effect.
*/

/* Vertex program that moves light and eye vectors into
texture tangent space at vertex */

void main_vp(float4 position   : POSITION,
             float3 normal     : NORMAL,
             float2 uv         : TEXCOORD0,
             float3 tangent    : TEXCOORD1,
             // outputs
             out float4 oPosition   : POSITION,
             out float2 oUv         : TEXCOORD0,
             out float3 oLightDir    : TEXCOORD1, // tangent space
             out float3 oEyeDir      : TEXCOORD2, // tangent space
             out float3 oHalfAngle   : TEXCOORD3, //
             // parameters
             uniform float4 lightPosition, // object space
```

```
            uniform float3 eyePosition,    // object space
            uniform float4x4 worldViewProj)
{
   // calculate output position
   oPosition = mul(worldViewProj, position);

   // pass the main uvs straight through unchanged
   oUv = uv;

   // calculate tangent space light vector
   // Get object space light direction
   float3 lightDir = normalize(lightPosition.xyz -  (position * lightPosition.w));
   float3 eyeDir = eyePosition - position.xyz;

   // Calculate the binormal (NB we assume both normal and tangent are
   // already normalized)
   // NB looks like nvidia cross params are BACKWARDS to what you'd expect
   // this equates to NxT, not TxN
   float3 binormal = cross(tangent, normal);

   // Form a rotation matrix out of the vectors
   float3x3 rotation = float3x3(tangent, binormal, normal);

   // Transform the light vector according to this matrix
   lightDir = normalize(mul(rotation, lightDir));
   eyeDir = normalize(mul(rotation, eyeDir));

   oLightDir = lightDir;
   oEyeDir = eyeDir;
   oHalfAngle = normalize(eyeDir + lightDir);
}

// General functions

// Expand a range-compressed vector
float3 expand(float3 v)
{
    return (v - 0.5) * 2;
}

void main_fp(float2 uv : TEXCOORD0,
    float3 lightDir : TEXCOORD1,
    float3 eyeDir : TEXCOORD2,
    float3 halfAngle : TEXCOORD3,
    uniform float3 lightDiffuse,
    uniform float3 lightSpecular,
    uniform float4 scaleBias,
```

```
        uniform sampler2D normalHeightMap,
        uniform sampler2D diffuseMap,
        out float4 oColor : COLOR)
{
    // get the height using the tex coords
    float height = tex2D(normalHeightMap, uv).a;

    // scale and bias factors
    float scale = scaleBias.x;
    float bias = scaleBias.y;

    // calculate displacement
    float displacement = (height * scale) + bias;

    float3 uv2 = float3(uv, 1);

    // calculate the new tex coord to use for normal and diffuse
    float2 newTexCoord = ((eyeDir * displacement) + uv2).xy;

    // get the new normal and diffuse values
    float3 normal = expand(tex2D(normalHeightMap, newTexCoord).xyz);
    float3 diffuse = tex2D(diffuseMap, newTexCoord).xyz;

    float3 specular = pow(saturate(dot(normal, halfAngle)), 32) * lightSpecular;
    float3 col = diffuse * saturate(dot(normal, lightDir)) * lightDiffuse +
        specular;

    oColor = float4(col, 1);
}
```

Listing 6-10. *ASM (Assembly) Program Targeting Pixel Shader 1.4, Available in*
Samples/Media/materials/programs/OffsetMapping_specular.asm

```
// Pixel Shader for doing bump mapping with parallax plus diffuse and
// specular lighting by nfz

// uv                       TEXCOORD0
// lightDir                 TEXCOORD1
// eyeDir                   TEXCOORD2
// half                     TEXCOORD3

// lightDiffuse             c0
// lightSpecular            c1
// Parallax scale and bias  c2
// normal/height map        texunit 0 - height map in alpha channel
// diffuse texture          texunit 1

ps.1.4
```

```
texld r0, t0                    // get height
texcrd r2.xyz, t0               // get uv coordinates
texcrd r3.xyz, t2               // get eyedir vector


mad r0.xyz, r0.a, c2.x, c2.y    // displacement = height * scale + bias
mad r2.xyz, r3, r0, r2          // newtexcoord = eyedir * displacement + uv

phase

texld r0, r2.xyz                // get normal N using newtexcoord
texld r1, r2.xyz                // get diffuse texture using newtexcoord
texcrd r4.xyz, t1               // get lightdir vector
texcrd r5.xyz, t3               // get half angle vector

dp3_sat r5.rgb, r0_bx2, r5      // N dot H - spec calc
dp3_sat r4.rgb, r0_bx2, r4      // N dot L - diffuse calc
+ mul r5.a, r5.r, r5.r
mul r0.rgb, r4, r1              // colour = diffusetex * N dot L
+ mul r5.a, r5.a, r5.a

mul r5.rgb, r5.a, r5.a
mul r5.rgb, r5, r5
mul r5.rgb, r5, r5
mul r5.rgb, r5, c1              // specular = (N dot H)^32 * specularlight

mad r0.rgb, r0, c0, r5          // colour = diffusetex * (N dot L)* diffuselight +
                                // specular
+ mov r0.a, c2.b
```

The programmable passes are performed only for one light (usually the first light in the scene). The vertex program is supplied with three automatically populated parameters: light position, eye position, and the current world-view-projection matrix (the three uniform parameters supplied to main_vp). The tangent data is supplied as an element in the vertex data (encoded in 3D UVW texture data), along with the vertex position, normal, and standard decal UV coordinate; these elements are the first four parameters to the vertex program. Tangent data typically is generated during an offline step, such as mesh export or during XML conversion, but you can build tangent vectors at runtime (for example, when creating mesh dynamically) with Mesh::buildTangentVectors(). main_vp provides its corresponding fragment program with five output parameters: the vertex position and four texture coordinate sets (the typical decal UV coordinates, and light, eye, and half 3-vectors in tangent space).

Ogre provides the fragment programs automatically with the diffuse and specular light colors, and your application can supply the height scale and bias data packed into a 4-vector (default values are supplied and used if it does not). The fragment program in either case takes as additional input (from the vertex program outputs earlier in the pipeline) the per-instance parameters defined in the pass, as well as the texture units defined in the pass and the output of the corresponding vertex program (the parameters marked out in main_vp in Listing 6-10). The fragment program then outputs the calculated pixel color, which is stored in the framebuffer.

The ASM and Cg fragment programs perform the same work; the reason that the PS 1.4 version is written in assembly instead of Cg has to do with limitations in earlier Pixel Shader versions; these earlier versions could not support dependent texture reads, where texture coordinates can be adjusted based on what was read from another texture. Adding this fragment program for PS 1.4 support allows this programmable technique to run on DirectX 8.1–level hardware (Radeon 8500 and up, for example).

▓**Note** Notice how texture coordinate sets are used to pass arbitrary data through to the fragment program. This usage pattern of unused texture coordinates is not specific to Ogre; it is a common method of storing otherwise anonymous data for use in a GPU program (either for sending data from the CPU to a vertex program or for passing data from the vertex program to the fragment program, as used in this example).

Conclusion

The Ogre material system is a very flexible, yet very straightforward way of managing the rendering properties of the objects in your scene. The goal of this chapter was to familiarize you with the ways that Ogre handles materials, and how it expects you to create and manage the materials for your project. This chapter was not intended to cover every single detail of all of the Ogre material attributes and directives: that would be exhausting and boring; the full set of directives and parameters for material scripting are provided in Appendix B. Instead, you should now be armed with the knowledge you need to create whatever material effect you need for your application. If you need information on all of the material directives and attributes available, Appendix B contains a material-scripting quick reference for your convenience.

In the next chapter, you will learn about the Ogre subsystem that, among other duties, finds and makes available your material scripts to your application: the Ogre resource management system.

■■■

## CHAPTER 7

Resource Management

Everything that Ogre uses to render your scene, it knows as a *resource*. Fonts, meshes, skeletons, materials, GPU programs—they are all resources to Ogre. *Resource management* is the term used to describe the organization strategy employed by Ogre to manage loading of and access to all of the files and data it needs.

Conceptual Overview

Back in Chapter 3, you learned a bit about how the Ogre resource management system operated in support of the rest of the API. For convenience, let's review that here.

The following types of resources are understood and supported directly by the stock Ogre distribution. While it is true that not all resources must exist as disk files, for the sake of brevity in this review, the assumption is that all resources start as disk files.

- **Material**: These `.material` script files contain the material definitions (techniques, passes, texture units, and so on).

- **Mesh**: Optimized binary `.mesh` files that contain the vertex, geometry, and some animation data.

- **Skeleton**: Optimized binary `.skeleton` files that contain the bone hierarchy and animation keyframe data used with skeletal animation in Ogre.

- **Font**: Textual `.fontdef` files that contain the font definitions, TrueType font references, and other font rasterization configuration data.

- **GPU programs**: GPU program definitions (for high-level HLSL, GLSL, or Cg programs, or low-level ASM GPU programs) are contained in `.program` files; the `.program` file is analogous to the `.material` file, but `.program` files are always parsed before any `.material` files.

- **Compositor scripts**: `.compositor` script files are very similar to `.material` files, except that they contain the definitions and directions for the Compositor framework (which you will learn about in Chapter 12).

- **Texture**: 2D images employed as texture data for use in texturing geometry during rendering. These files do not have any particular extension, other than their conventional extensions: `.jpg` or `.jpeg` for JPG files, `.tga` for Targa files, and so on.

Resource Management

You have many good reasons for using a resource management system as opposed to just loading a resource from a disk file as needed. One is speed: disk access is **slow** compared to memory access, so you do not want to exacerbate an already tight time budget per frame loading anything from the disk. Furthermore, not only is it faster to have (potentially compressed) data loaded, unpacked, and ready to go in memory, it is more efficient overall to swap out resources when they are no longer needed, and bring in resources at the time they are needed. Finally, with a resource management system, you do not need to load into memory, up front, every resource your application might ever need.

Resource Groups

Ogre can manage resources at two levels: in terms of the individual resources themselves or in named groups. Named groups have the advantage of being loadable and unloadable as a whole: you can treat all resources in a group as a unit when loading, unloading, and initializing them, rather than handling them individually (useful when you are loading dozens or hundreds of resources at a time, such as during game-level loading and initialization).

Resource group management is entirely up to the programmer. There is no performance benefit or detriment with using or not using resource groups; they exist entirely for your own organizational convenience. You cannot overwhelm a single group with resources; the resource search algorithm uses an O(1) complexity algorithm, so it can handle sizable resource counts with minimal performance degradation. If you add resource locations to the resource group manager without specifying a group name, they will end up in the General group, but if you do not care about organizing your resources into groups, then you do not need to care about this either.

Resource Groups and World Geometry

By default, Ogre places world geometry loaded by the scene manager into the General group. You can override this to allow management of the scene/world geometry resource data the same way you manage other resources. For example, you might not want to load world geometry until the resource group containing the world objects is loaded. Compatible scene managers will also provide a hint as to the number of steps required to load the world, allowing you a simple way to provide accurate loading progress feedback to your users during level loading, using the **ResourceGroupListener** callback class (example included later in the chapter in Listing 7-5).

Resource Locations (Archives)

Resource location refers to a place Ogre will look for resources to index. *Index* is defined the same here as it is with, say, an Internet search engine: resources in a location are mapped by their name for fast lookup when needed.

You can add and remove resource locations in your application at any time you want; you do not have to define them all up front. For example, you might have a particular resource group named World that contains all of your game's level data and resources. You can add and clear the World group as often as you like during your application's execution (for example, when the player moves from one level or mission to the next). This is also useful for tool authors, as users typically access resources located in different parts of their file system while using a tool, making it virtually impossible to define all resource group locations at application startup.

A resource location in Ogre is actually an *archive*, which is a fancy way of saying "a collection of files." When you provide Ogre with a location to add to the set of locations it will search for resources, you are giving it the top-level starting point of a potentially hierarchical file organization structure. If that sounds a lot like the definition of a file system, then you are correct: the file system on a hard disk drive is one type of archive that Ogre understands. However, you might have a potentially hierarchical organization of files contained within a single file on the file system: this is the more "classic" definition of an archive, and describes more accurately, say, a ZIP archive. The stock Ogre distribution can handle the ZIP archive format as well.

Archives can be any format you want: you just need to write the **Archive** class implementation to handle the format. Archives must

- Support enumeration of named *leaf* files at each node in the hierarchy (commonly known as a *directory listing* with disk file systems), with *wildcard* support (file name pattern matching, such as "*.gif")

- Support node recursion (for archives that support nodes containing other nodes, such as subdirectories in a file system)

- Provide Ogre with a stream containing the data in a file within the archive

Archives in Ogre are read-only; no writing of archive data is supported by the Ogre **Archive** interface. This is not to say that you cannot implement write capability in your **Archive** implementation, just that Ogre has no need for it, so no "write" methods exist in the interface.

Ogre's resource group manager uses the archive enumeration features to index the archive's contents. Ogre does not actually load any resources when it indexes an archive; that comes later.

Resource Life Cycles

Figure 7-1 outlines the life cycle of Ogre resources in the form of a state transition graph and the "events" that cause transitions. The events are Ogre API calls, some examples of which are given in the graph. Typically, you do not need to be concerned with managing resource states unless you are implementing a custom resource memory management scheme; Ogre will cause all transitions to happen "under the hood" and make your resources available in your application when they are needed.

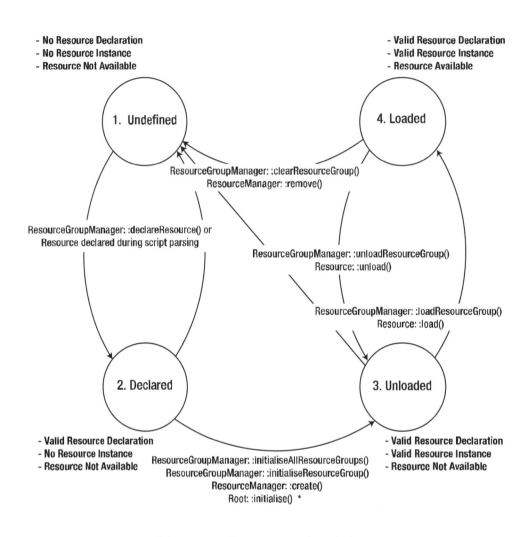

- No Resource Declaration
- No Resource Instance
- Resource Not Available

- Valid Resource Declaration
- Valid Resource Instance
- Resource Available

1. Undefined

4. Loaded

ResourceGroupManager: :clearResourceGroup()
ResourceManager: :remove()

ResourceGroupManager: :declareResource() or
Resource declared during script parsing

ResourceGroupManager: :unloadResourceGroup()
Resource: :unload()

ResourceGroupManager: :loadResourceGroup()
Resource: :load()

2. Declared

3. Unloaded

- Valid Resource Declaration
- No Resource Instance
- Resource Not Available

ResourceGroupManager: :initialiseAllResourceGroups()
ResourceGroupManager: :initialiseResourceGroup()
ResourceManager: :create()
Root: :initialise() *

- Valid Resource Declaration
- Valid Resource Instance
- Resource Not Available

* All resources and resource groups declared prior to
calling **Root: :initialise()** will be initialized when
Root: :initialise() is called.

Figure 7-1. *Resource life cycle*

If you are implementing a custom resource memory manager, then you should know a bit more about each state in a resource's lifetime, and what causes transitions from one state to another.

- **Undefined**: This is the default state of all resources at application startup; Ogre cannot know about any resources your application needs until they are declared, either manually in code with `ResourceGroupManager::declareResource()` or as a result of parsing a script file (such as a material script). In this state, your resources are using no memory at all.

- **Declared**: You declare a resource when you want to inform Ogre that you intend to load the resource as part of a bulk load (for example, with a call to `ResourceGroupManager::loadResourceGroup()`). The mechanism that allows you to declare a resource (namely, `ResourceGroupManager::declareResource()`) is always available (including prior to initializing a render system). This is in contrast to the `ResourceManager::create()` functionality, which depends on the placement of an initialized render system.

- **Unloaded**: Resources enter this state when they are initialized, by calling `ResourceGroupManager::initialiseAllResourceGroups()`, `ResourceGroupManager::initialiseResourceGroup()`, or `Root:initialise()` (which will also initialize any resources declared prior to its call). Your resource is using a small amount of memory now, enough to hold an instance of its definition, but the actual resource itself still is not loaded into memory. Resources can also become unloaded if you call `ResourceManager::unload()`, `ResourceManager::unloadAll()`, `ResourceManager::unloadAllUnreferencedResources()`, `ResourceGroupManager::unloadResourceGroup()`, or `Resource::unload()`. All of these will maintain the resource instance, but will remove the actual resource data from memory.

- **Loaded**: This is the "fully active" state of your resource: its data (for example, the actual texels in a texture resource) is available in memory, and you can use it in your application. Ogre will load resources automatically if they are not loaded (and their resource manager's memory quota has not been exceeded) when your application uses them (for instance, when adding an **Entity** to your scene with `SceneManager::createEntity()`). You can also force the loading of resources with `Resource::load()`, `Resource::reload()`, `ResourceManager::load()`, `ResourceManager::reload()`, `ResourceManager::reloadAll()`, `ResourceManager::reloadAllUnreferencedResources()`, and `ResourceGroupManager::loadResourceGroup()`.

Logical Resource Management

At this point, we depart the physical Ogre resource storage concerns and concentrate instead on the logical organization of Ogre resources. As mentioned, resources are organized at the top level into named groups. These groups each can contain any number of resource references to any type of registered resource (known resource types were enumerated earlier in this chapter in the section "Conceptual Overview").

Each type of resource gets its own resource manager, which is responsible primarily for loading and unloading resources of its type. Ogre does not implement any particular memory management scheme for its resources other than a configurable memory limit per manager; if you want to use, say, a least-recently-used scheme for a particular resource type, you will need to implement that in your code. Keep in mind that the video drivers already implement LRU management for the most important resources.

Resource Loading

Resources are loaded, if not already preloaded, when accessed. This access occurs most often deep within Ogre; for instance, when an entity is created, its mesh, material, and any skeleton are referenced (which loads them), and any GPU programs, textures, and/or fonts needed to render the entity are referenced (and loaded) as well.

The actual loading and unloading of a resource is delegated to the resource itself. The reason is that not all resources of a given type might come from the same place, or even from an archive.

Manual Resource Loading

Ogre supports the notion of a *manual resource loader* (as opposed to loading "automatically" from disk using the operating system API or from an archive file using its particular API). This makes it impossible to place the loading functionality in the resource manager layer, since a new implementation of the manager would have to exist for all manually loaded resources. The solution is to allow the actual resources to define how they are loaded, and fetch and assemble their data at this low level.

■**Note** This is a feature of *usage* and is not particular to any class. For example, a **Mesh** instance can be manually or automatically loaded, depending on the needs of the particular instance.

Normally, you do not need to worry about resources that exist on nonvolatile media such as a hard disk or CD-ROM not being there the next time you need them (for example, if the resource needs to be unloaded to make room for new resources and is later reloaded when it is needed again).

However, manual resources do not enjoy this advantage: the implementer of the manual resource loader has to be prepared to reload the resource at any time. This means that if the resource is procedural in origin, the manual loader code has to either cache the generated resource in memory somewhere or re-create it every time it is loaded by the resource manager. This is the primary caveat when dealing with manual resource loading; other than that, Ogre treats manually loaded and automatically loaded resources no differently.

Background Resource Loading

Ogre, by default, is not thread-safe.

■**Note** There are two very good reasons for this. First, modern GPUs are already inherently parallel architectures (sometimes massively so). Second, the drivers that bundle up your geometry and material data for rendering are single-threaded. Taking both of these points together, the case for making Ogre thread-safe (with the inherent and inevitable slowdown caused by the use of synchronization objects) is not a very strong one, although this does not stop users from regularly trying to make the case. This does not mean your application cannot be designed with concurrency in mind (most 3D applications benefit from concurrency), but you should view Ogre as a single thread in that design.

A compile-time #define does enable a limited form of thread-safety, but this thread-safety is limited solely to the resource management system and is used almost exclusively for the purpose of background resource loading.

You do not really want to try to load resources from disk during the middle of a frame setup; the tiniest latency in disk access will cause a noticeable "hiccup" in frame rate. You probably have noticed this in games you have played: when the disk activity light is on, the game is off. The solution is to load resources in another thread, separate from the main rendering loop: in the background, in other words.

Threaded Resource Management Ogre, as mentioned, does not implement this feature for you. However, if you enable thread-safety by setting

```
#define OGRE_THREAD_SUPPORT 1
```

in the header file OgreConfig.h, then the thread synchronization features in the resource management code are enabled, and you can manipulate the resource management classes and methods from a thread separate from the thread containing the **Root** instance. This will allow your intelligent resource loading scheme to run unhindered and direct Ogre to load and unload resources as needed by your application.

Nonthreaded Resource Management If you are not comfortable with threads, or if you feel the additional development bandwidth is not worth the gain for your application, then Ogre can accommodate you as well. As mentioned early in this book, the Ogre design contains plenty of examples of the *Observer* design pattern, and the resource management system is not exempt.

The **ResourceGroupListener** callback interface contains several methods that allow you to monitor the progress of resource loading at a very granular level and take whatever action you deem necessary at any step along the way. For example, you might perform only one of the ten stages of resource loading per frame, and execute the next step during the next frame, and so on, until the resource is loaded and initialized, and then move on to the next resource. In this way, you can implement a sort of lightweight, "cooperative multitasking" approach to loading resources in the background that does not involve multiple threads.

Resource Unloading

Resource data stays in memory once loaded until it is forcibly unloaded by the application (through the resource group manager or by releasing the resource directly). The resource group manager unloads resources at the group level, meaning that all resources in a group will be released when using the group manager to do so. In no case, group or otherwise, will Ogre remove a resource from memory automatically; in fact, you cannot force-unload resources until only the resource group manager and the resource manager have references to the resource.

Intelligent resource management for 3D applications is a research topic unto itself, and I will not debate the merits of one system over another here. It is enough to mention that Ogre will not manage your resources for you. Any further intelligence (for example, just-in-time loading/unloading policies) must be supplied by the developer. Luckily, Ogre allows a high degree of control over the lifetime of various resources, as you have seen in this chapter, so you can easily supply this intelligence.

Resource Management in Practice

Listing 7-1 provides an example (from the default Ogre SDK distribution) of the `resources.cfg` file that the Ogre demo application framework uses to initialize its resource locations.

Listing 7-1. *Contents of the* `resource.cfg` *File That Comes with the Ogre Demo Applications*

```
# Resource locations to be added to the 'bootstrap' path
# This also contains the minimum you need to use the Ogre example framework
[Bootstrap]
Zip=../../media/packs/OgreCore.zip

# Resource locations to be added to the default path
[General]
FileSystem=../../media
FileSystem=../../media/fonts
FileSystem=../../media/materials/programs
FileSystem=../../media/materials/scripts
FileSystem=../../media/materials/textures
FileSystem=../../media/models
FileSystem=../../media/overlays
FileSystem=../../media/particle
FileSystem=../../media/gui
Zip=../../media/packs/cubemap.zip
Zip=../../media/packs/cubemapsJS.zip
Zip=../../media/packs/dragon.zip
Zip=../../media/packs/fresneldemo.zip
Zip=../../media/packs/ogretestmap.zip
Zip=../../media/packs/skybox.zip
```

Listing 7-1 is fairly self-explanatory. Two resource groups are populated from this file: Bootstrap and General. General always exists, so when you add resources to this group, no new group is created. The Bootstrap group in this example has meaning only to the Ogre demo `ExampleApplication` framework; it is a completely arbitrary name (like any non-General resource group name), and not to be considered anything special like General.

`FileSystem` and `Zip` prescribe the archive type: `FileSystem` indicates a file-system–based resource location, and `Zip` indicates that the resource location is a standard ZIP file. If you implement a custom archive type, you could use the specifier here.

Resource Locations

One commonly asked question is, "How can I set resource locations without `resources.cfg`?" Let's look at the code from `ExampleApplication.h`, as shown in Listing 7-2, that reads the `resources.cfg` file shown earlier.

Listing 7-2. *Code Used in the* ExampleApplication *Framework to Parse the* resources.cfg *File*

```
// Load resource paths from config file
ConfigFile cf;
cf.load("resources.cfg");

// Go through all sections & settings in the file
ConfigFile::SectionIterator seci = cf.getSectionIterator();

String secName, typeName, archName;
while (seci.hasMoreElements())
{
   secName = seci.peekNextKey();
   ConfigFile::SettingsMultiMap *settings = seci.getNext();
   ConfigFile::SettingsMultiMap::iterator i;
   for (i = settings->begin(); i != settings->end(); ++i)
   {
      typeName = i->first;
      archName = i->second;
      ResourceGroupManager::getSingleton().addResourceLocation(
         archName, typeName, secName);
   }
}
```

■**Note** resources.cfg is a file that is used for the convenience of the demo applications only; you will not find any Ogre API calls that deal with a resources.cfg file. The **ConfigFile** class (and its nested classes), however, **is** part of Ogre; it is designed to read and parse file formats such as those used by resources.cfg. You can also use this class for your own configuration files if you wish; there is nothing in it specific to Ogre.

This is the code used in all of the Ogre demos to read and parse the resources.cfg file used by the Ogre demo applications. It simply iterates through each section in the file (in this case, the sections are also the group names, Bootstrap and General), and for each section iterates each name/value pair in the section. For each name/value pair, it calls the addResourceLocation() method of **ResourceGroupManager**.

The primary method to observe in Listing 7-1 is addResourceLocation(). It may be easier to observe the analogue between the code and the config file with a more hard-coded example (see Listing 7-3).

Listing 7-3. *Explicit, Hard-Coded Example of Performing the Same Actions As Listing 7-2*

```
ResourceGroupManager *rgm = ResourceGroupManager::getSingletonPtr();
rgm->addResourceLocation("../../media/packs/OgreCore.zip", "Zip", "Bootstrap");
rgm->addResourceLocation("../../media", "FileSystem", "General");
rgm->addResourceLocation("../../media/fonts", "FileSystem", "General");

// and so on, for the rest of the locations in the file
```

Note that in both Listings 7-1 and 7-2, we use relative pathnames to our resource locations. Ogre has no problem with using absolute pathnames, but if you do so, you run the risk of your application not working on machines other than the one on which you are developing it, since you cannot guarantee that everyone has their computer set up the same way as you. Do yourself a favor: get into the habit of using relative pathnames for your resource locations.

Resource Initialization

Once you have added a resource location, you have to initialize the group you placed it in before the resources in that location are available to your application (see Listing 7-4). You must also create at least one rendering window before initializing your resources, since parsing of scripts may create GPU resources, which require a rendering context in order to exist.

■Caution I wanted to highlight this because failure to perform this important second step is the reason for one of the top five most common questions asked in the Ogre support forums, and one of the simplest mistakes to prevent.

Listing 7-4. *Initializing Resource Locations*

```
// initialize all of the previously defined resource groups
ResourceGroupManager::getSingleton().initialiseAllResourceGroups();

// or, alternately, initialize the defined resource groups one at a time
ResourceGroupManager::getSingleton().initialiseResourceGroup("General");
ResourceGroupManager::getSingleton().initialiseResourceGroup("Bootstrap");
```

In Listing 7-4, the first example initializes all uninitialized locations, and the second example initializes them one at a time.

Resource Unloading

You can unload a resource (individually or by group) from memory at any time; if the resource is referenced elsewhere in your code when you unload it, it simply will be reloaded next time it is used. Ogre thus will prevent you from permanently unloading resources that are in use, thereby saving you from yourself in a potentially bad situation (at least in terms of 3D-related resources).

Unloading by Group Name

The following code shows pretty much the extent of resource unloading from the **ResourceGroupManager** interface:

```
ResourceGroupManager::getSingleton().unloadResourceGroup("Bootstrap", true);
ResourceGroupManager::getSingleton().
    unloadUnreferencedResourcesInGroup("Bootstrap", true);
```

As mentioned earlier, the interface loads and unloads resources a group at a time. This only unloads the resources' data from memory; it does not remove the resource instances. `ResourceGroupManager::unloadUnreferencedResourcesInGroup()` will only unload those resources for which no references exist (other than those held by the **ResourceGroupManager** and **ResourceManager**).

The `true` parameter we supplied indicates that Ogre should unload only resources that can be reloaded; those resources that were marked as nonreloadable when created will not be unloaded with this call. Supplying the default of `false` would unload everything in the group, regardless.

Clearing or Destroying Resource Groups

The difference between clearing a resource group and destroying it is subtle but important. Clearing the group will only unload and de-index all of its resources:

```
ResourceGroupManager::geSingleton().clearResourceGroup("Bootstrap");
```

Destroying the group will do the same as `clearResourceGroup()`, with the additional step of removing the group itself from the list of resource groups.

```
ResourceGroupManager::geSingleton().destroyResourceGroup("Bootstrap");
```

Unloading Individual Resources

If you wish to manage resource lifetimes at a level of smaller granularity, you can do so right on the resource itself, with the `unload()` method.

```
// assume that pEntity is a valid pointer to an instance of Entity
MeshPtr meshPtr = pEntity->getMesh();
meshPtr->unload();
```

Loading/Reloading Resource Groups

You can load all resources declared in a resource group with a single call.

```
ResourceGroupManager::getSingleton().loadResourceGroup("Bootstrap");
```

This method also takes a couple of additional parameters that control whether or not to load only "normal" resources, load world geometry, or both. For example, to load or reload only world geometry, the call would be

```
ResourceGroupManager::getSingleton().loadResourceGroup("Bootstrap", false, true);
```

and to load or reload only the "normal" resources in the group:

```
ResourceGroupManager::getSingleton().loadResourceGroup("Bootstrap", true, false);
```

Resource Group Loading Notification

Ogre will notify your application of resource group loading events if you register a listener for those events. This is useful for implementing a loading-progress-feedback UI, for performing preprocessing (or postprocessing) on loaded resources, and so on (see Listing 7-5).

Listing 7-5. *Simple Implementation of a **ResourceGroupListener** for the Purpose of Driving a Loading-Progress Meter UI Widget (the Fictional **ProgressMeter** Class)*

```cpp
// note: the ProgressMeter class used in this example is entirely
// fictional

class LoadingProgressListener : public ResourceGroupListener
{
public:
    LoadingProgressListener(ProgressMeter& meter) :
        m_progressMeter(meter) { m_currentResource = 0; }

    // ResourceGroupListener event methods

    // fired when a group begins parsing scripts
    void resourceGroupScriptingStarted(const String& groupName,
        size_t scriptCount) {}

    // fired when a script is about to be parsed
    void scriptParseStarted(const String& scriptName) {}

    // fired when the script has been parsed
    void scriptParseEnded() {}

    // fired when all scripts in the group have been parsed
    void resourceGroupScriptingEnded(const String& groupName) {}

    // fired when a resource group begins loading
    void resourceGroupLoadStarted(const String& groupName,
        size_t resourceCount) { m_resCount = resourceCount; }

    // fired when a resource is about to be loaded
    void resourceLoadStarted(const ResourcePtr& resource) {}

    // fired when the resource is done loading
    void resourceLoadEnded();

    // fired when a step in world-geometry loading has been started
    void worldGeometryStageStarted(const String& description) {}

    // fired when a step in world-geometry loading has been completed
    void worldGeometryStageEnded();

    // fired when a resource group is fully loaded
    void resourceGroupLoadEnded(const String& groupName) {}
```

```
private:
    int m_resCount;
    int m_currentResource;
    ProgressMeter &m_progressMeter;
};

void LoadingProgressListener::worldGeometryStageEnded()
{
    // increment the current stage counter
    m_currentResource++;

    // update the progress meter with the amount complete
    m_progressMeter.updateProgress((float)m_currentResource /
        (float)m_resCount);
}

void LoadingProgressListener::resourceLoadEnded()
{
    // increment the current stage counter
    m_currentResource++;

    // update the progress meter with the amount complete
    m_progressMeter.updateProgress((float)m_currentResource /
        (float)m_resCount);
}

//
// register the listener with the ResourceGroupManager somewhere in your code
//

// instantiate a listener using an existing instance of the ProgressMeter class
LoadingProgressListener listener(m_progressMeter);
ResourceGroupManager::getSingleton().addResourceGroupListener(&listener);
```

The code in Listing 7-5 is a simple example of how you might perform the update of a loading-progress meter in your application. In this example, we are interested in updating the meter only when a resource (whether a "normal" resource or world geometry loading stage) has completed loading; the rest of the **ResourceGroupListener** callback methods are stubbed out (since they are declared pure virtual in the interface, their implementation does not actually have to do anything other than exist).

This example utilizes a "fictional" **ProgressMeter** class; this class is entirely made up, assumed to exist for the purposes of this example, and not a part of Ogre at all.

Ogre Archives

By the most basic description, an archive is a collection of files stored in a single file. An archive might exist in compressed format, it might contain compressed files but the archive itself is not compressed, it might do both, and it might do neither. The archive exists solely to provide efficient access to the files contained within.

Ogre accesses its resource files via an archive abstraction, defined by the **Archive** interface. This interface is implemented by any class that wishes to provide the services of an archive to Ogre. In the stock Ogre distribution, as mentioned previously, the only true archive implementation provided is for ZIP files (archives, compressed or otherwise, stored in the public domain PKZIP format). Ogre also treats standard file system storage as an archive, and accesses plain disk files through the archive interface as well.

Both of these methods have their advantages. Accessing plain file system disk files is useful during the construction and testing of an application, as it allows you to alter and swap files quickly without having to rebuild a (potentially huge) archive file to iterate on testing and trial and error. However, production releases of an application typically use some form of archive file format to provide efficient access to application assets and resources.

Archive

You are not restricted to the choice between PKZIP compressed archive format or individual file storage in the file system. You can easily implement a new archive handler and make that archive type available to Ogre for your application. In fact, in keeping with Ogre convention of "everything is a plug-in, even the stock functionality," the **FileSystemArchive** and **ZipArchive** implementations do just that: they make great references if you wish to implement a custom archive type.

ArchiveManager

Making a new archive implementation available to Ogre is as simple as implementing a class that derives from **Archive** to handle the actual archive access and a class that derives from **ArchiveFactory** that creates instances of that archive when needed, and then supplying an instance of the **ArchiveFactory** to the **ArchiveManager** subsystem (see Listing 7-6).

Listing 7-6. *Registering a New Archive Type with Ogre*

```
class MyArchive : public Archive
{
    // Archive implementation here
};

class MyArchiveFactory : public ArchiveFactory
{
    // implement the ArchiveFactory (FactoryObj template) methods here
    // For example, createInstance()
    Archive* createInstance(const String& name) {
        return new MyArchive(name, "MyArchiveType");
    }
};
```

```
void function()
{
    MyArchiveFactory *factory = new MyArchiveFactory;

    ArchiveManager::getSingleton().addArchiveFactory(factory);
}
```

When Ogre encounters the type of archive you have registered (either while processing a `resources.cfg` file or when manually setting up resource locations), it will access the archive through the **Archive** class you just registered. For example, when the Ogre `ExampleApplication` framework encounters a `Zip` line in the `resources.cfg` file, it accesses that archive through an instance of **ZipArchive**. In the preceding example, when you specify a resource location of type MyArchiveType, it will use an instance of `MyArchive` to handle the archive.

Custom Resource Loading via Archive Implementation

Continuing our custom resource loader example from earlier, the same effect can be achieved by implementing a custom archive type instead. Understand that Ogre does not really care whether the data exists as an actual archive file or exists solely in memory, so long as it can obtain information about the contents of the archive and can access, by file name, the "files" contained within. You can pull off a complete fake archive that loads or creates "files" on demand (they do not even have to exist in any form until a load is requested) and maintains a skeleton table of contents that can be provided to Ogre when it indexes the archive. For example, many games use a large archive file known as a *wad* file for their deployed asset storage. One strategy would be to open the wad file as a memory-mapped file and maintain a completely independent table of contents for the wad. Then, supply Ogre with arbitrary "files" created on the fly by copying bits of the wad file through a memory buffer and providing that data to Ogre as if it were a newly opened disk file. This way you can maintain independent usage of or access to the wad file from other non–Ogre related parts of your application and still allow the file to contain Ogre-related resources, accessible via a standard mechanism satisfactory to Ogre.

Conclusion

Resource management in 3D applications is not a complex topic, but it is an important one. Poor resource management can lead to dismal performance and dissatisfaction among your user base. You should now have the tools and understanding you need to make intelligent decisions regarding the resource management strategy in your Ogre-based application.

In the next chapter, we will begin our transition into the more GPU-specific portion of this book, and start learning about how Ogre leverages the power and features available with common graphics acceleration hardware.

## CHAPTER 8

Ogre Render Targets

Ogre is not limited to rendering to the display device; to Ogre, the framebuffer that holds the color data that eventually makes its way to your LCD or CRT display is simply another render target. The *render target* in Ogre is an abstraction of an area in shared AGP or video memory that holds the two-dimensional result of a render of all or part of your scene.

The most common render target is of course the primary render window. This is your application's main window, the one that you can resize and minimize and Alt+Tab to and from. You do not need to do anything special to use this render target; just start up Ogre as described in earlier chapters, and it is created for you.

However, most interesting applications and games benefit from the ability to render all or part of the scene (even parts of the scene that are not visible) into a texture that can then be applied to polygons in the scene. Some examples of this include a rear-view mirror on a car in a racing game; a security monitor simulation that shows another part of your world on a quad near your player-character; reflections in a mirror or on the surface of water; precomputed data used as a lookup table in a later rendering pass; full-scene renders for use in a later postprocessing pass (such as for motion-blur effects). These are just a few examples of the utility of the *render-to-texture* (RTT) capability that multiple render targets provide. Note that while you certainly can render to a buffer that does not ultimately end up as a texture, the most common nondirectly displayed render is to a texture. This chapter will focus primarily on the render-to-texture aspect and usage of render targets.

Conceptual Overview

The target hardware buffer (framebuffer or otherwise) is abstracted in Ogre as a render target. The physical manifestation of the render target can be your application's main rendering window, or it can be a secondary window (perhaps used to show a different view of the scene or a view with different rendering properties enabled). As mentioned, the nonvisible manifestation of a render target can be a texture target: a texture, after all, is just a 2D "surface" like a rendering window's framebuffer.

Render targets are event sources as well. If your application registers to receive such events, Ogre will notify it at pre- and postrender times, providing your application an opportunity to alter, on a per-target basis, render settings, object visibility, and so on. It can also notify your application pre- and postrender at the viewport level, as well as when viewports are added and removed.

Ogre provides a small utility feature as part of the render target: it will calculate rendering stats for your convenience. Of course, you do not need to use these calculations, but if you wish to know how long a frame took to render (and even a running smoothed-average framerate) and/or how many triangles were rendered in a given render target, Ogre is more than happy to provide you these numbers. These numbers can be used for anything from simple stats over-lays (as in the Ogre Sample applications) to adaptive complexity reduction or framerate stabilization. For example, some developers prefer to limit their framerates during more idle periods to prevent the application from hogging the CPU unnecessarily.

Render Window

There is nothing mysterious about the render window in Ogre. It is a window in the operating system's windowing GUI, like any other window. It is created and managed by the render system implementation. Under Windows, it is a normal Win32 window (actually, a normal Win32 window when the Direct3D 9 render system is used). Under Linux, it can be a GLX window (default), GTK window, or SDL window (though SDL is deprecated in Ogre 1.2).

Ogre allows minimal configuration of the render window, typically limited to manipulat-ing its size and title bar text. The render window usually is not intended to be a full-fledged GUI window, with drop-down menus and so on. If you are developing an application that has menuing and toolbars and the like, and you want to have Ogre render into that window's client area, that is possible as well. Ogre will provide you the window system–specific handle to the render window, and also will allow you to provide the handle to a parent window. Ogre will then create the render window in the client area of that parent. Experienced users (espe-cially tool authors) often prefer to manage the window system hierarchy themselves and have Ogre render into the window context of their choice.

The first Ogre render window you create will be the *primary* window. This is the window to which the Direct3D device or OpenGL context will be bound. Any other additional render window you create is a *secondary* one, and its management is not as important as the first, pri-mary, window. For example, if your application creates three render windows, you need to shut down (destroy) the two secondary windows before destroying the first primary window in order for your application to clean up properly. Failure to observe this ordering will cause your application to lose its rendering context/device when the primary window is destroyed (your application effectively shuts down, in other words, possibly in a very nasty fashion).

Viewports

A render target contains one or more viewports. A *viewport* is a rectangle into which a scene manager renders its visible contents, from the perspective of a single camera. While viewports are "created" with reference to a particular camera, that is not a static property of the viewport; you can change the camera used to render the viewport at any time.

Each viewport in a render target occupies a single *z-order* (the "vertical" stacking order within the render target). Viewports with higher z-order are rendered on top of those with lower z-order (z-order 0 is nearly always occupied by a viewport covering the entire render target), and interesting effects can be achieved by careful organization and configuration of multiple overlapping viewports within a render target.

■**Caution** Other interesting, but unwanted, side effects can also be had by careless organization and configuration of multiple overlapping viewports. Ogre will clear a viewport's color and depth buffer contents by default; however, you can turn off these buffer clearings, and as a result, multiple overlapping viewports will share the contents of the render target's depth buffer. This can lead to unwanted depth fighting between the contents of two otherwise unrelated viewports.

The viewport is the single point of interaction between the render target (and therefore a particular render system such as the OpenGL render system) and the camera (and therefore a particular scene manager and its contents). The viewport is your "window into the scene," in other words.

Viewports do not have to occupy the entire render target's surface area, but in most cases, they will. Typically, your main rendering window likely will contain, at least most of the time, a single viewport covering the entire window. However, interesting effects can be achieved by using viewports smaller than the size of the render target. For example, a car-racing simulation will benefit from an additional viewport within the cockpit view of a rear-view (and/or side-view) mirror. The mirror would contain the rendered contents of a second camera pointing behind the vehicle. Another example might be a picture-in-picture "zoom" view in a combat simulator; the second viewport contains the rendered contents of a second camera placed closer to the target.

■**Note** One common mistake (at least from the standpoint of performance considerations), especially with non–picture in picture zoom views, is simply changing the camera's focal properties to effect a "closer" rendering (by narrowing the field of view, for example, as you learned in Chapter 4). After all, this is all that a real camera would do. The problem with this approach is that a 3D rendering camera is **not** a real camera, and since all geometry LoD calculations are done from the location of the camera in world space, the quality of the contents of the zoom view usually are less than stellar. If you encounter this and cannot figure out why, this is the reason. Use a second camera positioned closer to the target; the geometry LoD will begin to work as you expected.

Render Texture

The most interesting form of render target is the texture. The concept is simple: some (or all) of your scene is rendered to a texture, which is then used to render other bits of the scene later in the frame.

The steps in the process are also fairly straightforward: create a texture render target, configure its rendering properties, add that texture to the render target list, and set the texture to be used in some material. Ogre takes care of the rest; texture targets are updated (rendered) prior to all other render target types, so objects that use materials with RTT textures can be assured that the texture is current when the object is rendered. Render texture targets are textures like any other, and can be managed, handled, blended, etc., in the same way as any other texture. For texture targets that do not need to be updated every frame, you can turn off the automatic per-frame updating and update each target manually as needed.

Performance Considerations

Under the covers, texture targets are simply hardware buffers. For highest performance, treat them as write-only and static (in fact, you will not be writing to them at all on the CPU in most cases), and do not make a habit of reading rendered textures back from the hardware, and so on.

Render-to-texture is in fact a rendering of geometry in the scene. As such, it does take time to perform, and the time it takes each frame will reduce your application's framerate, sometimes considerably (especially if you have complex renderings to texture targets). However, some algorithms simply cannot be performed any other way. In Chapter 12, you will learn about one set of useful techniques used for real-time shadowing; these techniques rely exclusively on render-to-texture techniques. Real-time reflections also require RTT techniques to exist; static reflection solutions such as environment mapping cannot provide reflections of dynamic objects, such as the reflection of a boat moving on the surface of a body of water. Another interesting use for RTT materials is *3D GUI* techniques; solutions that map 2D GUI controls onto 3D objects in the scene, providing a novel alternative to the "same old boring GUI" found in many 3D games and applications. For example, you could map a dialog box or main menu onto a spinning cube or lateral wall, and your users could interact with the GUI widgets as if they were displayed in the "normal" 2D overlay fashion.

If you want to render your objects or scene to multiple textures at the same time (for example, if you want to render, say, your scene's normals to one texture and depth information to another), Ogre supports that functionality as well. Ogre will render to as many multiple render targets as the hardware supports. The only restriction on multiple texture render targets is that they must all be the same size. Apart from that, each target behaves normally like any other render target; it can contain multiple viewports, and so on.

Render Target Classes

Most of the classes you use in Ogre to manage and manipulate render targets are fairly self-evident. **RenderTarget** is the base class for the three types of render targets supported: **RenderWindow**, **MultiRenderTarget**, and **RenderTexture**.

Render Window by Example

RenderWindow is implemented in several subclasses: **D3D9RenderWindow**, **GLXWindow**, **GTKWindow**, **SDLWindow**, and **Win32Window**. Since Ogre on Linux uses only OpenGL and defaults to GLX for platform support, you will most often be using the **GLXWindow** variant under Linux. On Windows, you have the choice of the Direct3D 9 and OpenGL render systems, so you will be using either the **D3D9RenderWindow** or **Win32Window** classes, respectively. OpenGL uses the **Win32Window** version on Windows, since GLX is present only with an X Windows server; however, since XFree86 (now X.Org, http://www.x.org) runs on Windows as well (typically under the Cygwin platform layer: http://www.cygwin.com), it is possible to run Ogre applications under the GLX platform even on Windows.

Render windows are obtained from the **RenderSystem** that is chosen at application startup. Typically, the window is actually obtained from the **Root** object instance, in its capacity as a façade class (it simply delegates the call to the selected render system). Ultimately, however, the render window is produced by the createRenderWindow() method of **RenderSystem**:

```
RenderWindow* createRenderWindow(const String &name, unsigned int width,
    unsigned int height, bool fullScreen,
    const NameValuePairList *miscParams = 0);
```

This method will produce a windowing system window containing the rendering surface for your application. Through the `miscParams` name-value list parameter, you can set the following extended, often platform-specific, window options:

- **Window title**: Indicates the text that appears in the window's title bar (as well as the taskbar in windowing systems that use one). The default window title is "OGRE Render Window". Note that this is not the same as the `name` parameter passed in this method; that parameter is used for unique identification of the window within the render system, and does not have to be the same as the window title. Parameter key: `title`.

- **Window border**: Sets the style of border for the render window (applies only to windowed mode, nonparented/nonembedded render windows). Possible values are `none`, `fixed`, and `resize`. Default is `resize`. Parameter key: `border`.

- **Render window dimensions**: Indicates whether the window dimensions as specified in the `createRenderWindow()` width and height parameters apply to the entire window (including decorations) or the actual client rendering area (inner dimensions). Possible values are `true` (dimensions include decorations) and `false` (dimensions apply only to the client area). Default is `false`. Parameter key: `outerDimensions`.

- **Color depth**: Defines the bit depth for the rendering window, which can be 16 or 32. This parameter is specific to Windows only; Linux and Mac use the depth of the current "visual." The default on Win32 is also the desktop depth (as set in Display Properties). Parameter key: `colourDepth`.

- **Window position**: Serves as the only means to position the window on the desktop in terms of pixels (offset from upper-left corner of the desktop). Default behavior is to center the window on the desktop. Parameter keys: `top`, `left`.

- **Depth buffer**: Controls whether the window uses a depth buffer or not (valid values are `true` or `false`, default is `true`). DX9-specific. Parameter key: `depthBuffer`.

- **External window handle**: Embeds Ogre's rendering context in another window in the windowing system. For Windows, this value is the textual equivalent of the window handle (`HWND`). Under X Windows (GLX, Linux, Mac), this is either in the format "*A:B:C*" or "*A:B:C:D*", where *A* is the display pointer value (`XDisplay*`), *B* is the screen number (typically 0), *C* is the window handle, and *D* is an `XVisualInfo*` value. This is essentially a hack to allow platform-independent, window system–specific code, but it is really the most direct and simple way of providing this information. Convert the text strings to integers, and you are set. Default is 0. Parameter key: `externalWindowHandle`.

- **Parent window handle**: Has the same format, purpose, and default as the external window handle, except that this value contains the information for the render window's parent window in the window system. Parameter key: `parentWindowHandle`.

- **FSAA**: Specifies a different full-screen antialiasing factor. Possible values are 0, 2, 4, 6 . . . multiples of two. Default is 0. Parameter key: `FSAA`.

- **Refresh rate**: Specifies a different refresh rate for the render window. Possible values are valid values for the display settings. Applicable only in full-screen mode. Default is the desktop refresh rate. Parameter key: `displayFrequency`.

- **Vertical sync**: Turns on (or off) synchronization with the vertical blanking interval (which typically limits framerates to 60Hz on NTSC displays and 50Hz on PAL displays, but ensures that framebuffers are not displayed until they are fully drawn). Applicable only in full-screen mode. Possible values are `true` and `false`. Default is `false`. Parameter key: `vsync`.

- **NVPerfHUD**: Enables/disables rendering through the NVIDIA Performance Counter Overlays (known as NVPerfHUD). Requires installation of the NVIDIA Instrumented Driver (http://developer.nvidia.com/object/nvperfhud_home.html). Specific to Direct3D 9 and NVIDIA accelerated graphics hardware. Possible values are `true` and `false`. Default is `false`. Parameter key: `useNVPerfHUD`.

Listing 8-1 shows an example of render window creation. This window will be full screen, with a 75Hz refresh rate and 2X FSAA and vsync turned on.

Listing 8-1. *Creation of Full-Screen Render Window*

```
NameValuePairList params;   // is just a typedef std::map<std::string, std::string>

// set for 2x AA
params["FSAA"] = "2";

// turn on vsync
params["vsync"] = "true";

// set to 75Hz refresh rate
params["displayFrequency"] = "75";

RenderWindow* window = createRenderWindow("MyWindow", 800, 600, true, &params);
```

Tool creators often want to embed the Ogre rendering window inside another windowing system widget. This is accomplished easily with the same window creation call, as shown in Listing 8-2.

Listing 8-2. *Creation of Embedded Render Window*

```
NameValuePairList params;   // is just a typedef std::map<std::string, std::string>

// set external window handle -- assume that you have
// already created a window to embed the Ogre render window, and its handle is
// stored in an integer variable called "mParent"

params["externalWindowHandle"] = StringConverter::toString(mParent);

// window can be resized later to fit within parent client area if needed
RenderWindow* window = createRenderWindow("MyWindow", 800, 600, false, &params);
```

Render-to-Texture by Example

As you might expect, the collection of Ogre demos includes a render-to-texture example. Oddly enough, it is named *Demo_RenderToTexture*. Let's examine the critical parts of that application.

Demo_RenderToTexture

The render-to-texture demo application is fairly simple in concept. It creates a tilted plane centered at the origin and sets up a camera to render into a texture a reflection of the scene contents relative to that plane (the scene consists of an Ogre head and several torus knots), as you can see in Figure 8-1. The render texture is then blended with a static texture already applied to the plane, resulting in the simulation of real-time reflections (something that would only have been possible with an offline raytracing renderer in the not-too-distant past). This entire process is done without any GPU programming at all. Although it does not show up in the static screenshot of Figure 8-1, the reflection rendering also takes into account the animated skybox texture in a view-dependent manner (that is, when the camera moves, the skybox is reflected accurately in the render texture).

Figure 8-1. *The Ogre render-to-texture demo in action*

The code in Listing 8-3 is taken verbatim from the createScene() method of RenderToTextureApplication, RenderToTexture.cpp. I want to focus here on the section that sets up the render texture; the rest of the method is fairly common scene setup code (loading entities, creating the plane, and so on). Listing 8-3 will be used in the plane material later in the code. PF_R8G8B8 represents a 24-bit nonalpha pixel format.

Listing 8-3. *Creating a 512×512, 24-Bit 2D Render Texture Named* RttTex

```
TexturePtr rttTex = TextureManager::getSingleton().createManual("RttTex",
    ResourceGroupManager::DEFAULT_RESOURCE_GROUP_NAME,
    TEX_TYPE_2D, 512, 512, 0, PF_R8G8B8, TU_RENDERTARGET);
```

Listing 8-4 goes about the process of setting up a camera and viewport used to render scene contents into the texture.

Listing 8-4. *Creating the Camera and Viewport Used to Render the Texture*

```
{
    mReflectCam = mSceneMgr->createCamera("ReflectCam");
    mReflectCam->setNearClipDistance(mCamera->getNearClipDistance());
    mReflectCam->setFarClipDistance(mCamera->getFarClipDistance());
    mReflectCam->setAspectRatio(
        (Real)mWindow->getViewport(0)->getActualWidth() /
        (Real)mWindow->getViewport(0)->getActualHeight());


    Viewport *v = rttTex->addViewport( mReflectCam );
    v->setClearEveryFrame( true );
    v->setBackgroundColour( ColourValue::Black );
```

Note that the reflection camera is set up identically to the current main camera (the one used to render the whole scene). This is because the reflection camera will render from the same position as the main camera; we are not trying to pull off any fancy effects here, we just want to render the scene normally (only reflected at the plane).

We then add a viewport to the render texture and set it to clear every frame. This is important because otherwise the texture will contain the contents of the previous scene's render (useful if we want to implement a motion-blur effect for some reason, but wholly undesirable for our purposes in this demo). The viewport background color is set to black to ensure that the texture is devoid of color when we begin rendering into it each frame.

Listing 8-5 sets up the actual Ogre material that will be used on the plane that was set up in a previous (unshown) part of createScene().This material will be applied to the plane created earlier in the createScene() method.

Listing 8-5. *Creating the Material to Use the Render Texture*

```
MaterialPtr mat = MaterialManager::getSingleton().create(
    "RttMat", ResourceGroupManager::DEFAULT_RESOURCE_GROUP_NAME);
TextureUnitState* t = mat->getTechnique(0)->getPass(0)->
    createTextureUnitState("RustedMetal.jpg");
t = mat->getTechnique(0)->getPass(0)->createTextureUnitState("RttTex");
// Blend with base texture
t->setColourOperationEx(LBX_BLEND_MANUAL, LBS_TEXTURE, LBS_CURRENT,
    ColourValue::White, ColourValue::White, 0.25);
t->setTextureAddressingMode(TextureUnitState::TAM_CLAMP);
t->setProjectiveTexturing(true, mReflectCam);
rttTex->addListener(this);
```

This material is named RttMat, and includes a single technique with a single pass. This pass is given two texture units, one for the static texture (loaded from the image file RustedMetal.jpg) and the other, named RttTex, for the render texture. The two textures are set up to blend the render texture into the RustedMetal.jpg texture by 25% (meaning the render texture will have 25% of the intensity of the static texture when applied to the plane during rendering). You can see this difference in the blending in Figure 8-1.

Projective texturing is required for rendering a reflection texture to world geometry. TAM_CLAMP is used to prevent filtering over the edges of the render-to-texture (at the edges of the screen when projected).

Finally, the RenderToTextureApplication class instance is added to the render texture target as a listener (we will examine the callback methods shortly).

Listing 8-6 demonstrates an important step for the operation of this demo.

Listing 8-6. *Setting Up the Camera for Reflection and Assigning the Material from Listing 8-3 to the Plane*

```
// set up linked reflection
mReflectCam->enableReflection(mPlane);
// Also clip
mReflectCam->enableCustomNearClipPlane(mPlane);
}

// Give the plane a texture
mPlaneEnt->setMaterialName("RttMat");
```

In Listing 8-6, the camera is set to render a reflection of the scene. This reflection is relative to the plane; that is, the same plane that will receive the render texture in its material is also the plane that divides the scene for reflection. This is a common setup, used often for water reflections; it only makes sense, if you think of it in terms of reality: the plane that will show the reflections is the plane at which the reflections are referenced. Think of pictures you have seen of placid mountain lakes, where the reflection is mirrored on the lake surface. This is the same thing.

The use of a custom near clip plane might not be as readily understood. Without a custom clip plane, objects below the reflection surface will render as well (which is not what you want when rendering a reflection), and with the custom plane, you can conform the clipping to the reflection plane. Several reasons exist for altering the view frustum as opposed to using user-defined clip planes. For one, user-defined clip planes are not available on all hardware, while near clip planes are. Near clip planes also are faster than user-defined clip planes on all hardware. Finally, the loss of depth precision as a result of using a custom near clip plane usually does not impact the typical uses for custom near clip planes (namely, rendering reflections to a texture, as we are doing here).

The final step in Listing 8-6 sets up the plane to use the material we defined in Listing 8-5.

The other half of the equation happens each frame, when the scene contents are rendered into the texture, as shown in Listing 8-7.

Listing 8-7. *Hiding the Plane Before Rendering and Making It Visible Again After Rendering*

```
void preRenderTargetUpdate(const RenderTargetEvent& evt)
{
    // Hide plane
    mPlaneEnt->setVisible(false);

}
void postRenderTargetUpdate(const RenderTargetEvent& evt)
{
    // Show plane
    mPlaneEnt->setVisible(true);
}
```

Each time the texture is rendered, we want to use the plane to define the "mirror surface" for the reflection, but we do not actually want to render the plane itself. Therefore, we have to "turn it off" prior to rendering into the texture, and then turn it back on once the texture has been rendered. This is why we called addListener() method >rttTex->addListener() in Listing 8-5; the **RenderToTextureApplication** class implemented the **RenderTargetListener** callback interface, and addListener() registered the class with the texture target to be notified of these events.

One last thing worth mentioning is that each frame, the reflection camera is updated to have the same position and orientation as the main camera.

```
// Make sure reflection camera is updated too
mReflectCam->setOrientation(mCamera->getOrientation());
mReflectCam->setPosition(mCamera->getPosition());
```

The user can move the main camera around, and we want the reflection camera to render from the same perspective as the main camera; otherwise, the reflection would not look right.

Demo_Fresnel

The Fresnel example application (shown in Figure 8-2) demonstrates the calculation and usage of refractive Fresnel terms in photo-realistic rendering of water environments. The goal of this demo is to show the blending of the refractive and reflective Fresnel terms for a photo-realistic real-time scene rendering. The demo uses render-to-texture for the reflective and refractive textures, and blends them in a pair of GPU shaders (vertex and fragment programs, not shown).

Figure 8-2. *The Demo_Fresnel Ogre application*

The effect on viewing of objects beneath the surface of water as a function of the view angle was first observed and quantified by Augustin-Jean Fresnel in the early 19th century. While the primary focus of the *Demo_Fresnel* application is on this effect, it also uses RTT in much the same way that the *Demo_RenderToTexture* uses it. A second reflective camera is set up to render everything above the water for use in applying a reflection texture to the surface of the water. Furthermore, a third camera is used to render everything under the water as well, to a "refractive" texture.

Once the geometry under the water is rendered to a texture, it is no longer rendered in the scene at all. Instead, both the reflective and refractive textures are applied to the surface of the water, and both are then perturbed in a GPU fragment shader using a noise function; this is what gives the appearance of ripples on the water surface (the geometry of the water surface is not deformed at all). In addition (and this is the "Fresnel" part of *Demo_Fresnel*), the blending between the two render textures is not static; instead, the blending varies, conforming to a *Fresnel term*, which mathematically describes the relationship between the amount of reflection and refraction at varying viewing angles. Next time you are near a lake or other (relatively clear) body of water (or even a good-sized swimming pool), observe how different viewing angles affect the amount of reflection and refraction at the water surface; this is the Fresnel term in real life.

Conclusion

This chapter introduced the concept of render targets, a generalization that includes the functionality of render windows as well as render textures (useful for implementing a number of interesting effects, such as real-time reflections). You also learned about the relationship between render targets and viewports, and the purpose of viewports in the rendering process.

In the next two chapters, you will leverage the knowledge gained in this chapter as you learn about billboarding, particles, shadows, and the Compositor in Ogre.

## CHAPTER 9

Animation

Animation, in general, is no different in the computer age than it was when some artist first flipped quickly through pages containing a series of slightly different images and noticed that it gave the illusion of motion. In 1872, Eadweard Muybridge settled a bet (not his own) by rigging several cameras to take a series of photographs of a running horse (to prove that all four feet left the ground), and the resulting animation strip was the first documented instance of a sequence of images streaming to form the illusion of motion.

In the early 21st century, you do not have to rig up an elaborate Rube Goldberg of an apparatus to create the illusion of motion in your 3D Ogre scene: you simply move and/or deform bits of your scene a little each frame, and the illusion of motion is created. However, it is in fact just an illusion: Ogre does not keep track of an object's velocity and acceleration vectors, or whether your character's arm is raised or hanging akimbo. Ogre deals with positions and orientations on a frame-by-frame basis. What Ogre **will** do for you, however, is assist you in replaying animations you create in an offline tool, or procedurally at runtime, or even just fitting a curve to a series of positions to support a nice camera move (during a cutscene, for example).

Your scene is drawn from scratch every frame; nothing is saved between frames (apart from whatever resources might be needed that are already on the GPU from previous frames). Whether your scene includes animated characters or not, it is drawn anew each frame. The animation features in Ogre, as mentioned, are there only to help position and orient your characters (or other animated objects) as a function of some arbitrary variable (usually time, although any variable can act as a controller). Every frame, entities and animations under the control of the animation system in Ogre are moved or deformed in your scene a little bit, and the scene is redrawn. This is no different than the animation team at, say, Warner Brothers, drawing a cartoon rabbit 24 times in a row (in a slightly different pose or position each time) to give him one second of motion when the images are played back in sequence at standard cinematic speeds (24 frames per second). The only difference in Ogre is the automatic nature of the controllers at your disposal (semiautomatic, anyway, as you will learn in this chapter). So, let's get on with it.

Types of Animation Support in Ogre

In general, Ogre supports two different ways to manipulate objects on a functional basis. The first is *keyframed animation*, and the other is via a *controller*.

Animation

At the highest and most abstract level, an animation in Ogre is a collection of possibly (usually) related *tracks*. An animation track is a set of data values stored as a function of time. The pair of *time point* and *track value* composes a *keyframe* (a fancy way of saying "sample the position, orientation, and scale of all or parts of an object over time"). Ogre supports several types of keyframes, depending on the type of animation, as you will see shortly. Ogre also supports several types of tracks; the type of track used to store keyframes corresponds to the type of data being keyframed.

■Note The term *keyframe* comes from the days of hand-drawn animation (such as the animated rabbit mentioned previously) when master artists would provide the junior artists with a set of "key" frames in an animation. These keyframes provided the target poses and positions of various characters in the scene, and the junior artists would perform *tweening*, which is an odd way of saying "drawing the 'in-between' positions and poses of the characters," hence the name. I bring this up to illustrate the role Ogre plays in your 3D animations. In this case, you are the master artist, providing the keyframes, and Ogre is the junior artist, dutifully tweening your animations between the keyframes. In nearly 100% of the cases, you (or your artists) will be creating the keyframes in an offline 3D modeling tool such as Blender, SoftImage|XSI, Maya, or 3D Studio Max. Ogre then uses that keyframe data to interpolate, between keyframes, the various positions of bones in a skeleton or vertices in a mesh, allowing your animation to perform in the Ogre scene as it did in the offline tool.

The following types of animation tracks are supported in Ogre (note that all keyframes in a track must have a consistent type):

- **NumericAnimationTrack (NumericKeyFrame)**: Keyframes contain a single scalar value, of **AnyNumeric** type. **Any** is a special Ogre construct, similar to the variant type in COM, that allows polymorphic behavior at the data-type level. **AnyNumeric** restricts the range of possible data types to only those that are numeric (either real or integer).

- **NodeAnimationTrack (TransformKeyFrame)**: Keyframes contain two 3-vectors and a quaternion, representing (respectively) a node's position, scale, and orientation for that key frame.

- **VertexAnimationTrack (VertexMorphKeyFrame, VertexPoseKeyFrame)**: Keyframes contain (or reference in the case of pose animation) vertex position (and blend weight, in the case of **VertexPoseKeyFrame**) data at a particular point in time.

Animation State

The primary interaction between your application and an animation in Ogre is through an *animation state*. In your modeling tool, you can define multiple animations for a skeleton or mesh along a timeline. As part of the export process, different parts of the timeline in an object's animation can be given names; your code uses these names to "address" different animations on an entity. The object returned is an animation state that provides access to the following properties of the animation:

- **Length**: Get length, in seconds, of the animation segment.

- **Current position**: Set or get current position, in elapsed time (seconds) from the beginning of the animation segment (not from the beginning of all animations).

- **Animation name**: Since you can also get a list of all of the animations on an object, this provides (read-only) access to the animation's name in case it is unknown in advance.

- **Looping**: Set or get whether or not the animation will loop when it reaches the end of the segment.

- **Enabled**: Set or get whether or not this animation is enabled.

- **Weight**: Animations can be blended (with some restrictions, described next). This property sets or gets the amount of influence this animation has when blended with others.

Animation blend weights are processed differently depending on which type of animation is being blended:

- **Blend weight averaging**: When you instruct Ogre to use blend weight averaging (`ANIMBLEND_AVERAGE`), weights must always add up to 1.0. If the sum of all weights is not 1.0, then Ogre will normalize all of the present weights to sum up to 1.0. This can create unintended consequences, such as an intended weight of 0.3 behaving as 0.5, when it is blended only with one other animation of weight 0.3. Likewise for two animations blended, each with a weight of 1.0: both will have only half the intended influence on the overall animation when blended. Blend averaging is available only for skeletal animations, where it is the default blend type.

- **Blend weight accumulation**: When `ANIMBLEND_CUMULATIVE` is in effect, Ogre will simply accumulate the effects of all referenced weights, with no rebalancing. Blend accumulation is the only type of weight blending available for vertex animations (pose and morph) and is also available for use with skeletal animation.

The animation state is also where you add time to an animation to "push" it forward (or backward, by adding negative time). This is **always** a time *delta*, meaning that it is the time elapsed since the last call to advance the animation. Under the covers, there is no difference between adding a time delta and setting the time position directly (by adding your delta to the current position); that is what Ogre does anyway. Adding time to an animation is simply a handy shortcut alternative.

Skeletal Animation

Skeletal animation is probably the most common type of animation you will use. With skeletal animation, vertices in a mesh are bound (usually in a 3D modeling tool) to "bones" that make up a skeleton (like your muscles are bound to the bones in your body). The difference between your body and computer animation is that the "bones" in computer animation do not really exist; they are represented by "disembodied" transforms that define the bone's position, orientation, and scale. If you look at the exported skeleton data for an animated mesh, you will find no mention of geometry; the bones have none, as mentioned. However, instead of referring to the bones as transforms (or more accurately, as *matrix palettes* as they are technically named), we will continue to call them bones: now at least you know what they really are. In fact, the technical name for skeletal animation is *matrix palette skinning*, where the "skinning" refers to the fact that the bones are "skinned" with the vertices bound to them.

Skeletal animation operates by calculating the position of a vertex as a function of the transform matrix that represents the bone (or matrices, when a vertex is affected by more than one bone). The keyframes in a skeletal animation are simply relative offsets from the bones' rest positions, orientations, and scales. These are combined to form the bones at a given point along the animation's timeline.

Skeleton

A skeleton in Ogre defines a parent hierarchy. You know, "The foot bone is connected to the shin-bone, the shinbone is connected to the kneebone," and so on. Typically, all bones in a skeleton will have parents except one, which is the *root* bone. This bone can be whatever you want (whatever makes the most sense for the model that has the skeleton). Of course, you are not limited to only one root bone; the parenting hierarchy is used only to propagate transforms down the hierarchy to child bones. For example, if you move the hip bone, the child bones of the hip (the rest of the leg, in other words) have no choice but to adjust position and/or rotation as well. This is entirely analogous to an actual human skeleton.

■**Note** Right about this time you may be thinking about IK (inverse kinematics). You can stop thinking about it; Ogre does not do IK solving. You still need to sample your IK animations into keyframes that Ogre can use and interpolate. If you do not understand what IK is, visit Wikipedia: `http://en.wikipedia.org/wiki/Inverse_kinematics`.

In terms of transforms, bones in a skeleton hierarchy function much the same way as nodes in a scene hierarchy: changes to one bone affect the positions of all of the bone's children. As mentioned in the preceding note, however, Ogre will not do IK solving: when a bone moves, Ogre will not update the positions of its parent bones.

Vertex Binding

In order for the vertices in your model's mesh to move when a bone (or bones) in the model's skeleton move, the vertices must be "bound" to the skeleton. This operation, typically done in a 3D modeling tool, consists of assigning vertices to a particular bone along with a *weight*: the weight is the influence that bone has on a given vertex. If a bone is assigned to influence a vertex with 1.0 weight, then it will completely control the deformation of that vertex when the bone is moved. (*Deformation* is the term used to describe the process of displacing a vertex, usually as a result of outside influence such as bone movement, from its originally modeled position). If two bones are bound to a vertex, each with 0.5 weight, then each will exert the same amount of influence on the position of a vertex when the bone moves, but obviously will only have half the influence it would have had if it was the only bone bound to the vertex at 1.0 weight.

Assigning multiple bones to a vertex is a good way of approximating, say, the effect of muscle "bunching" when bones in a human skeleton are moved. The classic demonstration used to show the effect is simply for you to observe the shape of your shoulder with your arm hung at your side, and the increasingly "bunched" appearance of the shoulder muscles as you raise your arm. (The shoulder, incidentally, is one of the hardest parts of the human anatomy to model in a 3D computer character, for this reason.) The typical solution is a careful assignment of vertex weights to multiple bones.

Ogre supports only four bone assignments per vertex, but you can assign a bone to as many vertices as you like.

Vertex Animation

Vertex animation refers to the fact that instead of animating bones in a skeleton and calculating the positions of vertices as a function of those bones, the actual vertex positions are animated. As you might expect, vertex animation is a rather resource-intensive scheme, as it involves carrying around (in the mesh resource) an entire copy of animated vertex data for each morph target or pose in the animation. However, sometimes it is the only way to achieve a particular effect (especially convincing facial animation).

Vertex animations are managed at the animation track level. This means that you can animate different parts of your mesh using different vertex animation types. For example, you could animate your model's head and face using the more complex (but more flexible) pose animation (described in the upcoming section of the same name), and animate the rest of your model's mesh using the simpler but less flexible morph animation (described in the next section). However, you cannot use different types of animation on the same vertices: for example, you cannot have one track of pose animation for your character's mouth vertices and another track for morph animation in the same animation for the same mouth vertices.

Vertex animations reference entire sets of vertices on an all-or-none basis. This means that at the mesh level in your model, all of the "shared geometry" of the mesh comprises the vertex data in a vertex animation, and at the submesh level, all of the submesh's vertices make up the vertex animation's vertex data. This means that you cannot, for example, have just a few of a submesh's vertices participate in a vertex animation mix (e.g., have parts of a head submesh be morph animated and the rest pose animated).

Morph Animation

Morph animation is the simplest and most straightforward of the two vertex animation types to compute. Instead of computing the positions of vertices as a function of the positions of skeletal bone bindings, the actual vertex positions themselves are stored for a sequence of "snapshots" (*morph targets* in morph animation). This is almost identical to the cartoon animation process described earlier: the positions of mesh vertices in a scene are adjusted and a keyframe stored, containing the absolute position of each vertex in the animated meshes. As you might imagine, this can be incredibly resource-intensive, as each keyframe contains a complete copy of the vertex data (for the vertices that are animated). However, this makes for a computationally efficient animation process, as it is a simple matter to compute the "in-between" position interpolations for each vertex in the mesh from one frame to the next.

The primary drawback of morph animation is that you cannot blend multiple morph animations into one: the vertex positions are stored as absolute, which precludes blending of different animations on the same vertex data (for example, two tracks that animate the same hand). Of course, if you have two animations that affect nonintersecting sets of vertices (such as one for the hand and another for the arm on the same model), then you can certainly blend those two.

Pose Animation

Pose refers to the fact that various *poses* (similar to the morph targets of morph animation) in a model's animation are stored in the animation tracks. These poses can be blended to create a more complicated (and realistic) animation than is possible without blending. The biggest difference (and the enabling factor in blending poses) is that the mesh vertex positions, instead of being stored with absolute positions, are stored as offsets from the rest pose. Furthermore, only data for the vertices that changed are stored (as opposed to the simple snapshot of all vertices in a mesh or submesh as with morph animation). As a result, pose animation is not only more flexible than morph animation, but also more resource efficient.

In the *FacialAnimation* demo that comes with Ogre, multiple phonetic "sounds" are achieved by blending multiple poses in the pose vertex animation stream. Figure 9-1 demonstrates blending various poses from the *FacialAnimation* demo to create an entirely new facial expression.

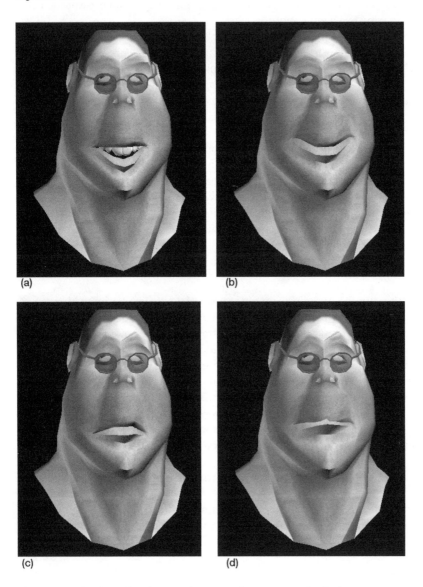

(a)   (b)

(c)   (d)

Figure 9-1. *The demo head in (a) the neutral (rest) pose, (b) the happy pose, (c) the sad pose, and (d) the sad-happy blend of the poses in (b) and (c)*

Figure 9-1 shows how multiple poses can be blended to create interesting, more complex facial expressions. In this instance, we have created a sort of sympathetic, sad-happy pose by blending both the sad and happy poses in the demo. Note how the position of the eyebrows was affected only by the sad pose; this position was left unchanged by the happy pose, since the happy pose did not change the position of the eyebrows, only the mouth (which was blended with the sad mouth vertex offsets to create a sort of pouty look).

The keyframes in pose animation refer to one or more pose tracks, and each reference has an influence weight for that pose. This influence weight determines how much the vertex offsets affect the final position of a vertex when poses are blended. These influences are also scaled by the overall weight of the animation. You do not have to reference a pose in every keyframe if you reference it in one; if a keyframe references a pose in keyframe *n* but not in keyframe *n+1*, the pose influence level is treated as zero in keyframe *n+1*.

There are practical limits to blending pose animations, however: every additional pose you blend in an animation costs that much more processing time. Also, blending across poses (say from Pose A and B to Pose C and D from one keyframe to the next) will actually involve four active tracks instead of two, as you might expect (this has more impact on hardware-accelerated pose animation, discussed shortly).

Blending Animations

You can blend most animation types together to create complex animations in your scene. The exception is that you cannot blend pose and morph animations together, nor can you blend multiple morph animations. The previous section covered the basics of blending pose animations, so we will not rehash that here.

When blending vertex and skeletal animations (regardless of type), Ogre will calculate/blend the vertex animations first, and then apply the skeletal deformations to the blended vertices.

The canonical application for blending pose and skeletal animation, to which we keep returning, is blending full-body skeletal animation with complex facial expressions for a realistically animated organic character. For example, you might animate the character's face vertices using pose animation, and the rest of the character (including the head mesh) using the more common (and more efficient) skeletal animation.

Blending two or more skeletal animations together (usually just two) is most useful to create transitions between one animation and the next. For example, your character might be performing its "run" animation loop and then need to stop (or go into its idle animation). It would look rather awkward to complete the run loop and then instantly transition into its idle animation, so you can blend the two, gradually phasing out the run and phasing in the idle.

Morph and skeletal animation blending is a good candidate for adding "canned" mesh deformation animations to a skeletally animated character or actor in your scene. For example, you could approximate the movement of a character's clothing with morph animation and blend the clothing animation with the character's actual skeletal movement, without having to endure the cost of actual real-time clothing simulation.

Hardware vs. Software Animation

All of the animation types covered so far can be (and are, by default) performed in software (on the CPU, in other words). However, each animation type alternately can be accelerated in a GPU vertex program. While this is a good way to balance the computation load between the CPU and the GPU, each type of animation comes with its own set of caveats when you move the load over to the GPU.

> ■**Caution** The most important thing to understand when you implement hardware animation acceleration is that **the hardware-animated mesh data cannot be used on the CPU**. This is **vitally** important if you are relying on the mesh data for other computations such as software shadow-volume generation or CPU- or PPU-based physical simulation. Once the vertex deformation calculations are moved to the GPU, consider the vertices as gone forever from the perspective of your code. If you need the deformed vertices on the CPU, you actually have to perform the same vertex deformation calculations on the CPU as well as on the GPU; you can tell Ogre to do this with `Entity::addSoftwareAnimationRequest()`.

Hardware-accelerated skeletal animations that blend with vertex animation types will need to have that blend performed in the vertex program as well. This provides the added benefit of control over the order of blending, if you do not care for the order used by Ogre as described previously (specifically, vertex then skeletal). However, it also means more complex (and longer) GPU programs, as well as the fact that **all** animation techniques must be hardware accelerated if any of the blended techniques are hardware accelerated (in other words, you cannot blend, for example, software-based vertex animation with hardware-accelerated skeletal animation).

Skeletal Animation

Skeletal animation is typically a good candidate for GPU acceleration in a vertex program. The performance increase over software skinning is substantial (especially for more than just a few skinned and animated objects in a scene). However, the gotchas must be considered carefully.

For starters, the nature of the skeletal animation algorithm is such that all of the bones' data for a skeleton must be provided for each vertex calculation. In terms of the limitations of various levels of graphics hardware, this means that older hardware might only support skinning passes with 24 bones or less (true of typical DirectX 8–level hardware such as the NVIDIA GeForce 3/4-Ti-series). Therefore, if you need a wide range of hardware support, your application will have to cater to the lowest common denominator (or raise your minimum spec a bit; the next level of hardware, the GeForce FX for example, supports up to 85 bones per skinning pass). The term *skinning pass* is used instead of *skeleton* because you could, if you need to get around the 24-bone limit mentioned earlier, split up your mesh into separate sections and skin them in multiple passes. Ogre only sends the bones referenced by a submesh to the skinning shader, rather than all the bones in the skeleton, making multiple skinning passes possible.

Along the same lines, in a nonbranching GPU program environment you have to maintain multiple vertex programs, one for each number of bone influences per vertex you have in your application. The reason is that each program has to be written to blend a specific number of bone influences when calculation a vertex's deformation. If you can set your application's minimum spec to require GPUs that support branching in their vertex programs, then this limitation obviously does not apply to you. In the end, it is probably simplest either to maintain multiple programs or instruct your artists to use a set number of bone influences per vertex. Of course, this does not mean you should blindly make that the highest possible number of influences; animations using fewer influences will be wasting GPU cycles unnecessarily.

Morph Animation

The primary benefit to interpolating vertex morph animation data on the GPU is the inherently parallel nature of the GPU. That is, multiple vertices' positions can be interpolated at once (as opposed to CPU-based morph animation, which can at most perform four interpolations concurrently in a dual-core hyperthreaded configuration). Beyond that, hardware morph animation is not particularly complicated. The primary input to a hardware morph vertex program is two vertex positions (the morph target will appear in the first free texture unit, supplied as a TEXCOORD parameter to the program) and an interpolation factor, from which the program generates the interpolated vertex position as output.

As mentioned previously, hardware-accelerated vertex animations blended with skeletal animation means that the skeletal animation must be hardware accelerated as well. Since you cannot pass the output of one vertex program to another vertex program (not directly, anyway), you must implement the matrix palette skinning in your morph animation program as well.

Pose Animation

Pose animation on the GPU is quite similar in concept to morph animation on the GPU, with the same restriction mentioned earlier about blending with skeletal animation. The primary difference is in the number of poses provided to the program, and how they are passed (along with the pose weights). The poses are found starting with the first free texture unit (same as the morph target earlier), and continuing to the number of poses supported by the program. The weights of each pose are found in one or more specially identified constant parameters to the program. For example, Listing 9-1 shows the Cg program source for the pose animation blending used in the *FacialAnimation* demo (the source of which can be found in Samples/Media/ materials/programs/Example_Basic.cg).

Listing 9-1. *Cg Program Used for Hardware Pose Animation in* Demo_FacialAnimation

```
void hardwarePoseAnimation(float3 pos : POSITION,
                float4 normal     : NORMAL,
                float2 uv         : TEXCOORD0,
                float3 pose1      : TEXCOORD1,
                float3 pose2      : TEXCOORD2,

                out float4 oPosition : POSITION,
                out float2 oUv       : TEXCOORD0,
                out float4 colour    : COLOR,

                uniform float4x4 worldViewProj,
                uniform float4 anim_t)
{
    // interpolate
    float4 interp = float4(pos + anim_t.x*pose1 + anim_t.y*pose2, 1.0f);

    oPosition = mul(worldViewProj, interp);
    oUv = uv;
    colour = float4(1,0,0,1);
}
```

In Listing 9-1, the two poses to be blended are passed in the second and third texture unit slots, and the weights for each pose are passed as components in the anim_t parameter.

Tag Points

Tag points are not a part of animation per se, but they are often used to link arbitrary objects (such as a weapon) to an existing animated model and skeleton (such as the player-character in a first-person shooter). I want to mention tag points in the context of animations because they are often considered as part of an object's animation (and they do involve a character's skeleton, after all).

The concept of the tag point is simple: it is a particular bone in the skeleton that can control the position and orientation of an object attached to it at runtime. You do not have to create tag points beforehand; you can attach movable objects to any named bone in a skeleton at runtime with the attachObjectToBone() method of the **Entity** class. Regardless, once an object is attached to a tag point, it will follow that tag point around. Note that the object is not actually attached to the tag point; it is attached instead to the **Entity** that is using the skeleton in question. If needed, when attaching an object you can apply an adjustment to the tag-point bone's transform to position the attached object properly.

Controllers

Where keyframed animation is how you animate your meshes, a controller would be what might move, say, the scene node to which your mesh is attached, around the scene, under the control of an arbitrary function.

Controller refers to the fact that the position, orientation, scale, etc., of one or more objects in your scene are controlled by a calculated value, instead of tracking toward keyframe data.

Animation vs. Controller

When would you use one or the other? Both can be used to manipulate an object's state in some way, on the basis of a one-dimensional input variable, and in the most general terms, both animation and controllers run an input variable through a function to produce an output value. In the case of animations, this input variable is always *time*. For controllers, the input variable can be anything you want.

Following is a list of animation characteristics:

- For animations, the output is produced by one of two built-in interpolation functions that calculate the value of an animation track at a given point in time (based also on the keyframes in the animation track). The output values drive, for example, the actual positions, rotations, and scale of bones or vertices in an animated skeleton or mesh, or the positions, rotations, and scale of a node in the scene, and so on.

- Animations are treated as a closed-end system; you set the input value, and Ogre takes it from there, updating the spatial properties of the associated object for you (animations **must** be associated with a node, "animate-able" object, or vertex data).

- The interpolation functions are set: either linear or cubic spline interpolation is used.

- Animations enjoy the full support of the Ogre toolchain (3D tool exporters and mesh/skeleton converter; see Appendix A).

And here are the controller characteristics:

- A controller has far more flexibility in how it calculates the output for a given input: the actual function used **must** be supplied, so the choice in algorithm is entirely up to you.

- Controllers also can be chained (the output of one used to drive the input of another), something not possible with animations (which produce no actual output value other than deformations to a mesh).

- Controllers do not actually move anything on their own; you have to do something with the output to make a controller actually control something. For example, you could have a controller's output drive the input of an animation, if that makes sense for your application. Another use is texture animation; all of the animated texture support in Ogre uses controllers to drive the processes.

- Controllers are all automatically updated each frame (whereas you manually have to "push" an animation forward or backward each frame in your code).

The point of the preceding comparison is not to try to say one is better than the other; controllers and animations are really two different things in Ogre, and when you use one or the other is entirely up to the needs of your application.

You might use a controller, for example, to control the motion of the earth around the sun in a celestial mechanics simulation. The controller input would be time, the function would mimic the quasi-ellipsoidal motion of the earth around the sun, and the output of the controller might be a 3-vector describing the earth's position in 3D world space for a particular time of the year.

Animation by Example

As you might expect, it is rather difficult to adequately demonstrate animations in a static medium such as the printed word, so we will have to satisfy ourselves with code examples based on some of the Ogre demos (which are up to you to run on your own to see what is going on). The primary areas I would like to cover by example are how to extract and use animation information and data from an **Entity**, and how to add hardware animation support to your application. Both can be accomplished by analyzing the *Demo_SkeletalAnimation* application.

Demo_SkeletalAnimation

An obvious place to start our tour of animation-related Ogre coding is the skeletal animation demo application that comes with Ogre (see Figure 9-2).

Figure 9-2. *Screenshot from the Demo_SkeletalAnimation application*

As Listing 9-2 shows, it is a straightforward application, creating six instances of a skeletally animated mesh (the *Jaiqua*, which is an animated model that comes with Softimage|XSI 5.*x*). Each Jaiqua runs repeatedly through her "Sneak" animation (which, somewhat unfortunately, is not animated-in-place so there is some explaining that needs to be done about the code).

■**Note** It is worth telling your artists that *animate-in-place* is far and away the preferred method of animating characters in their modeling tool. They might like to see them running around in their 3D modeler, but that simply wreaks havoc when it comes time to move the animated mesh around the scene via scene node. If you have animations that include translations or rotations of the model's rest pose, you will have to jump through far too many hoops to make the animation work in your application. The solution: animate-in-place.

Listing 9-2. *Demo_SkeletalAnimation Scene Creation Code.* NUM_JAIQUAS *is set to* 6

```
void createScene(void)
{
    mSceneMgr->setShadowTechnique(SHADOWTYPE_TEXTURE_MODULATIVE);
    mSceneMgr->setShadowTextureSize(512);
    mSceneMgr->setShadowColour(ColourValue(0.6, 0.6, 0.6));

    // Set up animation default
    Animation::setDefaultInterpolationMode(Animation::IM_LINEAR);
    Animation::setDefaultRotationInterpolationMode(
        Animation::RIM_LINEAR);
```

```
    // Set ambient light
    mSceneMgr->setAmbientLight(ColourValue(0.5, 0.5, 0.5));

    // Author note:
    // snipped animation fix-up code; see demo source for code
    // and explanation

    Entity *ent;
    Real rotInc = Math::TWO_PI / (float)NUM_JAIQUAS;
    Real rot = 0.0f;
    for (int i = 0; i < NUM_JAIQUAS; ++i)
    {
        Quaternion q;
        q.FromAngleAxis(Radian(rot), Vector3::UNIT_Y);

        mOrientations[i] = q;
        mBasePositions[i] = q * Vector3(0,0,-20);

        ent = mSceneMgr->createEntity("jaiqua" +
            StringConverter::toString(i), "jaiqua.mesh");

        // Add entity to the scene node
        mSceneNode[i] = mSceneMgr->getRootSceneNode()->
            createChildSceneNode();
        mSceneNode[i]->attachObject(ent);
        mSceneNode[i]->rotate(q);
        mSceneNode[i]->translate(mBasePositions[i]);

        mAnimState[i] = ent->getAnimationState("Sneak");
        mAnimState[i]->setEnabled(true);

        // manual loop since translation involved
        mAnimState[i]->setLoop(false);
        mAnimationSpeed[i] = Math::RangeRandom(0.5, 1.5);

        rot += rotInc;
    }

    // continue with the rest of the basic scene setup
}
```

The first thing this code does is set the models to cast modulative texture shadows. I will explain shortly why this is important. Then, the code loops six times, creating a new instance of the Jaiqua and placing each in a circle, 60 degrees apart and 20 units from the center of the circle (and facing outward).

The interesting parts of the code (in terms of animation) begin with the getAnimationState("Sneak") call. Note that the animation states and the animation speeds are kept in arrays sized to the number of Jaiquas in the demo; this is so the demo can manage each instance individually.

As mentioned earlier in this chapter, the animation state is how you typically manage the animations created for an entity: how you set the time position along the animation, and so on. In this demo, there are six Jaiquas, and each will have her own animation state. The code then enables each animation state (which turns the animation on) and turns off the animation looping (because the animation was not created in-place, and therefore the Jaiqua would warp back to her initial position when the loop restarted if it were left to run on its own). The animation speed is a factor that the demo code uses itself to modify the pace (or *scale*) at which the animations run (this is not a feature of the Ogre animation system, in other words). The frame listener code shows how this animation speed is applied (see Listing 9-3).

Listing 9-3. *Essential Frame Listener Code to Advance the Animations*

```
bool frameStarted(const FrameEvent& evt)
{
    for (int i = 0; i < NUM_JAIQUAS; ++i)
    {
        Real inc = evt.timeSinceLastFrame * mAnimationSpeed[i];

        // Author note:
        // animation fix-up code snipped

        mAnimState[i]->addTime(inc);
    }

    // Call default
    return ExampleFrameListener::frameStarted(evt);
}
```

Listing 9-3 shows how the demo application advances the "Sneak" animation we obtained for each Jaiqua instance during scene setup. The frame time is scaled by the animation speed factor also set during scene setup, which causes the animations to advance more slowly or more rapidly, depending on the factor set for each.

To this point, the demo application will run fine on any graphics hardware, whether that hardware supports vertex programs or not; the skinning can be done entirely in software if needed. However, there are two parts of this application that we have not yet seen that will enable not only hardware acceleration of the skeletal animation, but also the texture shadows I pointed out.

Skeletal Animation Material Script

Listing 9-4 provides the material script required to enable hardware skinning for a two-bone-per-vertex model.

Listing 9-4. *Jaiqua Vertex Program Declarations and Material Script*

```
vertex_program Ogre/HardwareSkinningTwoWeightsShadowCaster cg
{
```

```
        source Example_Basic.cg
        entry_point hardwareSkinningTwoWeightsCaster_vp
        profiles vs_1_1 arbvp1
        includes_skeletal_animation true
}
// Basic hardware skinning using two indexed weights per vertex
vertex_program Ogre/HardwareSkinningTwoWeights cg
{
        source Example_Basic.cg
        entry_point hardwareSkinningTwoWeights_vp
        profiles vs_1_1 arbvp1
        includes_skeletal_animation true
}

material jaiqua
{
        // Hardware skinning technique
        technique
        {
            pass
            {
                vertex_program_ref Ogre/HardwareSkinningTwoWeights
                {
                    param_named_auto worldMatrix3x4Array[0] world_matrix_array_3x4
                    param_named_auto viewProjectionMatrix viewproj_matrix
                    param_named_auto lightPos[0] light_position 0
                    param_named_auto lightPos[1] light_position 1
                    param_named_auto lightDiffuseColour[0] light_diffuse_colour 0
                    param_named_auto lightDiffuseColour[1] light_diffuse_colour 1
                    param_named_auto ambient ambient_light_colour

                }

                // alternate shadow caster program
                shadow_caster_vertex_program_ref
                    Ogre/HardwareSkinningTwoWeightsShadowCaster
                {
                    param_named_auto worldMatrix3x4Array[0] world_matrix_array_3x4
                    param_named_auto viewProjectionMatrix viewproj_matrix
                    param_named_auto ambient ambient_light_colour

                }

                texture_unit
                {
                    texture blue_jaiqua.jpg
                    tex_address_mode clamp
```

```
            }
        }
    }

    // Software blending technique
    technique
    {
        pass
        {
            texture_unit
            {
                texture blue_jaiqua.jpg
                tex_address_mode clamp
            }
        }
    }
}
```

Listing 9-4 actually contains relevant scripting from two different files; you will find the material definition in Example.material and the vertex program declarations in Examples.program.

The most important part of this scripting in terms of enabling hardware animation support is the line

```
includes_skeletal_animation true
```

in each vertex program declaration. Without this line in your program declaration, Ogre has no way of knowing it should do hardware instead of software skinning. The line

```
profiles vs_1_1 arbvp1
```

says that this program targets these profiles. This is important to note, since these profiles are the ones that support only 24 bones per skinning pass, as mentioned earlier in this chapter.

Skeletal Animation and Shadows

The shadow support when using skeletal animation is enabled by providing and referencing a second vertex program declaration that is designed solely to render shadows (in this case, the modulative texture shadows that were enabled in the scene way back in the createScene() method). Ogre will automatically use this second program when rendering the shadow pass; the only caveat is that the shadow will be rendered with a single color, which you must pass to the shadow caster program in the ambient_light_color parameter. If you do not provide a shadow caster program, Ogre will fall back to a fixed-function material for the shadow pass, which will not reflect any skeletal mesh deformations.

■**Note** With hardware skinning, you can use any type of shadow you want; texture shadows work with any mesh-deforming GPU program, and Ogre knows how to deal with stencil shadows for hardware skinning programs. It is only with vertex animations and stencil shadows that you are out of luck (unless you do not care that the stencil shadows will not reflect the deformed vertices from vertex animations).

Note the difference in parameters between the primary program and the shadow-caster program; all of the lighting information has been stripped because the shadow-caster pass does not need any of it. All that is needed is the `world_matrix_array_3x4`, which contains the matrix palette for the skinning (and of course the world-view-projection matrix and the `ambient_light_colour` parameter).

Conclusion

By this point, you should have a good working knowledge of the ins and outs of animation in Ogre. I have deliberately left off from this chapter any more discussion about controllers than you have seen thus far, because in the next chapter you will learn all about one of the two primary uses of controllers in Ogre: managing the lifetime and behavior of particles in Ogre.

■ ■ ■

## CHAPTER 10

Billboards and Particles

The twin topics of this chapter are closely related: in fact, the one depends on the other. Particle systems are a special utilization of billboards. But what are billboards?

Billboards

Think of the last time you drove down a major roadway. If you live somewhere like the USA, there is no doubt that you have seen billboards: those huge, ugly steel frames covered in garish colors, hawking whatever ware or service you did not know you needed as you make your way across the countryside at 65 miles per hour (or about 100 kph, as applies). Notice how they are always situated so that they are always facing you directly, lest you miss the tiniest nuance of the full impact of their urgent message.

The name "billboard" is not a coincidence. I may have laid on the sarcasm a bit heavy there, but the analog to billboards in 3D graphics is simple enough. A *billboard* in Ogre (and in 3D graphics in general) is simply a quad in your scene whose orientation is dependent on the camera. Usually this dependence means that the billboard will be rotated to align with the camera's view direction; this is an approximation of facing directly at the camera, but typically the results are indistinguishable. In some cases, you can trade performance for accuracy and orient the billboards to face directly at the camera, as you will learn shortly.

Figure 10-1 illustrates the *accurate-facing* alignment model.

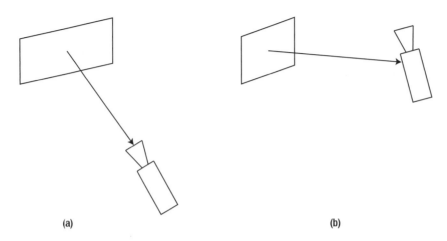

(a)   (b)

Figure 10-1. *Billboard is facing the camera in (a). In (b), the camera has moved and the billboard has rotated automatically to face the camera.*

Why is this useful? The answer is that you can place anything on a billboard that you might put, say, in an overlay, and put that billboard anywhere in your 3D scene, and it will always be facing the camera—text, a rendered texture, a set of images that when placed a certain way might look like a puff of smoke or a flame. If you have seen games where the characters run around with their names floating above their heads, chances are pretty good that those names are rendered in the scene with billboards. Likewise for just about any special effect such as an explosion or smoke: billboards are involved. Atmospheric effects such as clouds, rain, and lightning? Billboards. Billboarding is used to create vast low-cost areas of realistic vegetation such as trees and grass without having to render actual meshes (also known as *impostors*, a common performance-enhancing technique for densely populated scenes).

■**Note** For computational efficiency, billboards are aligned with the camera's view direction, not with the actual vector from the billboard to the camera. In most cases, this is not noticeable. However, for large billboards you might want the billboard aligned with the camera-billboard vector. You can enable this alignment if you wish, but be aware that it does incur a performance penalty. There is nothing magical about billboards themselves. They are just a simple mechanism provided primarily to create these special effects or other illusions in your 3D world. You certainly could manage the positions and orientations of the billboards yourself, but there is no need since Ogre is more than happy to oblige, and it is usually far more efficient to let Ogre handle the details.

Billboard Sets

Billboards cannot exist on their own; they are not renderable themselves, and must belong to a *billboard set*. The billboard set is sort of a manager for a group of billboards, which all have the same dimensions and material. The requirement for identical dimensions and material is so that Ogre can perform calculations on the set more efficiently when rendering. This is not something that would matter much for a set with just a few billboards, but it is something you begin to care about when you have hundreds of them in a set and in view on the screen. Note that you can alter the size of individual billboards in the set if you wish (for example, to render expanding puffs of smoke), but this is discouraged, as performance is affected negatively because the billboard set is optimized for billboards of all the same size.

Along those same lines, Ogre will treat the billboard set as a single unit: all of the billboards render or none of them render (all are culled, in other words), unless you enable individual culling. This is not something you would want to enable without good reason, due to the potential performance hit: smoke effects at the edge of the field of view is one possible good reason for individual culling; wide fields of grass impostors, where the likelihood is high for nonvisibility of significant numbers of billboards in the set, is another, but the performance penalty incurred with significant individual culling means you are probably better off with multiple billboard sets in this case.

Billboards in a billboard set are positioned relative to the scene node to which the set is attached. Since all of the billboards in the set share the same material, they can all be rendered in the same batch; this means that there is no real difference to the GPU between 200 and 2000 billboards in a set.

Billboard Creation

Billboards are described by an offset from the center of their set and a size (width and height). The direction, as mentioned, is calculated each frame as a function of the vector from each billboard to the camera. Figure 10-2 illustrates the principle.

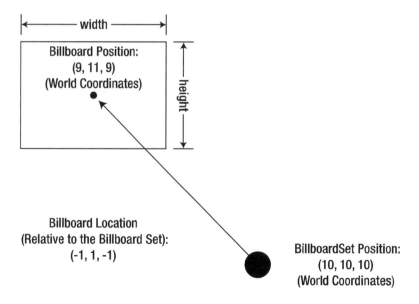

Figure 10-2. *Billboard creation parameters*

By default, the billboard is a *point* billboard. Point billboards **always** face the camera and are always upright. The billboard in Figure 10-1 is a point billboard, with its origin at the center (the default). You can change this origin to any of the nine canonical locations on the quads: top-left, top-center, top-right, middle-left, center (default), middle-right, bottom-left, bottom-center, bottom-right. This origin placement is as much for your convenience as it is for purposes of rotation, since the billboard will always face the camera.

The origin point is more important to rotation when you choose the second of three major billboard types, the *oriented* billboard. Oriented billboards will rotate either around their own Y axis (this is the *self* variety of oriented billboards) or around a common Y axis shared among all billboards in the set (the *common* variety of oriented billboard). There is also a third type of billboard, the *perpendicular* billboard. This type will align itself perpendicular to a direction vector (the vector between the camera and the billboard). This vector is either shared (*common*, the common direction provided by you) or is each billboard's own Z axis. Either way, the perpendicular billboard type requires a second "up" vector to determine how it should right itself. Figure 10-3 endeavors to clarify these additional four types.

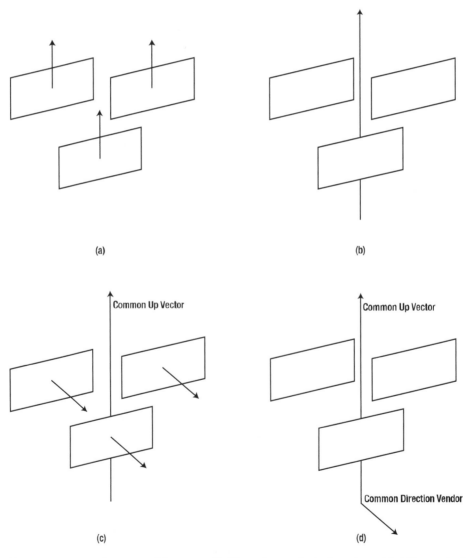

Figure 10-3. *(a) is the oriented "common" billboard type. (b) is the oriented "self" type. (c) is the perpendicular "common" type. (d) is the perpendicular "self" type.*

Point-type billboards do have an advantage over the other types. By default, Ogre generates a quad (four vertices, each with position and texture coordinates) for each billboard based on its creation parameters, and passes that geometry to the GPU for rendering. With point billboards, you can do away with three of those vertices per billboard and let the GPU sort out how to render the billboard based on point-rendering material attributes. Of course, this is a compromise, since hardware point rendering comes with a few limitations:

- Obviously, only the point-type billboard is supported, and for that, only the center origin is supported.

- Size and appearance are set in the material, not the billboard set. Size is also limited by the GPU, so point-rendered billboards cannot be as large as those you could create in software.

- Per-billboard size and rotation therefore are not supported. The only rotation possible is texture-unit rotation.

- Texture coordinates are set automatically in the GPU, from (0,0) to (1,1); you cannot use alternate texture coordinates as you can with software billboarding.

However, if you are willing to give up that little bit of control (or those limitations do not affect your application), then depending on the effect you are trying to pull off, you could see significant speedups with hardware-based point rendering.

Billboard Pools

The common way of creating billboards is to tell Ogre how many billboards you want in the set (the *pool* size, in other words) when you create the billboard set itself. Ogre will then create in the set as many billboards as you requested, ready to go when you need them. The billboards are kept in *active* and *free* lists, which makes allocation extremely fast. If you ask for a billboard and there are none left in the pool. Ogre will return a NULL. If you want Ogre to be able to allocate more as needed, then you can instruct the billboard set to do so, and it will double the pool size each time a billboard creation request would exceed the pool size. Be aware that this could potentially be expensive, and certainly not something you would want to do constantly, such as in a loop. The same goes for setting the pool size directly (apart from during billboard set creation). It is usually best to have a good idea how many you will need before you create the set and live with it.

Billboard Texture Coordinates

Billboards (especially when used for special purposes such as particles) can benefit from non–full range texture coordinate assignment. For example, let's say that you have a texture containing several subtextures, organized into rows (*stacks*) and columns (*slices*). Let's assume further that this texture contains uppercase members of the English alphabet, and you want to create several billboards, each with a different letter on them, taken from this texture.

You do this by creating an array of texture coordinate "rectangles" (each containing the coordinates for corner of a billboard quad), and providing this array to the billboard set. Then, when you create a billboard, you can set its texture coordinates by the *index* into this texture coordinate array. Figure 10-4 and Listing 10-1 provide an example.

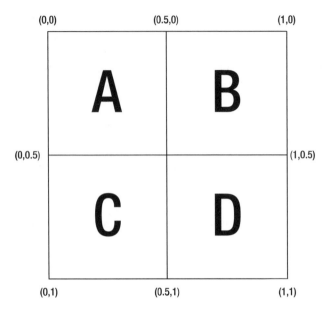

Figure 10-4. *A simple texture containing four letters of the English alphabet*

Listing 10-1. *Setting Custom Texture Coordinates for a Billboard Set*

```
// assume sceneMgr is already created and valid

// create a new billboard set with a pool of 4 billboards
BillboardSet* bbset = sceneMgr->createBillboardSet("BBSet", 4);

// create a texture coordinate array to address the texture in Figure 10-4
FloatRect texCoordArray[] = {
    FloatRect(0.0, 0.0, 0.5, 0.5),     // address the "A"
    FloatRect(0.5, 0.0, 1.0, 0.5),     // address the "B"
    FloatRect(0.0, 0.5, 0.5, 1.0),     // address the "C"
    FloatRect(0.5, 0.5, 1.0, 1.0),     // address the "D"
};

// provide this array to the billboard set
bbset->setTextureCoords(texCoordArray, 4);

// now create a billboard to display the "D"; this
// is the fourth entry in the array, index=3
Billboard* bb = bbset->createBillboard(Vector3(0, 0, 0));
bb->setTexcoordIndex(3);
```

Alternately, you could have simply passed an arbitrary rectangle of coordinates to the billboard instead:

```
FloatRect coords(0.5, 0.5, 1.0, 1.0);
bb->setTexcoordRect(coords);
```

The second version is useful for one-off texture assignment, but the first version is more flexible for dealing with large numbers of billboards that use the same texture. The texture used on the billboard is defined in the material assigned to the billboard set. This material can contain anything that a normal material script contains, but some material directives are particular to billboards and point rendering (Appendix B contains a listing of billboard-specific directives and parameters).

For simple billboard shading, you can just create each billboard with a particular single diffuse color.

Billboard Chains and Ribbon Trails

Billboard chains are useful for creating effects such as lightning, beams, streaks, and trails, or any effect where the billboards in a set need to "play follow-the-leader" instead of being a disconnected set of quads. Ogre even provides a ready-made ribbon-trail reference class that uses billboard chains to "chase after" a scene node, leaving a trail behind as it goes. Figure 10-5 is an example of ribbon trails (and, therefore, billboard chains) in action.

Figure 10-5. *Screenshot from the Ogre* Demo_Lighting *example application, which has been enhanced to include ribbon trails behind the light-attached scene nodes*

Billboard chains can exist in multiple segments, making them good candidates for effects such as lightning. The only drawback of billboard chains is that you have to update them manually; there is no auto-updating feature for the generic billboard chain. Instead, you can keep adding items to the tail of a chain segment: each segment has a maximum length, and if adding the item would exceed that length, the current tail item is removed and reused as the head of the segment. The ribbon trail behaves this way, removing elements from the tail as the head grows, and fading the trail along its length from head to tail.

BillboardChain Example

Listing 10-2 is the setupTrailLights() method from *Demo_Lighting* that sets up the ribbon trails shown in Figure 10-5 and attaches them to the animated light nodes.

Listing 10-2. setupTrailLights() *Method from* Demo_Lighting

```
void setupTrailLights(void)
{
    mSceneMgr->setAmbientLight(ColourValue(0.5, 0.5, 0.5));
    Vector3 dir(-1, -1, 0.5);
    dir.normalise();
    Light* l = mSceneMgr->createLight("light1");
    l->setType(Light::LT_DIRECTIONAL);
    l->setDirection(dir);

    NameValuePairList pairList;
    pairList["numberOfChains"] = "2";
    pairList["maxElements"] = "80";
    RibbonTrail* trail = static_cast<RibbonTrail*>(
        mSceneMgr->createMovableObject("1", "RibbonTrail", &pairList));
    trail->setMaterialName("Examples/LightRibbonTrail");
    trail->setTrailLength(400);


    mSceneMgr->getRootSceneNode()->
        createChildSceneNode()->attachObject(trail);

    // Create nodes for trail to follow
    SceneNode* animNode = mSceneMgr->getRootSceneNode()->
        createChildSceneNode();
    animNode->setPosition(50,30,0);
    Animation* anim = mSceneMgr->createAnimation("an1", 14);
    anim->setInterpolationMode(Animation::IM_SPLINE);
    NodeAnimationTrack* track = anim->createNodeTrack(1, animNode);
    TransformKeyFrame* kf = track->createNodeKeyFrame(0);
    kf->setTranslate(Vector3(50,30,0));
    kf = track->createNodeKeyFrame(2);
    kf->setTranslate(Vector3(100, -30, 0));
    kf = track->createNodeKeyFrame(4);
    kf->setTranslate(Vector3(120, -100, 150));
    kf = track->createNodeKeyFrame(6);
    kf->setTranslate(Vector3(30, -100, 50));
    kf = track->createNodeKeyFrame(8);
    kf->setTranslate(Vector3(-50, 30, -50));
    kf = track->createNodeKeyFrame(10);
    kf->setTranslate(Vector3(-150, -20, -100));
    kf = track->createNodeKeyFrame(12);
```

```
kf->setTranslate(Vector3(-50, -30, 0));
kf = track->createNodeKeyFrame(14);
kf->setTranslate(Vector3(50,30,0));

AnimationState* animState = mSceneMgr->createAnimationState("an1");
animState->setEnabled(true);
mAnimStateList.push_back(animState);

trail->setInitialColour(0, 1.0, 0.8, 0);
trail->setColourChange(0, 0.5, 0.5, 0.5, 0.5);
trail->setInitialWidth(0, 5);
trail->addNode(animNode);

// Add light
Light* l2 = mSceneMgr->createLight("l2");
l2->setDiffuseColour(trail->getInitialColour(0));
animNode->attachObject(l2);

// Add billboard
BillboardSet* bbs = mSceneMgr->createBillboardSet("bb", 1);
bbs->createBillboard(Vector3::ZERO, trail->getInitialColour(0));
bbs->setMaterialName("Examples/Flare");
animNode->attachObject(bbs);

// remainder of method is duplicate of above for second light node
}
```

The bits of interest in Listing 10-2 are those for the `trail->` methods. First, the **RibbonTrail** is created as two chains (one for each light node) with 80 elements max each and a trail length of 400 world units. Once the light node is created and its animation keyframes are set, the trail is set to have the same initial color as the light it follows and is also set to fade to black as the trail peters out. Finally, the trail is instructed to follow the node to which the light is attached with `trail->addNode()`.

Particle Systems

Particle systems are the foundation of most visual special effects in a 3D application. While you certainly do not need a particle system to pull of any particular visual effect, they do make life easier when you need an effect.

Particle System Basics

Particle systems are typically script based, as opposed to hard-coded, to enable fast prototyping and iteration. Like anything else in Ogre, however, you can create and configure a particle system fully in code if you wish. The particle system definitions in a particle script are actually templates, since the particle system they define can be reused throughout your application to create multiple actual instances of that particle system. In other words, if you are creating a particle system to define an explosion, you do not have to have a different particle script for every slight variation on that explosion in your application.

Particle Systems and the 3D Scene

Since particle systems are attached to scene nodes, they are subject to the node's translations, scaling, and rotations, which will affect the direction in which they emit. Furthermore, the particles, once emitted, are emitted into world space. This means that as the scene node moves, it takes the emitter with it, but the emitted particles remain behind (good, for example, if you are interested in leaving behind, say, a smoke trail). If you have need for the particles to travel or reorient with the node, you can set the particle system to emit particles into local space, which will carry along the emitted particles with the node.

Particle systems cannot emit particles without bound; they have to have a limit (*quota*). Once this limit is reached, the particle system will not emit any more particles until existing particles have expired (they have existed past their time-to-live setting). The default particle quota is ten, so if you are writing a particle script from scratch, you probably want to set this parameter to something significantly higher.

Particle System Bounds

The dynamic nature of particle systems means that their bounding boxes have to be recalculated regularly. This can be an expensive process to do every frame, which Ogre does by default; also by default, Ogre will stop updating bounds on its own after ten seconds. You can override this behavior and instruct Ogre to turn off bounds updating after a certain number of seconds with the `ParticleSystem::setBoundsAutoUpdated()` method. This method takes a `stopIn` parameter, which tells Ogre to stop updating the bounds after the supplied number of seconds. If you have a particle system that you know will not grow beyond a certain size, you can set the size of the bounds up front with `ParticleSystem::setBounds()`. Obviously, it is most efficient to set the bounds up front and leave them, but you can only do so if you know the extents in advance of particle system creation. `ParticleSystem::setBounds()` works in conjunction with `ParticleSystem::setBoundsAutoUpdated()` to provide a compromise; you can set an initial bounds size and let it update for a bit after particle system creation.

Particle System Updating

Ogre performs some mild heuristics when updating particle systems. For instance, when a particle system exits the view frustum, it will continue updating on the chance that it will reenter the view shortly after. This is important because it would be visually jarring if a particle system freezes as soon as it leaves the view, and when it comes back a few seconds later, it is in the same state as it was when it left.

However, for performance reasons, once a particle system has been outside the view for a set period of time, the particle system will in fact stop updating. This of course brings back the original problem of a frozen particle system suddenly reentering the view. As a result, Ogre offers (and uses) a "fast-forward" mechanism that allows the particle system to advance to its "current" state after being frozen. This feature can also be used to advance a newly created particle system's timeline forward by a set amount of time, with the `ParticleSystem::fastForward()` method.

Particle System Sorting

You can instruct Ogre to sort particles based on their distance from the camera. This feature is disabled by default. Obviously, sorting each particle on its distance from the camera has a performance impact, especially for larger particle systems, but sometimes there is no other way to achieve a particular effect.

For example, consider the particle system in Figure 10-6 (from the *Demo_Smoke* sample application). Figure 10-7 shows the same demo from 10-6 with sorting disabled, and Figure 10-8 is the demo with sorting enabled. In Figure 10-7, the fire at the bottom of the particle system shows clearly and unnaturally through the smoke, while Figure 10-8 illustrates the more expected view from above, where the smoke entirely obscures the fire. In this case the effect of particle sorting was worth the performance penalty.

Figure 10-6. Demo_Smoke *sample application*

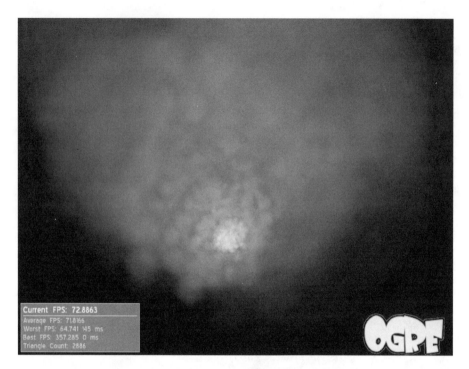

Figure 10-7. Demo_Smoke *sample application from Figure 10-6 with particle sorting disabled*

Figure 10-8. Demo_Smoke *sample application from Figure 10-6 with particle sorting enabled*

Emitters

A *particle emitter* is exactly what it sounds like: a "thing" that emits particles. The emitters that Ogre provides by default emit particles in an intuitive spatial way: *point* emitters emit all particles from a single point in space; *box* emitters emit particles from anywhere in a defined rectangular volume; *cylinder* emitters emit particles from within a defined cylindrical volume; *ellipsoid* emitters emit from an ellipsoidal volume, while *hollow ellipsoid* emitters emit from the shell of an ellipsoidal volume; and *ring* emitters emit from the edges of a planar ring.

The rate, velocity, and direction in which particles will be emitted are completely configurable. Particle systems are attached to nodes in the scene, and therefore so are emitters, which will have a position relative to their parent node.

Particles are not typically emitted in a straight line; usually they are emitted in a "cone" around the direction of the emitter, defined by the `angle` parameter to the emitter. If you actually want your particles emitted in a straight line, this parameter should be 0, and if you want them emitted in all directions, this parameter should be 180. A value of 90 will emit randomly in a hemisphere around the direction vector.

The rate at which particles are emitted is defined in terms of particles/second. The particles can emit either with a set velocity or with a random velocity within a range. Likewise, they can have a single time-to-live (TTL, in seconds) or have the emitter pick randomly from a TTL range for each particle. The duration of emission (the length of time the emitter is on) can be either set or random within a range, as can the delay before emission begins again. Color also can be set at emission time, both single valued and ranged.

You can plug in custom emitters at runtime, and this is probably the simplest way to extend Ogre's particle system.

Affectors

Again, *affectors* do to particles exactly what you might think they do: they affect the particle's path and lifetime once it has been emitted into the world. For example, you can impose "gravity" on particles, you can impose "wind" on them, and so on (these are both examples of the **LinearForce** affector, by the way). Since each affector is specialized unto itself, let's examine each one briefly.

LinearForce

LinearForce applies a force to the particles in the system. Since a force is a vector, it has a direction and a magnitude. The magnitude is actually the magnitude of the force vector definition, so `force_vector 0 50 0` will have the same direction but half the magnitude as `force_vector 0 100 0`. Since forces left unchecked can quickly result in huge velocities, you can set how the force is applied with `force_application`. `force_application average` will asymptotically stabilize the particles' velocities by setting the velocity to the average of the force and the particle's current velocity. `force_application add` will allow the velocity to increase (or decrease) forever.

ColourFader

ColourFader modifies a particle's color while it exists. The color definition is in terms of "component change per second," so the following code will fade the color by half each second:

```
affector ColourFader {
    red -0.5
    green -0.5
    blue -0.5
    alpha -0.5
}
```

Note that this does not mean an infinite regression; the "half" in this example is not half of the current value. Instead, 0.5 means that the color component will reduce in intensity by 0.5 each second, so if you start with the color white, it will fade to black in two seconds.

ColourFader2

ColourFader2 is similar to **ColourFader**, except that it will switch to a new fade function when a certain amount of time remains in a particle's lifetime. For example, you could fade a color gradually (say, from full to 60% intensity) for two seconds and then snuff it out quickly over the next half second.

ColourInterpolator

ColourInterpolator is similar to **ColourFader** and **ColourFader**, except that it will allow any number of stages up to six. It can be seen as a relative generalization of the other color affectors.

Scaler

Scaler sets a uniform (equally applied to both X and Y) scale factor to the particles' size as a function of time. This scaling factor is proportional to the particles' current size.

Rotator

Rotator rotates the particles' textures either by a set random amount or at a certain random speed. Both of these quantities are defined in terms of ranges. The defaults for all are zero (indicating no rotation).

ColourImage

ColourImage provides a means by which you can get the color changes not from a defined fade factor, but from an actual image file (such as a .png, .gif, .jpg, and so on). The only parameter is for the name of the image file, and the only direction is horizontal (from left to right) across the file. This is an ideal use for a one-dimensional texture, where the far-left extent of the texture is the color at birth of the particle, and the far-right extent is the color at particle death.

Particle System Renderers

With your new knowledge of the how and why of billboards, you already have more than half of what you need to know to understand particles in Ogre. The reason is that the default particle system renderer for the particle system plug-in that comes with Ogre is billboard based.

The *Demo_Smoke* sample application introduced earlier is a good example to examine for how particle systems are specified and created. Figure 10-9 is the `Example/smoke` particle script loaded in the Ogre Particle Editor. Listing 10-3 contains the particle script that defines the particle system, and Listing 10-4 is the material script used by the particle system.

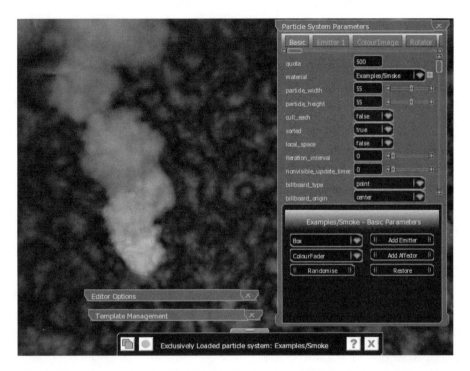

Figure 10-9. *Community-developed particle editor available for fast protoyping of Ogre particle systems (available in the Downloads section of the Ogre web site,* `http://www.ogre3d.org`*)*

Listing 10-3. `smoke.particle` *Script Corresponding to the Particle Effect in Figure 10-9*

```
Examples/Smoke
{
    material            Examples/Smoke
    particle_width      55
    particle_height     55
    cull_each           false
    quota               500
    billboard_type      point
    sorted              true

    // Area emitter
    emitter Point
    {
        angle                   11
        emission_rate           15
        time_to_live            4
```

```
        direction                0 1 0
        velocity_min             150
        velocity_max             240
    }

    affector ColourImage
    {
        image        smokecolors.png
    }

    affector Rotator
    {
        rotation_range_start        0
        rotation_range_end          360
        rotation_speed_range_start    -60
        rotation_speed_range_end      200
    }

    affector Scaler
    {
        rate    100
    }
}
```

Listing 10-4. *Material Script Used in the* smoke.particle *Template*

```
material Examples/Smoke
{
    technique
    {
      pass
      {
          lighting off
          scene_blend alpha_blend
          depth_write off

          texture_unit
          {
              texture smoke.png
              tex_address_mode clamp
          }
      }
    }
}
```

The Examples/Smoke particle script in Listing 10-3 begins by referencing the Examples/Smoke material in Listing 10-4. This material is an unlit, alpha-blended material (common for particles as they typically use transparency in their textures). Indeed, the smoke.png smoke-puff texture in Figure 10-10(a) is a texture with transparency.

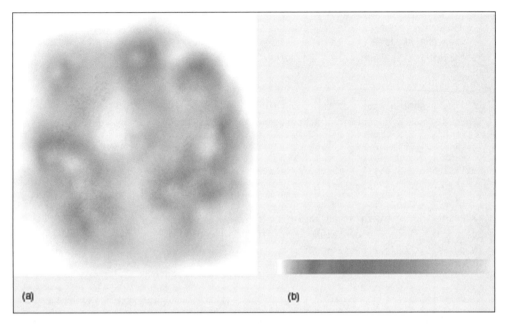

Figure 10-10. *The textures used for the smoke particles. (a) is the smoke puff texture; (b) is the 64×4 texture used for the fire colors.*

Listing 10-3 then continues by defining the particle width and height to 55 units, and sets a particle quota of 500. Point-type billboards are specified, and individual culling is turned off (since this is a relatively small particle system). Particle sorting, however, is enabled, for reasons discussed earlier in the chapter.

The particle script includes a single emitter and three affectors. The emitter creates particles that move along the local +Y axis, at a rate of 15 particles per second, emitted within an 11-degree cone around the +Y axis. The particles live for four seconds each, and leave the emitter at a rate of between 150 and 240 units per second.

The first affector is responsible for changing the base particle color along the color gradient in Figure 10-10(b) over the lifetime of the particle. The second affector is responsible for making each particle complete full rotations, at a speed ranging from –60 rotations per second to 200 (which has the effect of making some of the particles rotate in the reverse direction). Finally, the third affector causes the particles to grow by 100 units per second over their lifetime.

The code that causes this particle system to enter the scene in *Demo_Smoke* is provided in Listing 10-5.

Listing 10-5. createScene() *Method from the Source for* Demo_Smoke

```
void createScene(void)
{
    // Set ambient light
    mSceneMgr->setAmbientLight(ColourValue(0.5, 0.5, 0.5));

    // Create a skydome
    mSceneMgr->setSkyDome(true, "Examples/CloudySky", 5, 8);


    // Create shared node for two fountains
    mFountainNode = mSceneMgr->getRootSceneNode()->createChildSceneNode();

    // smoke
    ParticleSystem* pSys2 = mSceneMgr->createParticleSystem(
        "fountain1", "Examples/Smoke");

    // Point the fountain at an angle
    SceneNode* fNode = mFountainNode->createChildSceneNode();
    fNode->attachObject(pSys2);
}
```

■**Note** The Particle Editor shown in Figure 10-9 is not officially part of the Ogre distribution but is highly recommended if you need a particle editor to develop effects for Ogre-based applications. It is well-designed, easy to use, and spits out Ogre-ready .particle scripts.

Conclusion

Particle systems are the meat and potatoes of any visual effects in a 3D application. In this chapter, you learned the basics of particles and hopefully now have an idea of how to use a particle system to create special effects in your applications.

CHAPTER 11

▪▪▪

Dynamic Shadows

Shadows are an important spatial cue in 3D scene rendering. For example, can you tell how far the Athene model is above the rock floor in Figure 11-1? How about in Figure 11-2?

Figure 11-1. Demo_Shadows *with no shadows drawn at all*

Figure 11-2. Demo_Shadows *with modulative stencil shadows enabled*

The visual cues provided by shadows in a 3D scene are extremely important to the scene's perceptual realism factor and contribute greatly to the user's satisfaction with the scene as a whole. However, real-time shadowing in 3D graphics is still a computationally expensive proposition, even with strong hardware acceleration. Many shadowing techniques have existed for some time to obtain a big payoff for relatively little effort (such as "baked-in" static shadow maps for use on terrains or level geometry), but these techniques are not dynamic: the shadows in a static shadow map do not update as a function of the arrangement of dynamic scene contents.

This chapter explores the dynamic shadowing support in Ogre and provides a wealth of hints, tips, and tricks you can use to improve the visual quality of your 3D applications while at the same time preventing them from looking more like slide shows than interactive real-time applications.

Before we get started, I would like to add that this chapter is devoted to the *fixed-function* dynamic shadow support in Ogre. That means the shadowing functionality you get simply by setting the technique you want to use and marking which objects cast and receive shadows in your scene; the stuff Ogre can do for you, automatically and almost completely without your involvement.

When I say "supported by Ogre" in this chapter, it is this functionality I mean. You are of course free to create or implement and use in your application whatever shadowing algorithm you can imagine, with the use of the programmable GPU pipeline and GPU programs. When I say "not supported by Ogre," that is what I mean: Ogre does not provide any particular advanced

GPU-based shadowing support to your application; you have to write the shaders yourself for advanced techniques. Ogre has full support, therefore, as a result of its full support for the programmable GPU pipeline, for any of the shadowing techniques you might encounter in the *GPU Gems* (Addison-Wesley) or *Game Programming Gems* and *ShaderX* (Charles River Media) series of books, or from an online source, and so on. Now that we have that clear . . .

Shadow Techniques

At the time of this writing, Ogre supports two main types of dynamic shadow generation—stencil and texture shadows—and two variants within each: modulative and additive. The four permutations of these techniques are all fully compatible with a fixed-function graphics pipeline, and therefore require no programmable GPU support at all. However, they all can be accelerated using GPU programs, and as you saw in the last chapter, some GPU-accelerated techniques could require that the dynamic shadow generation be performed in a GPU program (for example, when a skeleton is skinned in a GPU program).

■**Note** Also at the time of this writing, Ogre has no direct support for real-time soft/subtle shadowing techniques such as ambient occlusion. You can add this support yourself through the use of GPU programs, and books such as *GPU Gems 2* by Matt Pharr and Randima Fernando (Addison-Wesley, 2005) even have entire chapters devoted to the calculation of real-time ambient occlusion. However, Ogre does not perform any of the preprocessing needed to support those techniques.

Shadowing in 3D graphics, in general, is a highly complex topic with a wide variety of gotchas and performance trade-offs. We will examine these pitfalls and compromises over the course of this chapter. However, Ogre also provides you a very simple way to enable and use shadows in your application with a minimum of fuss and often with only the most trivial of changes to your objects' materials (sometimes not even any changes at all). Of course, you still need to be aware of the implications of the shadowing techniques you choose to employ, but it is entirely possible to enable shadows in your scene with a single method call, and Ogre will take it from there.

Overview

Before we review the different types of shadow techniques in Ogre, you need to know a few things about shadows and Ogre in general:

- You can only use one technique or another in your scene, and you should set the technique to be used prior to rendering your scene (ideally, when you create your scene manager instance).

- You **should** set the shadow technique for your scene prior to assembling your scene. This means calling SceneManager::setShadowTechnique() with one of the following: SHADOWTYPE_STENCIL_ADDITIVE, SHADOWTYPE_STENCIL_MODULATIVE, SHADOWTYPE_TEXTURE_ ADDITIVE, or SHADOWTYPE_TEXTURE_MODULATIVE.

- Shadows are disabled by default.

- Casting and receiving of shadows is controlled in the material for an object; you can also control shadow casting on the object itself. The default is for all objects to cast shadows when shadows are enabled. Objects that have translucency or transparency do not cast shadows by default, although you can set translucent materials to cast shadows.

- As a consequence of the nature of the stencil shadow algorithm, translucent/transparent objects either cast full, solid stencil shadows or they cast none at all; you cannot get a semitransparent shadow unless you are using texture shadows (which handle transparency by default).

- Lights can be set **not** to cast shadows. This is done on a per-light basis. The compatibility between different light types and shadow techniques is described in Table 11-1.

Table 11-1. *Compatibility Matrix Between Light and Shadow Technique Types*

Shadow Technique	Point Light	Spot Light	Directional Light
Additive Stencil	Yes	Yes	Yes
Modulative Stencil	Yes	Yes	Yes
Additive Texture	Yes*	Yes	Yes
Modulative Texture	Yes*	Yes	Yes

* Point light support for texture shadows is approximated by rendering with spot lights. Avoid bringing objects near a point light (and do not enclose the point light in an object) for texture shadows.

Stencil Shadowing

Stencil shadowing is very simple in concept. The shape of the shadow thrown by a shadow-casting object in your scene is defined by the object's silhouette from the perspective of a given light. Figure 11-3 illustrates the principle. Note that Ogre provides a handy debugging feature that draws the shadow volume when enabled.

Figure 11-3. Demo_Shadows *with modulative stencil shadows and shadow debugging mode enabled*

The Shadow Volume

The *shadow volume* is the volume in space created by extrusion of the edges of the silhouette, bounded on one end by the model, with the other end bounded using the following rules:

- If programmable graphics hardware is available, vertex programs are used to project the shadow volume infinitely.

- If vertex programs are not available, the shadow volume is bounded on the far end by the light attenuation settings (for point and spot lights) or by the `SceneManager::setShadowDirectionalLightExtrusionDistance()` method.

■**Caution** If you do not have vertex programs available and Ogre has to use finite shadow volumes, then you should avoid letting objects draw too closely to light sources, or you run the risk of the wider shadow volume not properly shadowing objects within its volume.

The shadow volume is used to create a *stencil* in screen space, inside which all pixels on an object are drawn in shadow, and all pixels outside are unshadowed. When the shadow volume intersects an object (such as the floor plane in Figure 11-4), the stencil buffer (a buffer on the GPU similar to the depth buffer) is updated to reflect whether pixels on the screen should be rendered "in shadow" or "out of shadow."

Figure 11-4. Demo_Shadows *with debug shadows enabled, showing the intersection of the shadow volume and the floor plane object*

In Figure 11-4, only the pixels inside the stencil defined by the intersection of the floor and the shadow volume will be shaded darker; everything else will be rendered normally.

Due to the nature of the stencil shadow volume, stencil shadows possess sharply defined edges to the shadow: a pixel is either in shadow or out of shadow, with no in-between. This is a bonus in that stencil shadows can project over long distances with no loss in fidelity (such as objects that cast shadows at dusk or dawn), but also means that the actual polygon edges typically will be visible in the shadow (especially with long shadows). Ogre has no "make my shadows soft" switch; indeed, it is practically impossible to soften stencil shadows. The nature of texture shadowing allows for softening of texture shadows. The *Demo_Shadows* sample application we have been using in this chapter employs one such technique.

Keep in mind that edge lists are required for stencil shadow support in Ogre. The standard toolchain (exporters and OgreXMLConverter) will create edge lists while generating the binary mesh file, but you can also create them in your code using Mesh::buildEdgeList() (which you would need to do if you are creating mesh in code as opposed to using mesh created in an offline model- ing tool). You must call this method before trying to use an object's mesh with stencil shadows; ideally, you would do this while exporting your mesh, or during the offline XML-to-mesh conver- sion step, but as mentioned, if you are creating mesh dynamically you do not have that option. If no edge lists exist in your mesh, Ogre will assume you do not want it to cast stencil shadows.

Stencil Shadowing and GPU Programs

Stencil shadows will take advantage of programmable vertex GPU processing for infinite shadow volume extrusion when available. This behavior does not affect any GPU vertex programs you may write because the extrusion is done only during the automatic shadow generation pass (when your program would not be used anyway).

The problem, however, is that since stencil volume generation is a CPU-only process, there is no simple way to adjust this volume on the basis of geometry deformations that happen on the GPU in a vertex program. For hardware skinning, as described in the previous chapter, Ogre will duplicate the vertex skinning in software (which is unfortunate but unavoidable). However, for arbitrary algorithms implemented in a vertex program, Ogre has no way of knowing what the deformed geometry will look like. Therefore, if you use any other geometry-deforming vertex programs, you will have to live with the shadows not exactly reflecting the actual silhouette of your geometry when using stencil shadows. This may be enough reason to use texture shadowing instead.

Stencil Shadow Optimizations

Ogre can and does perform some generalized optimizations for you when rendering stencil shadows. As mentioned, vertex programs are used when available, to accelerate shadow volume extrusion. Ogre can do a good job of detecting which lights might affect the frustum (based on direction and range) and avoid constructing shadow geometry that is not needed. Ogre will also use a scissor test to save fillrate if a point or spotlight does not cover the entire viewport. Ogre supports the two-sided stencil and stencil-wrapping extensions that can prevent unnecessary primitive setup and driver overhead. Finally, Ogre uses the less expensive Z-Pass algorithm instead of the more expensive (but more robust) Z-Fail algorithm when the Z-Fail is not required (Z-Fail is most useful when the camera passes through a shadow volume).

However, this does not mean that you can just toss whatever you want at the shadowing support and let Ogre sort it out. You should be aware of the various gotchas particular to stencil shadows, in order to be able to optimize your usage of them in your scene.

- Shadow volumes are not affected by occluding geometry. This means that you can see shadows on the other side of what should be an occluding object (assuming that the occluding object is not set to cast shadows). Figure 11-5 shows this artifact; notice that the shadow is cast on the floor even though the cube should have blocked it (in the real world, that is). If the cube were instead a wall, and you could see both sides of the wall, then you would see the shadow cast through the wall and affecting objects on the other side as well.

- Offscreen shadow casters can cast shadows into the view frustum. If these casters are far away (such as those casting shadows at dawn or dusk, when the shadows are rather elongated), then the geometry that creates those shadows must be rendered, even if it is nowhere near the viewable portion of the scene.

- Avoid letting objects pass near or through lights if your target hardware does not include graphics accelerators capable of running vertex programs.

Figure 11-5. *Shadow volumes are not occluded by geometry.*

Texture Shadowing

Texture-based shadows are calculated entirely differently than stencil shadows and have their own benefits and drawbacks. Texture shadows are generated by rendering the scene to a texture from the point of view of the light. This texture is then projected onto shadow *receivers* in the scene during normal screenbuffer rendering. This is one of the primary differences between the Ogre mechanics of stencil and texture shadows: the use of shadow casters and receivers. Another is that fixed-function texture shadow casters cannot self-shadow: objects are either casters or receivers, but not both, and if an object is not a shadow caster, then it is a shadow receiver (unless this is disabled with the receive_shadows option in the object's material). Ogre does not yet support an alternate texture shadow technique called *depth shadow-mapping* that would allow self-shadowing with texture shadows. Figures 11-6 and 11-7 demonstrate the difference.

Figure 11-6. *Stencil shadows. Note the self-shadowing on the Athene's right arm and left leg.*

Figure 11-7. *Texture shadows. Note the **lack** of self-shadowing on the Athene's right arm and left leg with the texture technique.*

Texture shadows typically are a faster alternative to stencil shadow volumes, primarily at the cost of fidelity. Because the shadows are rendered to a texture, they possess a set resolution and do not respond well to extensive projective stretching: jagged edges, which can be filtered somewhat (but not enough to make them go away), are readily visible in the applied shadow. Figures 11-8 and 11-9 demonstrate the difference.

Figure 11-8. *Stencil shadows. Note the "sharpness" of the stencil shadow.*

Figure 11-9. *Texture shadows. Note the aliasing in the texture shadow; it is especially noticeable in the shadow of the Athene's staff. You can also see the difference in the nonmoving shadow cast by the sun at the right edge of the screenshot.*

However, texture shadows **are** fast, and they can be computed entirely in hardware (which enables a whole new world of versatility and fidelity not possible with fixed-function texture shadow maps). In many cases the decrease in fidelity is more than offset by the increase in performance and the ability to offload the entire shadowing process to the GPU. It is up to you which is the more important for your application.

Limitations

The increase in performance also comes with some limitations. While you theoretically could have as many texture shadows as you like, texture memory size and fillrate define the practical upper limit on the number of shadow textures in a frame. Ogre allows you to manage the upper limit on the number of shadow textures active in a frame with the `SceneManager::setShadowTextureCount()` method. Since Ogre uses one texture per light in a frame, it will use these textures on a first-come-first-served basis, essentially assigning the textures to the n nearest lights (where n is the number of textures supplied in `SceneManager::setShadowTextureCount()`). Any more lights in the frame are ignored.

You have at your disposal several tweaks to adjust the visual quality and aesthetics of your texture shadows. For spot lights, which have a natural frustum due to their radial falloff characteristic, shadow textures have a definite boundary, usually relatively small (in terms of the size of your scene). However, shadows for directional lights are typically large, and project over large areas of your scene. Ogre provides tweaks for the resulting artifacts caused by projecting texture shadows long distances:

- If you cannot increase the texture size to improve the visual quality of a elongated texture shadow, you can decrease the far projection distance so that the shadow terminates closer to the light. The drawback is of course a potentially less realistic shadow, but the quality of the shadow can be much improved.

- You can also "move" the shadow relative to the camera. By default, Ogre places the shadow such that 60% of the shadow is in "front" of the camera's line-of-sight. You can adjust this value up or down with `SceneManager::setShadowDirLightTextureOffset`, but be aware that you run the risk of inadvertently rendering the edges of the texture at extreme angles if you set this value too high (too much of the shadow is ahead of the camera, in other words).

- Shadows do not end abruptly; Ogre will fade the edges of a texture shadow to prevent a jarring change from shadow to no shadow. You can alter the radius at which the fade starts and stops from its defaults of 0.7 and 0.9 (normalized), respectively. You should avoid using 1.0 for the fade stop distance due to the "square peg, round hole" problem of radial lights and square textures; your texture shadows simply will always be circular or ellipsoidal.

Texture Shadows and GPU Programs

Texture shadows, since they are calculated on the GPU, do not suffer the same problems as do stencil shadows when it comes to shadowing GPU-deformed geometry. However, you do need to take some extra steps to enable your deformed geometry to be shadowed correctly. Ogre can properly take care of fully fixed-function shadow generation, but it needs some help when you involve GPU vertex programs in the shadow caster and/or receiver objects' materials.

Ogre provides a means to duplicate your geometry deformation in the shadow-casting pass with the `shadow_caster_vertex_program_ref` material directive.

```
shadow_caster_vertex_program_ref skinningOneWeight_ShadowCaster {
    param_named_auto    world_view_proj_3x4    worldviewproj_matrix
    param_named_auto    ambientColor           ambient_light_colour
}
```

Listing 11-1 shows the single-weight hardware skinning programs in `Example_Basic.cg`.

Listing 11-1. *Single-Weight Hardware Skinning Programs, One for Geometry and Lighting, and the Other for the Texture Shadow Map Generation Pass*

```
void hardwareSkinningOneWeight_vp(
    float4 position : POSITION,
    float3 normal   : NORMAL,
    float2 uv       : TEXCOORD0,
    float  blendIdx : BLENDINDICES,
```

```
    out float4 oPosition : POSITION,
    out float2 oUv       : TEXCOORD0,
    out float4 colour         : COLOR,
    // Support up to 24 bones of float3x4
    // vs_1_1 only supports 96 params so more than this is not feasible
    uniform float3x4   worldMatrix3x4Array[24],
    uniform float4x4 viewProjectionMatrix,
    uniform float4   lightPos[2],
    uniform float4   lightDiffuseColour[2],
    uniform float4   ambient)
{
    // transform by indexed matrix
    float4 blendPos = float4(mul(worldMatrix3x4Array[blendIdx], position).xyz, 1.0);
    // view / projection
    oPosition = mul(viewProjectionMatrix, blendPos);
    // transform normal
    float3 norm = mul((float3x3)worldMatrix3x4Array[blendIdx], normal);
    // Lighting - support point and directional
    float3 lightDir0 = normalize(
        lightPos[0].xyz - (blendPos.xyz * lightPos[0].w));
    float3 lightDir1 = normalize(
        lightPos[1].xyz - (blendPos.xyz * lightPos[1].w));

    oUv = uv;
    colour = ambient +
        (saturate(dot(lightDir0, norm)) * lightDiffuseColour[0]) +
        (saturate(dot(lightDir1, norm)) * lightDiffuseColour[1]);

}


/*
  Single-weight-per-vertex hardware skinning, shadow-caster pass
*/
void hardwareSkinningOneWeightCaster_vp(
    float4 position : POSITION,
    float3 normal    : NORMAL,
    float  blendIdx : BLENDINDICES,


    out float4 oPosition : POSITION,
    out float4 colour    : COLOR,
    // Support up to 24 bones of float3x4
    // vs_1_1 only supports 96 params so more than this is not feasible
    uniform float3x4   worldMatrix3x4Array[24],
    uniform float4x4 viewProjectionMatrix,
    uniform float4   ambient)
```

```
{
    // transform by indexed matrix
    float4 blendPos = float4(mul(worldMatrix3x4Array[blendIdx], position).xyz, 1.0);
    // view / projection
    oPosition = mul(viewProjectionMatrix, blendPos);

    colour = ambient;

}
```

In Listing 11-1, notice that the program signatures (the parameter lists) are identical; Ogre simply substitutes the standard program for the one marked for shadow-casting passes when rendering the shadow texture. Notice, however, that all the shadow-caster pass does is calculate the vertex position and pass the ambient color value through to the rasterizer; this enables the shadow generation pass to reflect the vertex positions accurately.

The ambient color value is required because modulative shadow techniques need a color with which to draw the shadow (additive techniques work differently, as you will see shortly). That is why we need to supply the ambient parameter to the vertex program.

As mentioned, shadow receivers need special attention as well, if they use vertex programs. The shadow_receiver_vertex_program_ref directive specifies an alternate shadow-receiving program.

```
shadow_receiver_vertex_program_ref skinningOneWeight_ShadowReceiver {
    param_named_auto    world_view_proj_3x4    worldviewproj_matrix
    param_named_auto    texProjMatrix          texture_viewproj_matrix
}
```

This program should

- Accept a texture_viewproj_matrix auto parameter with which it can transform the vertex texture coordinates properly

- Deform the vertices as normal

- Place the transformed texture coordinates into texture coordinate sets 0 and 1 (since some techniques use two texture units)

- For modulative shadows, render the output color as white so as not to alter the color of the shadow

Additive texture shadows must go even one step further: since the shadow pass render is actually the lighting render, if you use a fragment program on the object (for example, a parallax/offset mapping per-pixel fragment program that simulates perturbations in the surface of the object), you will need a special shadow receiver fragment program as well to simulate those perturbations in the shadow; this program is specified with the shadow_receiver_fragment_program_ref directive.

```
shadow_receiver_fragment_program_ref fragmentProgram_ShadowReceiver {
    param_named_auto    diffuse    light_diffuse_color 0
}
```

Projected shadow coordinates will come from the receiver vertex program, and the shadow texture will always appear in texture unit 0 (pushing any other textures up by one).

Modulative Shadow Blending

Modulative shadow blending is simple in theory: all of the colors that are in shadow in a normally rendered scene are multiplied (modulated) by the shadow color to create the darkened, shadowed color. This has the effect of "subtracting" light from an already-rendered scene.

In practice, however, several issues arise. First, the areas in shadow when modulative shadows are used are darkened uniformly, regardless of the amount of light that may have fallen on the area. This is an inaccurate shadow technique, since it does not account for the falloff inherent in point or spot light illumination (the shadow receiver surface is darkened the same regardless of the distance from the light), but it does provide acceptable results for a lower cost than the more accurate additive shadow masking. Finally, the multiplicative effect on the shadowed area can lead to unacceptably dark shadows when multiple lights cast shadows on the same area, so using modulative shadows for more than one light is inadvisable.

Modulative shadows do combine well with static shadow maps (such as those computed offline, like ambient occlusion or precomputed radiance transfer).

Additive Shadow Masking

Additive shadow techniques differ from modulative in that they "accumulate" the results of multiple shadow passes, each of which renders from the perspective of a single light. More "correct" shadows result from the fact that each light is prevented from affecting shadowed areas it cannot see, which allows accumulation of light from other lights in shadowed areas, something not possible with the modulative technique. The primary difference between the two techniques is that modulative shadowing affects only the areas that are in shadow, and additive shadowing affects only the areas that are lit (not shadowed), which is a more natural type of lighting technique.

Two costs accompany this enhanced visual quality. The first is simply logistic: you cannot combine additive shadow techniques with modulative "baked-in" lighting shadow maps (the technique used in games such as Quake 3) because there is no way to remove light that exists in a map generated using modulative techniques. You would have to use additive as your only shadow technique, for both the static map and dynamic shadows, and you can of course achieve some very realistic dynamic-only lighting solutions.

The computational cost for this realism, of course, is the number of passes required to perform additive shadow calculations. The cost is, in fact, $n+2$, where n is the number of lights in your scene. The reason for this is that Ogre splits up your passes (regardless of whether they are programmable or fixed function) into three passes:

- **Ambient**: Even if there are no unlit objects in your scene, Ogre will run an ambient-only pass to set up the depth buffer as well as apply any ambient and emissive colors to the scene. No textures are rendered in this pass.

- **Diffuse and specular**: This pass is rendered once per light. Areas in shadow from this light are not affected (are "masked" from the light). The unmasked areas are blended (scene_blend add) with the rest of the scene. No decal textures are used here either.

- **Decal**: This is the pass where any decal textures are applied (scene_blend modulate) with the accumulated color from the previous stage of passes.

Additive Shadows and GPU Programs

Ogre can and does perform this pass splitting on its own very well for fixed-function materials, but when programmable passes are involved, it needs a little help. In fact, you need to split up your programmable additive shadow materials for Ogre and mark them in certain ways so that it knows how to classify each. See Listing 11-2, which is a material script found in `Example-Advanced.material`; note that the real material also contains a fallback technique not shown here.

Listing 11-2. *Material Is Manually Partitioned, and Each Pass Marked So That Ogre Knows How to Categorize Each Pass*

```
// Any number of lights, diffuse
material Examples/BumpMapping/MultiLight
{

    // This is the preferred technique which uses both vertex and
    // fragment programs, supports coloured lights
    technique
    {
        // Base ambient pass
        pass
        {
            // base colours, not needed for rendering, but as information
            // to lighting pass categorisation routine
            ambient 1 1 1
            diffuse 0 0 0
            specular 0 0 0 0
            // Really basic vertex program
            // NB we don't use fixed function here because GL does not like
            // mixing fixed function and vertex programs, depth fighting can
            // be an issue
            vertex_program_ref Ogre/BasicVertexPrograms/AmbientOneTexture
            {
                param_named_auto worldViewProj worldviewproj_matrix
                param_named_auto ambient ambient_light_colour
            }

        }
        // Now do the lighting pass
        // NB we don't do decal texture here because this is repeated per light
        pass
        {
            // base colours, not needed for rendering, but as information
            // to lighting pass categorisation routine
            ambient 0 0 0
```

```
    // do this for each light
    iteration once_per_light

    scene_blend add

    // Vertex program reference
    vertex_program_ref Examples/BumpMapVP
    {
        param_named_auto lightPosition light_position_object_space 0
        param_named_auto worldViewProj worldviewproj_matrix
    }

    // Fragment program
    fragment_program_ref Examples/BumpMapFP
    {
        param_named_auto lightDiffuse light_diffuse_colour 0
    }

    // Base bump map
    texture_unit
    {
        texture NMBumpsOut.png
        colour_op replace
    }
    // Normalisation cube map
    texture_unit
    {
        cubic_texture nm.png combinedUVW
        tex_coord_set 1
        tex_address_mode clamp
    }
}

// Decal pass
pass
{
    // base colours, not needed for rendering, but as information
    // to lighting pass categorisation routine
    lighting off
    // Really basic vertex program
    // NB we don't use fixed function here because GL does not like
    // mixing fixed function and vertex programs, depth fighting can
    // be an issue
    vertex_program_ref Ogre/BasicVertexPrograms/AmbientOneTexture
    {
        param_named_auto worldViewProj worldviewproj_matrix
```

```
                    param_named ambient float4 1 1 1 1
            }
            scene_blend dest_colour zero
            texture_unit
            {
                texture RustedMetal.jpg
            }


        }
    }
}
```

In Listing 11-2, the depth-setup ambient-only pass is marked as such by setting the diffuse and specular colors to black. The per-light iterative pass is marked as such by its black ambient color, and by the `iterate once_per_light` directive. This directive also tells Ogre that the fragment program in the pass should be executed for each light; if this directive were not present, Ogre would not run the fragment program for each light because it would assume that the fragment program was performing decal work. Finally, in the decal pass, we turn off lighting to mark the decal pass and simply modulate the texture with the rest of the scene. Figure 11-10 illustrates the material in practice.

Figure 11-10. Demo_Dot3Bump *with ogrehead mesh, using the material in Listing 11-2*

Conclusion

Shadowing in 3D graphics, in reality, is a system of hacks and illusions that end up with some very pleasing results. The hacks and illusions, however, require that you wade through seas of tips, tricks, and gotchas in order to balance your application's requirements for realistic shadows with your application's need to perform at acceptable framerates. After completing this chapter, you should be ready to navigate that sea, armed with all of the details you need to arrive at your destination safely.

In the next chapter, we will address a much calmer topic, that of 2D support in Ogre. The next chapter will also introduce a new feature of Ogre, the Compositor framework.

CHAPTER 12

▪▪▪

Ogre 2D and Compositing

It might seem odd talking about two-dimensional graphics in a programming guide for a 3D API. However, many things simply are done better or easier in 2D. A graphical user interface (GUI), for example, often is more simply processed by the application and more intuitively understood by the user if it is presented as a two-dimensional screen. Application feedback mechanisms (such as the *heads-up display*, or HUD) in a game or training simulation often are best presented as a two-dimensional "overlay" to the 3D scene. Certainly you can engineer a fully 3D user interface, and many games and applications have done just that with mixed results, but even so, there is always a place in 3D applications for a two-dimensional framework.

This chapter also will cover a new concept in Ogre, that of the *Compositor*, which is a scriptable system for full-viewport effects such as motion blur, heat haze, transitional effects such as swirl—anything you can think of to do to an entire scene. It is called "Compositor" because its function is very similar to that of techniques used in traditional two-dimensional media such as film and television, and that is why I have included it in this chapter.

Ogre in Two Dimensions

2D in Ogre typically lives in the "overlay" render queue. There is nothing particularly special about this render queue except that everything that is rendered in that queue automatically is rendered after everything else ("on top" of the 3D scene, in other words). You can have 3D objects rendered in the Overlay queue; for example, a rotating rendering of a targeted object in a game HUD.

Overlays

Overlay is a sort of catch-all term that means exactly what it sounds like: an overlay "lays over" everything else in a scene, as do the stats window in the lower left and the Ogre logo in the lower right of Figure 12-1.

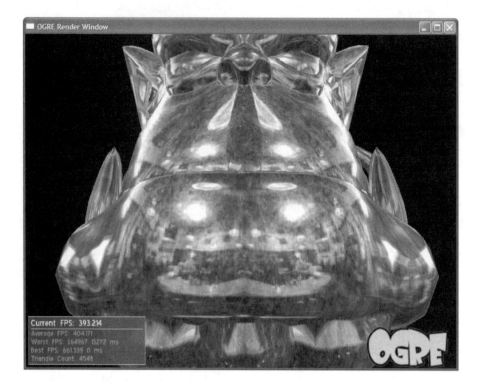

Figure 12-1. Demo_EnvMapping *with the "debug" overlays*

The stats window is drawn with a bit of transparency; if you look closely you can see the Ogre head showing through the stats window background. (You can find the script that defines this stats window in the OgreCore.zip file in the Samples/Media/packs directory).

Overlay Objects

Overlays in Ogre can be classified into two main types: those with the support of the Ogre framework (*managed*), and those without (*unmanaged*). The first type of overlay can be fully scripted and often is used for simple textual output or display. The second type encompasses any sort of GUI or generalized UI functionality your application might have (such as in-game HUD, UI menuing, and so on). Unmanaged overlay elements, in practice, are simply textured and shaded quads rendered in the overlay render queue; it is completely up to you how to draw, shade, and texture them.

■**Note**   Ogre comes with no GUI input management or event generation; overlays in Ogre are entirely noninteractive unless you wish to provide the functionality to make them interactive (for example, you might wish to add mouseover animations to an overlay that looks like a push button, as well as generate a "button-clicked" event if the user presses a mouse button while the button is active.

However, you are probably very much better served by using the CEGUI UI library for this purpose instead. It is a fully functioning GUI library that has native support for rendering to the Ogre overlay render queue. CEGUI 0.4.1 (the version supported by the version of Ogre covered by this book) is included in the Ogre samples, as well as with the Ogre SDK. Visit the CEGUI web site at `http://www.cegui.org.uk` for more information. You can also see how to use CEGUI with an Ogre application by looking at the source for the *Gui*, *FacialAnimation*, or *Ocean* Ogre demos.

Ogre Overlay Framework

Several Ogre API objects cooperate to make your managed overlay happen, whether it is a text overlay, a part of your application's HUD, or a UI widget. Whole overlays are managed by the **OverlayManager**, which is a standard Ogre resource manager of the scriptable variety (like the managers for Compositors, fonts, materials, and particle system resources).

The primary objects in an overlay are *containers* (**OverlayContainer**) and *elements* (**OverlayElement**, although this is simply a base class for the specialized functionality available in **PanelOverlayElement**, **BorderPanelOverlayElement**, and **TextAreaOverlayElement**). And obviously, if you are rendering text, you need a font to use for the text; fonts are handled by a class separate from the overlay framework, in **Font** and **FontManager**.

The root object in a defined overlay must be an OverlayContainer. Containers can be nested and can also contain elements. Each OverlayElement, regardless of subtype, in a container is positioned relative to its parent container, as illustrated in Figure 12-2. Note that TextAreaOverlayElement2 is the only object in the overlay positioned in relative terms, instead of pixels.

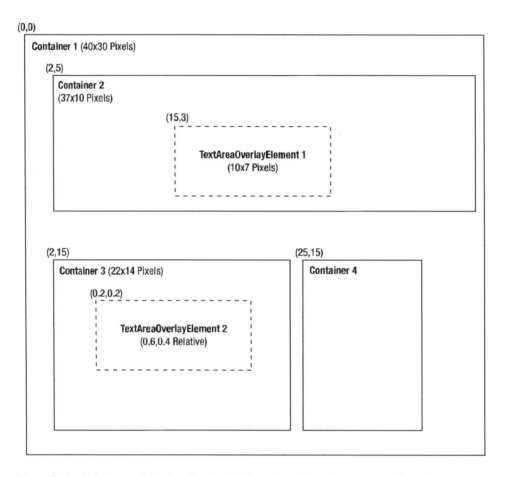

Figure 12-2. *Relative positioning (in pixels) of overlay objects in a managed overlay*

The overlay layout in Figure 12-2 is created by the overlay script in Listing 12-1.

Listing 12-1. *Overlay Script to Create the Overlay Layout in Figure 12-2*

```
TestOverlay
{
    zorder 500

    container Panel(Container1)
    {
        metrics_mode pixels
        left 0
        top 0
        width 40
        height 30
```

```
container Panel(Container2)
{
    metrics_mode pixels
    left 2
    top 5
    width 37
    height 10

    element TextArea(TextAreaOverlayElement1)
    {
        metrics_mode pixels
        left 15
        top 3
        width 10
        height 7

        font_name StarWars
        char_height 0.05
        colour 1.0 1.0 1.0
        caption TextAreaOverlayElement 1
    }
}

container Panel(Container3)
{
    metrics_mode pixels
    left 2
    top 15
    width 22
    height 14

    element TextArea(TextAreaOverlayElement2)
    {
        metrics_mode relative
        left 0.2
        top 0.2
        width 0.6
        height 0.4

        font_name StarWars
        char_height 0.05
        colour_top 1.0 1.0 1.0
        colour_bottom 0.5 0.5 1.0
        caption TextAreaOverlayElement 2
    }
}
```

```
      container Panel(Container4)
      {
         metrics_mode pixels
         left 25
         top 15
         width 10
         height 14
      }
   }
}
```

Assuming the root container in Figure 12-2 is positioned at (0,0) on the screen, the TextAreaOverlayElement1 would be positioned at (17,8) on the screen, since its parent is positioned at (2,5) and the text element at (10,3) relative to its parent.

Metrics

Element positioning can be done in terms of pixels, or in terms of normalized screen coordinates: (0.0,0.0) for upper left of the screen to (1.0,1.0) for lower right. You must use the same metrics for positioning and sizing in a particular element or container, but an element's metrics are not restricted by its parent container's metrics. For example, in Figure 12-2, TextAreaOverlayElement1 uses pixels metrics, and TextAreaOverlayElement2 uses relative metrics.

Use of relative metrics will make your overlays resolution-independent. For example, your application will not have to track whether the user is running your application at 800×600 or 1920×1200; your overlays will size properly regardless. However, if you use images in the materials for your overlay containers (see the next section), these may be stretched when the resolution changes.

Materials

Overlay elements are just quads, and as such, can use materials like any other geometry in your application. The only restriction is that when you use a material on an overlay element, lighting and depth checking are automatically turned off, so do not use the same material script on an overlay element as you would a normal 3D object in the scene.

Different overlay elements apply the material differently. A Panel element treats the material as the definition for the background, while a BorderPanel treats the material as the definition for the center area only; the border area material is defined with the border_material parameter.

If you define a material to be used for an overlay element in script, you must also define the material in a script as well (so that the material is defined when the overlay script is parsed). Materials are defined in an overlay element block with the material directive, in the form material <material_name>.

Element Alignment

Alignment of elements within a container can be managed in both directions; vertical alignment, using the vert_align directive, can be set to top, center, or bottom; and horizontal alignment, with the horiz_align directive, can be set to left, middle, or right. The defaults are top and left.

One effective trick with alignment operations is to use **negative** values for top and/or left position values with pixel metrics, to clamp an element to the edges of the screen. In order to make this work, you would need to use horiz_align right and vert_align bottom alignment operations.

Z-Order

Items in an overlay each have a "depth" associated with them, much like the objects in a 3D scene. In two dimensions, this depth is called *z-order* and the meaning is the same: items with greater depth (lower z-order) will be drawn first, possibly partially or fully obscured by items drawn with less depth (higher z-order). Therefore this depth determines the draw order of the items in the Overlay queue.

The depth of 2D items is independent of the depth of objects in the 3D scene (to a point; you should keep the depth values used for overlay elements in the range 0 to 650). All objects rendered in the overlay render queue will draw on top of everything else on the screen. You can blend overlays with the rest of the scene (for instance, alpha blend as used in the stats overlay in Figure 12-1), but only the scene as a whole, not individual objects in the scene. If you want to create complex visualizations combining parts of your 3D scene with overlay elements, you need to render only the desired 3D objects to a texture and apply that texture to your target overlay elements.

Fonts

A font in Ogre is not a renderable object itself; instead, a **Font** is used primarily to texture **TextAreaOverlayElement** objects (although you can use an Ogre font for whatever purpose you need). You can create fonts for use in your application in one of two ways: you can use an existing TrueType font, and Ogre will generate the glyphs for you on load, or you can use a font texture you created yourself.

Each method has its benefits and drawbacks. A wide variety of TrueType fonts probably are available to you for fast prototyping, but you will pay a loading-time penalty of the time it takes Ogre to generate the font texture. However, it takes some up-front time as well to create your own font texture. A good compromise is to use TrueType fonts for development and switch to custom fonts for production use. The decision primarily is whether you need multicolor fonts; Ogre will render a TrueType font to a texture in a single color. With your own hand-created font textures, you can use whatever colors you like.

■**Caution** TrueType fonts such as those that come with Microsoft Windows are **not** freely redistributable. In fact, some commercial fonts can cost hundreds or thousands of dollars to license for commercial use. Your application is allowed to use fonts that are installed on a user's system, but you are not allowed to redistribute most TrueType fonts with your application (without paying for them, anyway). The exception to this is freely available or open source fonts; it is your responsibility to ensure that any fonts you distribute with your application are "unencumbered" by licensing requirements or active patents.

Font Definition File

The font texture is generated for a certain screen resolution (in dots per inch) and a certain font size (in points). These definitions can be scripted in files that end with the .fontdef extension, such as the sample.fontdef file that comes with Ogre in the Samples/Media/fonts directory (same place you will find the solo5.ttf TrueType font file mentioned earlier). The contents of this file are given in Listing 12-2.

Listing 12-2. *Contents of* `sample.fontdef`

```
StarWars
{
    type            truetype
    source          solo5.ttf
    size            16
    resolution      96
}
```

The file format is fairly self-explanatory. This font is referred to in your code with the name "StarWars". For example, the following is sufficient to load the font defined in this file and make it ready for use in your application:

```
FontPtr font = FontManager::getSingleton().getByName("StarWars");
font->load();
```

The normal warnings apply regarding the `.fontdef` file containing the font definition being somewhere in your defined resource locations; a font is a resource like any other in Ogre, and its existence must be made known to Ogre if you plan to use it. Of course, like every scriptable resource in Ogre, you can also create a font definition entirely in code if you like (useful if you have a custom font definition scheme you prefer to use).

Fonts can come in one of two varieties for use with Ogre: TrueType or "image," the latter used when you have created your own texture containing the font glyphs. `source` is the file name of the font, regardless. `size` is the size of the font in points, and `resolution` is the intended dots-per-inch. Note that if you use font texture generated for the StarWars font defined in this file at any resolution other than 96 dpi, you will get aliasing, possibly severe, from either compressing or stretching the texture too much (same as you would get with abusing any other texture beyond its intended resolution).

For `image` type font definitions, you must provide the UV mappings for each glyph in the `.fontdef` file. These are of the form `glyph <character> <u1> <v1> <u2> <v2>`, one per line, where `U1` is the upper-left corner of the glyph in the texture and `U2` is the lower-right corner. Try to maintain a common height per character; width can vary for purposes of proper kerning.

For `truetype` type font definitions, you have an additional parameter available to antialias the colors (useful if you are color blending instead of alpha blending, which is the default). The parameter name is `antialias_colour`, and the possible values are `true` or `false` (the default is `false`). If in doubt, leave this parameter off, as it can lead to odd blending artifacts if you are using alpha blending.

Runtime Overlay Example

Overlays are most useful when you can update them from code. Listing 12-3 will update the caption for TextAreaOverlayElement1 from the overlay defined in Listing 12-1.

Listing 12-3. *Update **TextAreaOverlayElement** Caption from Code*

```
void setOverlayText(const String& newText) {
    OverlayManager *pOverlayManager = OverlayManager::getSingletonPtr();
```

```
OverlayElement* pText = static_cast<OverlayElement*>(
    pOverlayManager->getOverlayElement("TextAreaOverlayElement1"));

pText->setCaption(newText);
}
```

The same pattern used in Listing 12-3 applies to any overlay element or container: obtain a pointer to the object and then update its contents. The same properties available in script are available via similarly named API methods.

Compositor Framework

The Ogre Compositor framework is a set of APIs and scripting commands that support multi-pass rendering at the render-target level, in order to assist you with creating visual effects such as motion blur, heat haze, "infrared vision," or any per-fragment effect or postprocessing task you can imagine. At its core, the Compositor framework can be seen as a method of flexibly managing one or more passes through the graphics-rendering pipeline (whether programmable or fixed-function). These passes are performed on full-screen renders of your scene.

Compositor Example

It is far simpler to show how the Compositor framework works than to try to describe it. Figure 12-3 is a screenshot of the *Demo_Compositor* base scene, and Figure 12-4 is the same scene with the HDR Compositor applied.

Figure 12-3. Demo_Compositor *base scene (shiny gold-shaded torus spinning in the streets of a European village)*

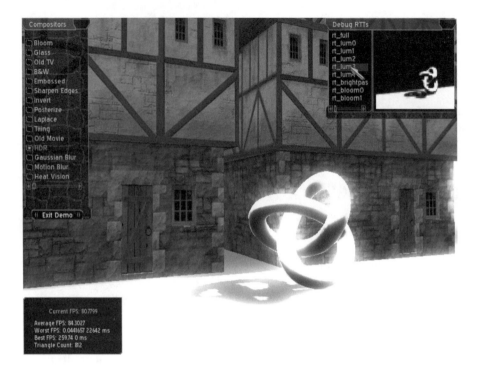

Figure 12-4. Demo_Compositor *base scene with the fake HDR filtering applied*

■**Note** Before we go much further, I would like you to notice the difference in framerates between the base scene and the composited scene; these screenshots were gathered on a Pentium 4 3.4GHz machine with an ATI X600 GPU. The Compositor framework is not magic, and not without cost; it runs additional rendering passes over your scene, and each pass takes additional rendering time. Of course, intelligent use of GPU features can reduce the time required to render each frame.

Listing 12-4 is the Compositor script that implements the HDR effect shown in Figure 12-4. You can find this script in Samples/Common/Media/materials/scripts/Examples.compositor. I should add that this is not really "HDR" as technically defined: *High Dynamic Range*, which uses higher-precision and higher-range floating-point source textures throughout the rendering process for much greater detail, especially in low-light situations. The source scene (and its textures) still use "normal" 8-bit integer textures; it is only the multiple passes through this Compositor that approximate the effect of using HDR in your original scene.

Listing 12-4. *HDR Compositor Script from the File* Samples/Media/materials/scripts/Example. compositor

```
compositor HDR
{
    // floating point only for now
```

```
technique
{
    // Temporary textures

    // Fullsize HDR render target, used as tone mapping source
    texture rt_full target_width target_height PF_FLOAT16_RGB

    // Targets used for luminance evaluation (3x3 downsample, point filtering)
    texture rt_lum0 1 1 PF_FLOAT16_RGB
    texture rt_lum1 4 4 PF_FLOAT16_RGB
    texture rt_lum2 16 16 PF_FLOAT16_RGB
    texture rt_lum3 64 64 PF_FLOAT16_RGB
    texture rt_lum4 128 128 PF_FLOAT16_RGB

    // Bright-pass filtered target (tone mapped)
    texture rt_brightpass 128 128 PF_R8G8B8

    // Bloom filter targets
    texture rt_bloom0 128 128 PF_R8G8B8
    texture rt_bloom1 128 128 PF_R8G8B8


    target rt_full
    {
        // No input, render differently
        input previous

        // Use float target HDR material scheme (unclamped shaders)
        // HDR scheme renders to FP textures, getting around [0..1]
        // limit on oer-channel texture values
        material_scheme HDR

        pass render_scene
        {
        }

    }

    // Downsample the original HDR scene to extract luminance value
    target rt_lum4
    {
        input none
        pass render_quad
        {
            // Downsample using a 2x2 filter and convert to grayscale
            material Ogre/Compositor/HDR/Downsample2x2Luminance
            input 0 rt_full
```

```
            identifier 994
        }
    }
    target rt_lum3
    {
        input none
        pass render_quad
        {
            // Downsample using a 3x3 filter
            material Ogre/Compositor/HDR/Downsample3x3
            input 0 rt_lum4
            identifier 993
        }
    }
    target rt_lum2
    {
        input none
        pass render_quad
        {
            // Downsample using a 3x3 filter
            material Ogre/Compositor/HDR/Downsample3x3
            input 0 rt_lum3
            identifier 992
        }
    }
    target rt_lum1
    {
        input none
        pass render_quad
        {
            // Downsample using a 3x3 filter
            material Ogre/Compositor/HDR/Downsample3x3
            input 0 rt_lum2
            identifier 991
        }
    }
    target rt_lum0
    {
        input none
        pass render_quad
        {
            // Downsample using a 3x3 filter
            material Ogre/Compositor/HDR/Downsample3x3
            input 0 rt_lum1
            identifier 990
        }
    }
```

```
target rt_brightpass
{
    input none
    pass render_quad
    {
        // Downsample using a 3x3 filter, hi-pass and tone map
        material Ogre/Compositor/HDR/Downsample3x3Brightpass
        input 0 rt_full
        input 1 rt_lum0
        identifier 800
    }
}

target rt_bloom1
{
    input none
    pass render_quad
    {
        // Blur horizontally
        material Ogre/Compositor/HDR/GaussianBloom1
        input 0 rt_brightpass
        identifier 701
    }
}
target rt_bloom0
{
    input none
    pass render_quad
    {
        // Blur horizontally
        material Ogre/Compositor/HDR/GaussianBloom0
        input 0 rt_bloom1
        identifier 700
    }
}

// Final output combines tone mapping of the original scene, with an
// exposure setting passed in as a GPU parameter, and an additive bloom
// effect
target_output
{
    input none
    pass render_quad
    {
        material Ogre/Compositor/HDR/ToneMapping
        input 0 rt_full
        input 1 rt_bloom0
```

```
                 input 2 rt_lum0
             }
         }
     }
}
```

Listing 12-4 starts by defining nine separate render texture targets that will be used to perform the rendering passes for the HDR rendering demo. Each target (beyond the first) disregards any existing contents in a render target; the first pass takes in the existing contents of the primary framebuffer, which contains the output of the nonprocessed rendered scene. Instead, each target runs a single pass that takes one or more rendered textures as source data and operates on that instead.

Figure 12-5 maps the progress of the script passes through these render targets, and Figure 12-6 shows the output of each rendering pass.

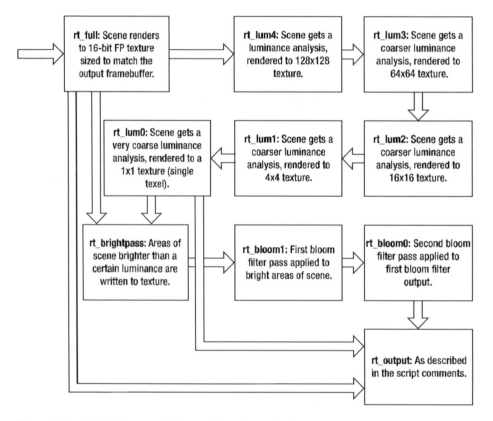

Figure 12-5. *Block diagram of the pass flow through the HDR Compositor script*

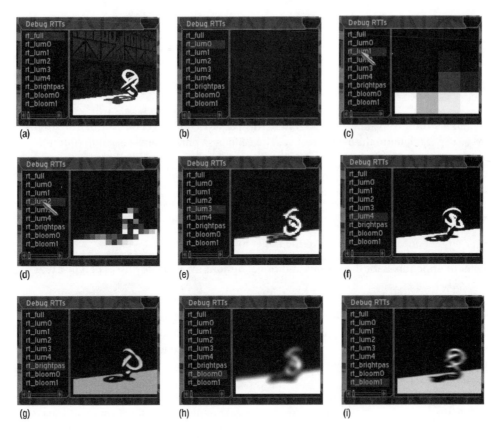

Figure 12-6. *Output of each rendering pass: (a) is the base scene before any composition passes; (b), (c), (d), (e), and (f) are the luminance analysis averaging steps; (g) is the bright-pass step to extract pixels greater than a particular luminance; (h) and (i) are bloom-filter steps to add a bit of "glow" to the final output.*

The actual materials that run these passes are somewhat involved; if you like to see them, they are available in Samples/Media/materials/scripts/hdr.material. Some of the passes use GPU fragment programs; others simply use the fixed-function pipeline (such as the render of the original scene into the rt_full target). In all cases, this Compositor example renders its intermediate output to textures and combines the textures in subsequent passes.

You can use more than one pass per Compositor target. Each input parameter specifies a texture unit index and a named input texture (using the name given at the top of the script). For example, the following tells the Compositor that this target wants to ignore any existing contents of the viewport with input none:

```
target rt_brightpass
{
    input none
    pass render_quad
    {
        // Downsample using a 3x3 filter, hi-pass and tone map
```

```
            material Ogre/Compositor/HDR/Downsample3x3Brightpass
            input 0 rt_full
            input 1 rt_lum0
            identifier 800
        }
    }
```

It then instructs the Compositor to render this pass to a full-target quad with the render_quad parameter to the pass directive. The valid pass parameters are

- render_quad: Render to the entire render target.

- render_scene: Perform a normal scene render to the target.

- stencil: Perform a stencil buffer setup pass (including configuring stencil operations).

- clear: Set one or more buffers in the target to a fixed value.

Refer to Appendix B for the various additional options available to passes of type clear and stencil.

The pass then instructs the Compositor to use the material named Ogre/Compositor/HDR/Downsample3x3Brightpass to render this pass; if you examine the pass in the material script file mentioned, you can see that this pass performs the filter in a pair of GPU programs. You are free to use whatever technique you need to achieve the needed effect; since this is just a normal Ogre material, all material functionality (such as technique fallback) is available to your Compositor passes.

Ogre/Compositor/HDR/Downsample3x3Brightpass expects two texture units to be prepared for its use; the texture units supplied to this material are defined in this Compositor pass definition as well:

```
input 0 rt_full
input 1 rt_lum0
```

The first input line specifies that the texture rendered to rt_full should be provided as the first (zero-based indexed) texture unit in the material, and that rt_lum0 should be provided as the second.

The identifier is an application-defined and application-interpreted unsigned integer that Ogre will use when calling back into registered Compositor pass listeners, so that you can know which pass is being rendered in your code (in the event that you wish to do some sort of special processing, or change GPU program parameters, in between or during Compositor rendering passes).

Compositor Chains

Compositor Chain is the term used to describe applying the output of one Compositor script as the input to another Compositor enabled on the same viewport. *Demo_Compositor* implements Compositor Chains; each Compositor effect you see listed on the left side of the demo is added to the chain for the demo viewport. At runtime, you can enable various effects; the effects will be applied to the scene in the order in which they appear in the demo (top to bottom), with the exception of the HDR effect, which is placed first in the chain.

Compositor Chain Design

One of the more important design traits to understand about the Compositor is that it is not an actual part of the Ogre viewport; instead, it is a set of classes that act on viewport instances. The origin of all Compositor Chain functionality in code begins with the **CompositorManager**, which is populated with instances of **CompositorInstance** based on Compositor scripts loaded at Ogre initialization. You can attach an instance to a viewport, which will include the instance in the **CompositorChain** that the **CompositorManager** manages for that viewport. All of the operations and sections available in Compositor scripts are available from the **CompositorInstance**: **CompositionTechnique**, **CompositionPass**, **CompositionTargetPass**. Each of these classes corresponds to a similarly named section in a Compositor script file.

Compositor Chain Example

Compositor Chains are the reason for the input parameter to Compositor target declarations; when this parameter is set to previous, the target will use the contents of the viewport as output from the previous Compositor in the chain (or will use the rendered scene if this is the first Compositor in the chain). Listing 12-5 shows an example.

Listing 12-5. *Code to Assemble a Two-Part Compositor Chain*

```
// assume vp points to the current Viewport
CompositorManager* cMgr = CompositorManager::getSingletonPtr();

// add Compositor from example script -- will be put first in chain
cMgr->addCompositor(vp, "Bloom", -1);

// enable the Compositor
cMgr->setCompositorEnabled(vp, "Bloom", true);

// do same for Motion Blur Compositor
CompositorInstance* ci = cMgr->addCompositor(vp, "Motion Blur", -1);
cMgr->setCompositorEnabled(vp, "Motion Blur", true);

// make Motion Blur take Bloom's output for target pass 0
ci->getTechnique()->getTargetPass(0)
    ->setInputMode(CompositionTargetPass::IM_PREVIOUS);
```

Listing 12-5 uses two of the Compositors defined in scripts (parsed during Ogre startup). These Compositors are chained back to back (by virtue of the order in which they were added), with the Motion Blur Compositor using the output of the Bloom Compositor as its input.

You can specify the order in which Compositors are processed for a viewport by managing the third parameter to addCompositor(); a value of -1 instructs Ogre to place it at the end of the list, but you can supply any position between 0 and size-1, where size is the current length of the viewport's Compositor list. You can get the length of the viewport's Compositor list with CompositorChain::getNumCompositors():

```
size_t len = cMgr->getCompositorChain(vp)->getNumCompositors();
```

Notes on Compositor Usage

The Compositor framework in Ogre is extremely flexible and powerful, but you should be aware of a few different features in its usage.

Rendering Your Scene During Compositor Passes

You can render your entire scene again into a render target during Compositor passes, if you wish. Of course, input previous provides access to your rendered scene at any time (or to the output of a previous Compositor in the chain defined for the viewport). The most common reason to render your scene again is to limit which render queues are invoked during this scene render, by specifying the starting and ending queues by their queue ID (you will need to examine the OgreRenderQueue.h header file to obtain this information). For example, the following renders only the "normal" object queue (disregarding skies, background, world geometry, and overlays):

```
pass render_scene {
    first_render_queue 50
    last_render_queue 50
}
```

The defaults for first and last render queue are 5 and 95, respectively, which renders everything.

Likewise, you can also set the visibility_mask parameter to instruct a Compositor target to render only objects whose flags match the mask provided to this parameter. The mask is simply an unsigned integer, which is a bitwise mask defined and understood by you and the application.

Compositor Callbacks

As mentioned, you can have Ogre notify your application when it is about to set up a material for a Compositor pass, and when it is about to start rendering the pass. The **CompositorInstance:: Listener** interface provides two methods, notifyMaterialSetup() and notifyMaterialRender(), that your callback object must implement. These methods both take the same parameters: the ID that you specified in script for a pass and the name of the material in question. This allows you to manage the material properties during Compositor operations at a very fine level if you wish.

Compositor Materials

As mentioned, the material scripts used with the Compositor follow the same rules as the materials you use during normal scene rendering. Within a pass render_scene block, you can specify different material schemes and so on for each Compositor target that uses a material. See Appendix B for more on the various per-target material metadata you can use.

Compositor Techniques

Compositor scripts use techniques, and the meaning and mechanics of *technique* is the same with Compositor as it is with regular Ogre materials: a Compositor technique is simply an "alternate way of pulling off a post-processing effect," and multiple techniques for a Compositor script are evaluated for preference in the order they appear in the script.

Techniques in the Compositor also can use "fallbacks" like material techniques. The difference is how the "best" technique is chosen for a given Compositor script.

First, since all Compositor passes use materials, the material specified for a pass must have at least one valid technique (determined by the normal material technique evaluation processes). Then, if there is at least one valid technique in the material, the Compositor examines the texture formats requested in the technique; if the technique uses one or more invalid or unsupported pixel formats (unsupported by the graphics hardware, that is), then the technique is discarded.

However, the hardware will "downgrade" unsupported formats to formats it supports, but you do not always want this; for example, your Compositor technique might rely on floating-point texture formats that the hardware does not support, and you might want to provide an alternate technique in this case. Therefore, the Compositor framework will not let the hardware downgrade your pixel format request the first time through, and instead search your defined techniques for fallbacks. If it does not find any, it will go through the list again from the top, this time letting the hardware downgrade your pixel format request. And only then, if no techniques you have defined match the hardware's ability to fulfill your requests, will Ogre discard your Compositor script with an exception. This is unlikely, however, since Ogre and the hardware usually will find some combination of materials and pixel formats that will allow your Compositor to be processed.

Conclusion

Two-dimensional topics in a book on 3D graphics might seem a bit odd, but as you have learned in this chapter, two-dimensional graphics and postprocessing can be fun and interesting, and even add that final special touch to your application's visual quality in a way not possible with 3D-only techniques.

This wraps up our coverage of the Ogre 3D rendering API and its capabilities and features. The appendix that follows will introduce the various Ogre tools and add-ons available to enhance your productivity when working with Ogre, but you are now equipped with the basic knowledge you will need to leverage OGRE 3D in your application.

Enjoy!

■ ■ ■

Ogre Tools and Add-Ons

As feature-rich and powerful as Ogre is (as you have learned in the rest of this book), it is rather useless unless it has something to render. This "something" almost always is created in an offline tool, or is made available to Ogre by some formal, systematic means, and that means a toolchain must exist in order to prepare your digital assets for use with Ogre.

This appendix is dedicated to introducing you to the various mature and supported (meaning actively maintained and developed) tools and add-ons available for Ogre. These tools and add-ons cover a wide range of functionality, from simple export of mesh data to Ogre's native format, to plug-ins for live streaming video and custom scene management.

Note Several of the projects and tools introduced here are available as *Ogre Addons*. The Ogre Addons are projects not part of the Ogre core that can add various types of functionality or bindings to Ogre-based applications. These add-ons are most often available in source form only, by CVS access, to the `ogreaddons` project at the same CVSROOT given in Chapter 2.

Official Tools and Utilities

The Ogre Team directly develops and maintains several tools and utilities for use in making content available to Ogre. These tools and utilities are available for download on the main Ogre site's Downloads page.

Exporters and Plug-Ins

Ogre reads only one binary mesh/animation format: its own. This means that whatever 3D modeling tool you are using, you will need to export your mesh/material/animation data to Ogre's format. In some cases, this is a two-step process, where the mesh/animation data is exported first to an intermediate XML format and then converted (with a command-line tool) into the binary loadable formats.

Almost all exporters, whether "official" or community-supported, handle animation export the same way. In short, you assign a name to a range of animation keyframes. This name is then used to reference the animation sequence in code when you obtain an **AnimationState** instance.

The following exporters are developed and supported directly by the core Ogre Team.

Blender

Blender is an open source 3D modeling package, with many features rivaling those of commercial modeling packages. It is freely available, and you can get it at `http://www.blender3d.org`. The Blender exporter supports full Ogre mesh, material, and animation (skeletal, morph, and pose) export, and is kept in synch with the Blender versions as they are released.

The Blender exporter is also actually an importer as well—it can read binary `.mesh` and `.skeleton` files into Blender, making Blender a useful tool (even if you do not use it for actual modeling) to import Ogre mesh data for which you do not have the original source assets.

Versions supported: 2.37a, 2.4*x*, and above

Softimage|XSI

Softimage was the first commercial tool vendor to recognize the importance of the Ogre library and community and offer direct support to the Ogre Team to create an Ogre exporter for their XSI modeling package. XSI is a full-featured commercial 3D modeling tool, with every feature you could think of and many you haven't. You can find out more about Softimage and XSI at `http://www.softimage.com/products/xsi`.

Versions supported: 4.2, 5.*x*, and above

Discreet 3D Studio Max

Discreet (now Autodesk) is one of the original 3D modeling tool vendors, and is the most recent to offer the Ogre Project support for development of an official Ogre 3D Studio Max exporter. 3D Studio Max is used to create at least some content for just about every game on the store shelves, in large part due to its Character Studio animation suite. You can find out more at `http://www.discreet.com/3dsmax`.

Versions supported: 6/7/8 and above

MilkShape 3D

MilkShape 3D is one of the original 3D modeling tools, period. It is a favorite of many modelers for its ease of use and features at a very reasonable price. You can find out more at `http://www.milkshape3d.com`.

Versions supported: 1.6.*x* and 1.7.*x*

Command-Line Tools and Utilities

OgreXMLConverter

As mentioned earlier, exporting mesh and animation data for use by Ogre sometimes is a two-step process. The second step of that process involves the conversion of an intermediate XML format to the binary `.mesh` and `.skeleton` formats. The **OgreXMLConverter** is the utility that performs this second step.

The **OgreXMLConverter** does more than just convert the XML to binary format (as well as binary to XML). It also saves the data with a preoptimized layout that makes for efficient data loading, as well as pregenerate edge lists for stencil shadow volumes and preferred platform-specific color formats (Direct3D on Windows, OpenGL on non-Windows). All of these default behaviors can be disabled at the command line.

The **OgreXMLConverter** can perform the following additional calculations (activated or configured by command-line switches):

- **Tangent generation**: The converter will generate tangents for tangent-space normal mapping (useful for view-independent lighting calculations).

- **Removal of redundant tracks and keyframes**: The converter can optimize out redundant animation data.

- **Automatic level-of-detail generation**: The converter can generate LoD mesh data automatically for you and allow you to set the number of levels, the level distances, and the percentage triangle reduction per level (relative to the previous level).

The **OgreXMLConverter** is available in the Tools ➤ Command-Line Tools download on the Ogre Downloads page.

■**Note** Direct-to-binary exporter authors can use the **MeshSerializer**, **SkeletonSerializer**, and **MaterialSerializer** classes; these are part of the Ogre core. See the **OgreXMLConverter** source code (included in the Ogre source distributions under Tools/) for more on how you can use these classes in your exporter.

MeshUpgrader and MaterialUpgrader

Also included in the Ogre source and in the Command-Line Tools package are MeshUpgrader and MaterialUpgrader, two utilities for upgrading older mesh or material file formats to the version suitable for the current Ogre version.

Third-Party Tools and Utilities

Exporters and Plug-Ins

The following exporters and plug-ins are not developed or maintained by the Ogre Project Team directly, but instead are actively developed and maintained by community members, and most of them are available in the Ogre Downloads or Addons (those that are not are indicated as such).

Note that most existing 3D modeling tools have some level of Ogre support developed for them. However, many of them are in unknown states of repair, and without knowing about their levels of development and maintenance, I cannot cover them too much here apart from mentioning them. Packages such as Newtek Lightwave 3D (http://www.newtek.com), Caligari trueSpace (http://www.caligari.com), and Wings 3D (http://www.wings3d.com) all have exporters or converters available for them (and a converter for Lightwave 3D and an exporter for Wings 3D in fact are available from the Ogre Tools Downloads page); trueSpace and Lightwave 3D both have exporters developed for them in various states of completeness (trueSpace exporter in Ogre Addons, Lightwave 3D exporter available by search in the Ogre forums).

Alias|Wavefront Maya

Alias|Wavefront (now Autodesk) Maya is a top-tier 3D modeling and animation package used, like Softimage|XSI and 3D Studio Max, for creating digital content for film, television, games, and more. The exporter is developed and maintained by an active member of the Ogre community, and the plug-in builds are available in the Ogre Tools Downloads.

Versions supported: 6/6.5/7 and above

oFusion for 3D Studio Max

The oFusion 3D Studio Max plug-in was developed by an Ogre community user for a third party; the Community Edition has since become the "gold standard" for Ogre digital content creation tools (in fact, an effort for a similar plug-in for Softimage|XSI is underway and could be available by the time you read this).

This plug-in allows artists to see how their model(s) looks in-engine with an Ogre viewport (an actual Ogre render window) in Max: materials are translated in real-time into Ogre materials, and animations can be previewed in the Ogre viewport at the same time they are previewed in a standard Max viewport. The oFusion plug-in also supports GPU shaders, and full model and scene export from Max directly to the Ogre binary skeleton and mesh formats. You can even drop your entire scene into an Ogre application using an available scene importer—your artists do not even need to involve an engineer to test their content in your application. It is the single biggest leap in toolchain support for Ogre in its history.

You can find the oFusion plug-in at `http://ofusion.inocentric.com`, and oFusion also has support forums in the Ogre Addons forums.

Google SketchUp

With SketchUp, Google has provided a 3D modeling tool, as Ogre founder Steve Streeting puts it, "for the rest of us." It is a lightweight, easy-to-use modeling tool that provides nontechnical artists the ability to mock up and prototype 3D scenes very quickly with a minimum of learning curve. You can find SketchUp at `http://sketchup.google.com` and its Ogre exporter in the Ogre Addons.

Digital Content Creation

Particle Editor

The Ogre particle system is very flexible and powerful, but it is easiest to use with an interactive editor such as the Ogre Particle Editor. This editor allows editing of existing particle systems and creation of new ones, with full control over all particle parameters via intuitive GUI. The editor is implemented in an actual Ogre application, so you can see exactly what your visual effects will look like in your application.

The Particle Editor is available from the Ogre Tools Downloads page.

Mesh Viewer

Similar to the Particle Editor, the Ogre Mesh Viewer is a simple application that allows to you load and preview your meshes and animations in an actual Ogre application, without having to load them into your full application. This allows for rapid iteration on 3D content creation when a modeling tool embedded Ogre viewport is not available (such as that with oFusion).

The Ogre Mesh viewer is called *CEGUIMeshViewer*, referring to the GUI library it uses, and is available on the Ogre Tools Downloads page.

ATI RenderMonkey Exporter

ATI's RenderMonkey is a shader development environment and set of modeling tool plug-ins, aimed at making the development of GPU shaders easier by reducing iteration time and allowing real-time preview of the effect of the shader on an object. The Ogre RenderMonkey exporter converts the RenderMonkey data to an Ogre native material file, readily usable in Ogre. RenderMonkey is available from ATI at `http://www.ati.com/developer/rendermonkey`, and the exporter is available in the Ogre Addons (you will need the RenderMonkey API, available on the ATI page, in order to build the exporter).

Ogre Addons

COLLADA

COLLADA is an important initiative in the 3D graphics industry, intended to develop a "common format" that all digital content creation tools in the industry can understand. This format exists in the form of an XML Schema, and an Ogre COLLADA plug-in is in active development. This plug-in will allow Ogre to load COLLADA files directly. The Ogre COLLADA plug-in is compliant, at this writing, with the 1.3.1 version of the COLLADA specification, and as the specification grows, the Ogre COLLADA plug-in is expected to grow with it.

Paging Scene Manager

The Paging Scene Manager is an Ogre scene manager plug-in designed to enable the efficient rendering of large (meaning more than one page) heightmapped landscapes. The plug-in is a "geo-mipmapping" scene manager that manages LoD at terrain page scope, allowing the use of large amounts of viewable terrain such as found in flight simulators. You can leverage the terrain paging scene manager for any large environment, like those found in sprawling urban games such as Grand Theft Auto.

The plug-in comes with a mapsplitter tool that helps you cut your large heightmap into smaller pages that the scene manager plug-in can sew back together and use for level-of-detail management. The entire package is available in the Ogre Addons, and I highly recommend first visiting the support forum in the Ogre Addons forums.

Streaming Video

One member of the Ogre Team developed a Theora-based streaming texture-source plug-in to enable the playing of video (even live streaming video) in your application. Theora is a widely used streaming video library available at `http://www.theora.org`.

The Ogre plug-in is called *videoplugin*, and is available in the Ogre Addons. Support is available at `http://www.wreckedgames.com/forum` in the Theora Plugin forum.

Physics Library Connectors

Connectors are implementations of the *Adapter* design pattern, and they serve to bridge the gap between a physics simulation library and Ogre. For the most part, the physics library does the "driving" of object transforms and updates the associated Ogre Entity instances on the basis of collision resolution in the physics world (which is maintained separately from Ogre's scene graph). This adapting removes from the developer the need to perform these updates manually.

OgreODE

ODE is an actively developed and maintained open-source physics library with all of the functionality of its commercial counterparts. **OgreODE** is maintained by active members of the Ogre MVP and user community. ODE can be found at `http://www.ode.org`, and **OgreODE** can be obtained from the Ogre Addons.

NxOgre

Novodex AG was a commercial physics library vendor who offered a product called *Novodex*. Novodex was acquired by Ageia, who produces a physics coprocessor unit (PPU) called *PhysX*. Ageia leveraged the Novodex API for the PhysX PPU's API, and renamed it "PhysX API" as well. The Novodex (PhysX) API is free for noncommercial use, but only for Win32.

NxOgre is a very actively developed and maintained connector for the Novodex physics library, and has a plethora of documentation and sample code. You can obtain PhysX (Novodex) from Ageia at `http://www.ageia.com`, and **NxOgre** itself from `http://www.nxogre.org`. **NxOgre** also has support forums in the Ogre Addons forums.

OgreNewt

The Newton Game Dynamics physics library is another free-for-noncommercial-use physics SDK with active development and maintenance. **OgreNewt** is the connector developed to adapt Newton to Ogre. Newton is available at `http://www.newtondynamics.com`, and **OgreNewt** is available in the Ogre Addons. **OgreNewt** has support forums in the Ogre Addons forums.

Script Bindings

Several scripting languages have been bound directly to Ogre. This list is not exhaustive; many of the existing binding efforts are in various states of completeness and maintenance levels. The bindings listed here are considered relatively "complete" and "mature" (meaning that you can most likely use them for your applications with little fuss).

PyOgre

PyOgre is a complete set of Python bindings for Ogre, allowing for fast prototyping and application development without the need to compile code. It exposes the Ogre classes and methods to a Python application, which enables any Python application to utilize Ogre for 3D rendering. It is available in the primary Ogre Downloads section under SDKs, and support is available in the **PyOgre** Addons forum at `http://www.ogre3d.org/phpBB2addons`.

OgreDotNet

While not technically a scripting language per se, the .NET Framework is a common language runtime that can run any program written in a language that can target the CLR. Bindings for Ogre to enable it as a CLR package and namespace exist in the **OgreDotNet** project. **OgreDotNet** is available in the Ogre Addons and support is available in the **OgreDotNet** Addons forum at `http://www.ogre3d.org/phpBB2addons`.

External Projects Using Ogre

The following projects use or leverage Ogre in one form or another, and are included for further study if you wish to investigate them.

Ogre4J

Java bindings for Ogre, making Ogre available to Java applications: `http://www.ogre4j.org`.

Yake

Game engine framework using Ogre for rendering: `http://www.yake.org`.

APPENDIX B

■■■

Script Attribute Reference

This appendix contains a complete listing of all attributes available for all scriptable Ogre features: materials, compositor, layouts, particle systems, and fonts.

Material Script Attributes

Top-Level Material Attributes

These attributes are used inside a `material` block.

Attribute Name	Value Format	Description
lod_distances	\<d1\> [\<d2\> ... \<dn\>]	Detail-level distance list
receive_shadows	\<on\>|\<off\>	Whether shadows are cast upon this object (default on)
transparency_casts_shadows	\<on\>|\<off\>	Whether transparent objects cast shadows (default off)
set_texture_alias	\<alias_name\> \<texture_name\>	Rename texture (used with material copying)

Technique Attributes

These attributes are used inside a `technique` block.

Attribute Name	Value Format	Description
scheme	\<name\>	Scheme to which this technique belongs (default Default)
lod_index	\<number\>	Detail level in which this technique is used (default 0)

Pass Attributes

These attributes are used inside a pass block.

Attribute Name	Value Format	Description
ambient	`<r> <g> <b> [<a>]` | `<vertex color>`	Ambient color value for this pass (default 1.0 1.0 1.0 1.0).
diffuse	`<r> <g> <b> [<a>]` | `<vertex color>`	Diffuse color value for this pass (default 1.0 1.0 1.0 1.0).
specular	`<r> <g> <b> [<a>] <shininess>` | `<vertex color> <shininess>`	Specular color value for this pass (default 0.0 0.0 0.0 0.0 0.0).
emissive	`<r> <g> <b> [<a>]` | `<vertex color>`	Emissive color value for this pass (default 0.0 0.0 0.0 0.0).
scene_blend	`<add>` | `<modulate>` | `<alpha_blend>` | `<colour_blend>`	How to blend this pass with the rest of the scene (default is opaque, no blending).
scene_blend	`<src_factor> <dest_factor>`	Advanced control of scene-blend function. Possible values for factors are one, zero, dest_colour, src_colour, one_minus_dest_colour, one_minus_src_colour, dest_alpha, src_alpha, one_minus_dest_alpha, one_minus_src_alpha (default one zero).
depth_check	`<on>` | `<off>`	Enable depth-buffer check for this pass (default on).
depth_write	`<on>` | `<off>`	Enable depth-buffer write for this pass (default on).
depth_func	`<func>`	Function to use for depth-buffer testing. Possible values are always_fail, always_pass, less, less_equal, equal, not_equal, greater_equal, greater (default less_equal).
depth_bias	`<offset>`	Depth bias offset for this pass (default 0).
alpha_rejection	`<func>`	Enable alpha-reject for this pass. Possible function values are same as for depth_func (default always_pass).
cull_hardware	`<clockwise>` | `<anticlockwise>` | `<none>`	Set vertex winding order for hardware backface culling (default clockwise).
cull_software	`<back>` | `<front>` | `<none>`	Set vertex winding order for software normal-based culling (default back).
lighting	`<on>` | `<off>`	Enable dynamic lighting for this pass (default on).

Attribute Name	Value Format	Description
shading	\<flat> | \<phong> | \<gouraud>	Set local dynamic lighting model for this pass (default gouraud).
polygon_mode	\<solid> | \<wireframe> | \<points>	Set type of rendering for this pass (default solid).
fog_override	\<true> | \<false> [\<type> \<colour> \<density> \<start> \<end>]	Override fog settings for this pass. type is one of none, linear, exp, exp2; colour is an RGB color value (component values 0.0 to 1.0) in the form \<r> \<g> \<b>; density for exp and exp2 is a floating-point value; start and end are the linear distance in world units from the camera (default is fog_override false).
colour_write	\<on> | \<off>	Enable color write for this pass (default on).
max_lights	\<number>	Number of dynamic lights to consider for this pass (default 8).
iteration	\<once> | \<once_per_light> [light_type]	Whether or not this pass is iterated, and if once_per_light, for which type of light (point, directional, spot) (default once).
iteration	\<number> [\<per_light> [light_type]]	Alternate form of pass iteration directive, either number times or number times per light (default 1).
point_size	\<size>	Point size for point list or point sprint rendering for this pass (default 1.0).
point_size_attenuation	\<on> | \<off> [constant linear quadratic]	Whether point size is attenuated with view-space distance for this pass; optional parameters determine attenuation function (default off).
point_size_min	\<size>	Minimum point size after attenuation (if used) for this pass (default 0).
point_size_max	\<size>	Maximum point size after attenuation (if used) for this pass (default 0).
point_sprites	\<on> | \<off>	Enable hardware point-sprite rendering for this pass (default off).

Texture-Unit Attributes

These attributes are used inside a `texture_unit` block.

Attribute Name	Value Format	Description
`texture_alias`	`<alias>`	Alias name for this texture unit (defaults to `texture_unit` name).
`texture`	`<name>` `[<type>]` `[unlimited` `|` `numMipMaps]` `[alpha]`	Static texture name for this texture unit; type is one of `1d`, `2d` (default), `3d`, `cubic`; `numMipMaps` is used to limit the number of mips automatically generated (default `unlimited`); `alpha` means load single-channel texture into the *alpha* and not the *red* channel.
`anim_texture`	`<base_name>` `<num_frames>` `<duration>`	Set images to be used in animated texture; construct `num_frames` image names from `base_name` and zero-based frame index; `duration` is length of animation, determines FPS for the texture animation (default is no texture animation).
`anim_texture`	`<frame1>` `<frame2>` `...` `<duration>`	Set images to be used in animated texture; supply list of frame image names; `duration` is length of animation, determines FPS for the texture animation (default is no texture animation).
`cubic_texture`	`<base_name>` `<combinedUVW|` `separateUV>`	Set images to be used in cubic (6-sided) texture; supply list of cube-side image base names; `combinedUVW` uses hardware cube-map capability and 3D addressing, `separateUV` uses individual textures and a single texture layer: supply images in order using file name suffixes `_fr`, `_bk`, `_up`, `_dn`, `_lf`, `_rt`.
`cubic_texture`	`<front>` `<back>` `<up>` `<down>` `<left>` `<right>` `separateUV`	Alternate means to set images to be used in cubic (6-sided) texture; `separateUV` as described in preceding entry.
`tex_coord_set`	`<index>`	Define texture coordinate set to use for this texture layer (default `0`).
`tex_address_mode`	`<wrap>` `|` `<clamp>` `|` `<mirror>` `|` `<border>`	Define texture addressing mode to use for this texture layer (default `wrap`).
`tex_border_colour`	`<r>` `<g>` `<b>` `[<a>]`	Define color to use for `border` texture addressing mode (default `0.0 0.0 0.0 1.0`).
`filtering`	`<none>` `<bilinear>` `<trilinear>` `<anisotropic>`	Define texture filter type (default `bilinear`).

Attribute Name	Value Format	Description
filtering	`<minification> <magnification> <mip>`	(Advanced) Define texture filter type; `minification` and `magnification` are one of `point`, `linear`, `anisotropic` (default `linear linear point`); `mip` is one of `none`, `point`, `linear`.
max_anisotropy	`<degree>`	Maximum degree of anisotropy to filter (default 1).
colour_op	`<replace>` | `<add>` | `<modulate>` | `<alpha_blend>`	Type of texture layer blending (default `modulate`).
colour_op_ex	`<operation> <source1> <source2> [<manual_factor>] [<manual_colour1>] [<manual_colour2>]`	(Advanced) Type of texturelayer blending; `operation` is one of `source1`, `source2`, `modulate`, `modulate_x2`, `modulate_x4`, `add`, `add_signed`, `add_smooth`, `subtract`, `blend_diffuse_alpha`, `blend_texture_alpha`, `blend_current_alpha`, `blend_manual`, `dotproduct`, `blend_diffuse_color`; `source1` and `source2` are one of `src_current`, `src_texture`, `src_diffuse`, `src_specular`, `src_manual`; values for `manual_factor`, `manual_colour1`, and `manual_colour2` are dependent on `operation`, `source1`, and `source2` values.
colour_op_ multipass_fallback	`<src_factor> <dest_factor>`	Fallback texture blending to use when multitexturing not available; `src_factor` and `dest_factor` values same as for `scene_blend`.
alpha_op_ex	(See `colour_op_ex`.)	Same as `colour_op_ex` but determines how alpha values are combined.
env_map	`<off>` | `<spherical>` | `<planar>` | `cubic_reflection` | `cubic_normal`	Enable this texture layer as an environment map (default `off`).
scroll	`<x> <y>`	Set fixed scroll offset for this texture.
scroll_anim	`<x_speed> <y_speed>`	Set fixed-speed animated scroll for this texture.
rotate	`<angle>`	Set fixed rotation (counterclockwise in degrees) for this texture.
rotate_anim	`<rev_per_second>`	Set fixed-speed animated rotation for this texture.
scale	`<x_scale> <y_scale>`	Set fixed scaling for this texture.
wave_xform	`<xform_type> <wave_type> <base> <freq> <phase> <amplitude>`	Set transformation for this texture; `xform_type` is one of `scroll_x`, `scroll_y`, `rotate`, `scale_x`, `scale_y`; `wave_type` is one of `sine`, `triangle`, `square`, `sawtooth`, `inverse_sawtooth`.

Continued

Attribute Name	Value Format	Description
transform	<m00> <m01> . . . <m32> <m33>	Apply static 4×4 transform to this texture.
lod_index	<number>	Detail level in which this technique is used (default 0).

GPU Program Attributes

This section applies to vertex_program_ref, fragment_program_ref, shadow_caster_vertex_program_ref, and shadow_caster_vertex_program_ref blocks. Each of these can take param_named, param_indexed, param_named_auto, and param_indexed_auto attributes.

GPU Program Parameters

The following attributes are used for the param_named_auto and param_indexed_auto directives in GPU program references. Most of these attributes also have available inverse, transpose, and inverse-transpose (or other precomputed) versions of the primary attribute to help you save GPU cycles in your vertex and fragment programs.

param_named_auto and param_indexed_auto are of the form

```
param_indexed_auto <index> <attribute_name> <optional>
param_named_auto <name> <attribute_name> <optional>
```

where <name> is one of the names listed in the following table and <optional> is an attribute-specific optional parameter.

Attribute Name	Description
world_matrix	Target object's world transform.
inverse_world_matrix	Inverse of world_matrix.
transpose_world_matrix	Transpose of world_matrix.
inverse_transpose_world_matrix	Inverse transpose of world_matrix.
world_matrix_array_3x4	Array of 3×4 world matrices, used for GPU skinning.
view_matrix	The current view matrix.
inverse_view_matrix	Inverse of view_matrix.
transpose_view_matrix	Transpose of view_matrix.
inverse_transpose_view_matrix	Inverse transpose of view_matrix.
projection_matrix	The current projection matrix.
inverse_projection_matrix	Inverse of projection_matrix.
transpose_projection_matrix	Transpose of projection_matrix.
inverse_transpose_projection_matrix	Inverse transpose of projection_matrix.
worldview_matrix	Concatenation of the current world and view matrices.
inverse_worldview_matrix	Inverse of worldview_matrix.
transpose_worldview_matrix	Transpose of worldview_matrix.
inverse_transpose_worldview_matrix	Inverse transpose of worldview_matrix.

Attribute Name	Description
viewproj_matrix	Concatenation of the current view and projection matrices.
inverse_viewproj_matrix	Inverse of viewproj_matrix.
transpose_viewproj_matrix	Transpose of viewproj_matrix.
inverse_transpose_viewproj_matrix	Inverse transpose of viewproj_matrix.
worldviewproj_matrix	Concatenation of the current world, view and projection matrices.
inverse_worldviewproj_matrix	Inverse of worldviewproj_matrix.
transpose_worldviewproj_matrix	Transpose of worldviewproj_matrix.
inverse_transpose_worldviewproj_matrix	Inverse transpose of worldviewproj_matrix.
render_target_flipping	−1 if the render target requires texture flipping, +1 otherwise.
light_diffuse_colour	The diffuse color of the zero-based nth closest light to this object (n provided in <optional>). Directional lights are always first in the list and always present. If no lights affect the object, this parameter will be set to black.
light_specular_colour	Similar to light_diffuse_colour but for specular color.
light_attenuation	A float4 containing the four light attenuation variables for a given light.
light_position	The position of the nth light in world space (n provided in <optional>). The parameter is provided as a 4-vector. Point lights have the form (pos.x, pos.y, pos.z, 1.0f) and directional lights the form (-dir.x, -dir.y, -dir.z, 0.0f).
light_direction	This attribute is deprecated; use light_position instead.
light_position_object_space	light_position in object space.
light_direction_object_space	light_direction in object space. Deprecated except for spotlights.
light_position_view_space	light_position in view space.
light_direction_view_space	light_direction in view space. Deprecated except for spotlights.
light_power	Power scaling for nth light (n provided in <optional>). Useful for HDR rendering.
ambient_light_colour	Ambient light color for the scene.
fog_colour	Fog color for the scene.
fog_params	Fog parameters in the form (exponential_density, linear_start, linear_end, 1.0/(linear_end - linear_start)).
camera_position	World-space camera position.
camera_position_object_space	Object-space camera position.
time	The current time, scaled by <optional> (1.0 otherwise).

Continued

Attribute Name	Description
time_0_x	Single repeating float time value. "Cycle time" provided in <optional>.
costime_0_x	Cosine of time_0_x.
sintime_0_x	Sine of time_0_x.
tantime_0_x	Tangent of time_0_x.
time_0_x_packed	4-vector of time0_x, sintime0_x, costime0_x, tantime0_x.
time_0_1	time0_x scaled to [0..1].
costime_0_1	costime0_x scaled to [0..1].
sintime_0_1	sintime0_x scaled to [0..1].
tantime_0_1	tantime0_x scaled to [0..1].
time_0_1_packed	time0_x_packed scaled to [0..1].
time_0_2pi	time0_x scaled to [0..2_].
costime_0_2pi	costime0_x scaled to [0..2_].
sintime_0_2pi	sintime0_x scaled to [0..2_].
tantime_0_2pi	tantime0_x scaled to [0..2_].
time_0_2pi_packed	time0_x_packed scaled to [0..2_].
frame_time	Current frame time scaled by the <optional> (1.0 otherwise).
fps	Current frames per second.
viewport_width	Current viewport width in pixels.
viewport_height	Current viewport height in pixels.
inverse_viewport_width	1.0/viewport_width.
inverse_viewport_height	1.0/viewport_height.
viewport_size	4-vector of (viewport_width, viewport_height, inverse_viewport_width, inverse_viewport_height).
view_direction	Object-space view direction vector.
view_side_vector	Object-space X axis view vector.
view_up_vector	Object-space Y axis view vector.
fov	Vertical field of view in radians.
near_clip_distance	Near clip limit (world units).
far_clip_distance	Far clip limit (in world units), or 0 for infinite far clip.
texture_viewproj_matrix	Applies only to "shadow receiver" alternate vertex programs; provides the current shadow projector view/projection matrix.
pass_number	Active zero-based pass number. Useful for multipass techniques that need to know the pass number.
pass_iteration_number	Similar to pass_number except that this is the iteration number on a particular pass (single-iteration passes will always have pass_iteration_number of zero).

Attribute Name	Description
`animation_parametric`	Used with hardware vertex animation. See Chapter 9 for more.
`custom`	Maps a custom parameter on an individual renderable to a parameter on a GPU program.
`optional`	Contains the index used in the **Renderable:: setCustomParameter** method.

GPU Program Syntaxes/Profiles/Targets

The following attribute values are valid for GPU program targets (HLSL), syntaxes (assembler), and profiles (Cg).

Syntax Name	Description
`vs_1_1`	DirectX 8.1 vertex shader (Radeon 8500+, NVIDIA GeForce 3+)
`vs_2_0`	DirectX 9 vertex shader (Radeon 9600+, NVIDIA GeForce FX 5+)
`vs_2_x`	DirectX 9 vertex shader (Radeon X series, NVIDIA GeForce 6 series)
`vs_3_0`	DirectX 9 vertex shader (NVIDIA GeForce 6 series)
`arbvp1`	OpenGL vertex programs (roughly equivalent to DirectX `vs_1_1`)
`vp20`	NVIDIA-specific OpenGL vertex shader syntax (superset of `vs_1_1`)
`vp30`	NVIDIA-specific OpenGL vertex shader syntax (superset of `vs_2_0`)
`vp40`	NVIDIA-specific OpenGL vertex shader syntax (superset of `vs_3_0`)
`ps_1_1`, `ps_1_2`, `ps_1_3`	DirectX 8.1 fragment program (Radeon 8500+, NVIDIA GeForce 3+)
`ps_1_4`	DirectX 9 fragment program (Radeon 8500+, NVIDIA GeForce FX 5+)
`ps_2_0`	DirectX 9 fragment program (Radeon 9600+, NVIDIA GeForce FX 5+)
`ps_2_x`	DirectX 9 fragment program (Radeon X series, NVIDIA GeForce 6+ series)
`ps_3_0`	DirectX 9 fragment program (NVIDIA GeForce 6+ series)
`ps_3_x`	DirectX 9 fragment program (NVIDIA GeForce 7+ series)
`arbfp1`	OpenGL fragment programs (roughly equivalent to `ps_2_0`)
`fp20`	NVIDIA-specific OpenGL fragment syntax (superset of `ps_1_3`)
`fp30`	NVIDIA-specific OpenGL fragment syntax (superset of `ps_2_0`)
`fp40`	NVIDIA-specific OpenGL fragment syntax (superset of `ps_3_0`)

GPU Program Animation Attributes

You indicate support for a given type of hardware-accelerated animation in a GPU program by adding one of the following to a program reference:

- `includes_skeletal_animation true`

- `includes_morph_animation true`

- `includes_pose_animation true`

Compositor Script Attributes

Technique Attributes

The following attribute is available in a technique block in a Compositor script.

Attribute Name	Description
texture	Declare a render texture for use in subsequent target passes. Format is texture <name> <width> <height> <pixel format>.

Target Attributes

The following attributes are available in target and target_output blocks in a Compositor script.

Attribute Name	Description
input	Target input mode, one of none (default) or previous.
only_initial	Execute this pass only once at start, either off (default) or on.
visibility_mask	Visibility mask for render_scene passes, defaults to 0xFFFFFFFF.
lod_bias	Set LOD bias for render_scene passes, defaults to 1.0.
material_scheme	Set material scheme for render_scene passes, defaults to Default.

Pass Attributes

The following attributes are available in pass blocks in a Compositor script. pass blocks take an outer parameter, one of render_quad, clear, stencil, or render_scene.

Attribute Name	Parameter Format	Description
input	<sampler> <name>	Applicable only to passes of type render_quad, define mapping of local render textures to the quad; sampler defines the texture sampler to use, name defines the local render texture name.
material	<name>	Applicable only to passes of type render_quad, define the material used to render the quad.
identifier	<num>	Application-specific identifier for this pass (default 0).
first_render_queue	<num>	ID of first render queue included in render_scene passes (default 5).
last_render_queue	<num>	ID of last render queue included in render_scene passes (default 95).
clear	N/A	See clear attributes in the section "Clear-Pass Attributes."
stencil	N/A	See stencil attributes in the section "Stencil-Pass Attributes."

Clear-Pass Attributes

The following attributes are available in pass blocks of type clear in a Compositor script.

Attribute Name	Description
buffers	Set buffers to be cleared by this pass, one or more of depth, colour, or stencil (default colour depth).
colour_value	For buffers colour, clear buffer to this color (default 0.0 0.0 0.0 0.0).
depth_value	For buffers depth, clear buffer to this depth (default 1.0).
stencil_value	For buffers stencil, clear buffer to this value (default 0.0).

Stencil-Pass Attributes

The following attributes are available in pass blocks of type stencil in a Compositor script.

Attribute Name	Description
check	Enable/disable stencil check, one of on or off (default off).
comp_func	One of always_fail, always_pass (default), less, less_equal, not_equal, greater_equal, greater.
ref_value	Value used to compare this pass against the function in comp_func (default 0.0).
mask	Mask used to compare this pass against the function in comp_func (default 0xFFFFFFFF).
fail_op	What to do with the current value of the stencil buffer if the stencil and depth tests both fail; is one of keep, zero, replace, increment, decrement, increment_wrap, decrement_wrap, invert (default keep).
depth_fail_op	What to do with the current value of the stencil buffer if the stencil test passes but depth test fails; possible values as with fail_op.
pass_op	What to do with the current value of the stencil buffer if both the stencil and depth test pass; possible values as with fail_op.
two_sided	Enable/disable inverse stencil operations to back-facing polygons (default off).

Particle Script Attributes

The following script attributes and parameters are available in particle system scripts.

Particle System Definition Attributes

These attributes are available at the top-level particle system block.

Attribute Name	Value Format	Description
quota	<max_particles>	Maximum number of particles at one time in the system (default 10).
material	<name>	Name of material used by all particles in the system (default none).
particle_width	<width>	Width of particles in world coordinates (default 100).

Continued

Attribute Name	Value Format	Description
particle_height	<height>	Height of particles in world coordinates (default 100).
cull_each	<true> | <false>	Cull particles individually (default false).
renderer	<name>	Particle rendering system (default billboard).
sorted	<true> | <false>	Sort particles by depth from camera (default false).
local_space	<true> | <false>	Emit particles into local space (default false).
billboard_type	<point> | <oriented_common> | <oriented_self> | <perpendicular_common> | <perpendicular_self>	Billboard-renderer-specific attribute (default point).
billboard_origin	<top_left> | <top_center> | <top_right> | <center_left> | <center> | <center_right> | <bottom_left> | <bottom_center> | <bottom_right>	Billboard-renderer-specific attribute (default center).
billboard_rotation_type	<texcoord> | <vertex>	Billboard-renderer-specific attribute (default texcoord).
common_direction	<x> <y> <z>	Billboard-renderer-specific attribute (default 0 0 1).
common_up_vector	<x> <y> <z>	Billboard-renderer-specific attribute (default 0 1 0).
point_rendering	<true> | <false>	Billboard-renderer-specific attribute (default false).
accurate_facing	<on> | <off>	Billboard-renderer-specific attribute (default off).
iteration_interval	<interval>	Fixed particle-system update rate (default 0).
nonvisible_update_timeout	<timeout>	Stop updating the particle system when it has not been visible in a while (default 0).

Particle Emitter Definition Attributes

These attributes are available in the emitter block. An emitter block takes a single type parameter, one of Point, Box, Cylinder, Ellipsoid, Hollow Ellipsoid, or Ring.

Attribute Name	Value Format	Description
angle	`<degrees>`	Maximum angle of deviation of emitted particles (default 0)
colour	`<r> <g> <b> [<a>]`	Static color of emitted particles (default 1.0 1.0 1.0 1.0)
colour_range_start	`<r> <g> <b> [<a>]`	Random color-range bound of emitted particles (default 1.0 1.0 1.0 1.0)
colour_range_end	`<r> <g> <b> [<a>]`	Random color-range bound of emitted particles (default 1.0 1.0 1.0 1.0)
direction	`<x> <y> <z>`	Parent-space direction of emitter (default 1 0 0)
position	`<x> <y> <z>`	Parent-space position of emitter (default 0 0 0)
emission_rate	`<rate>`	Particles per second from the emitter (default 10)
velocity	`<rate>`	Particles velocity in world units per second (default 1)
velocity_min	`<rate>`	Lower bound on random emission velocity (default 1)
velocity_max	`<rate>`	Upper bound on random emission velocity (default 1)
time_to_live	`<seconds>`	Particle lifetime in seconds (default 5)
time_to_live_min	`<seconds>`	Lower bound on random particle lifetime (default 5)
time_to_live_max	`<seconds>`	Upper bound on random particle lifetime (default 5)
duration	`<seconds>`	Emitter active period lifetime in seconds (default 0, or infinite)
duration_min	`<seconds>`	Lower bound on random emitter duration (default 0, or infinite)
duration_max	`<seconds>`	Upper bound on random emitter duration (default 0, or infinite)
repeat_delay	`<seconds>`	Emitter inactive period in seconds (default 0)
repeat_delay_min	`<seconds>`	Lower bound on emitter inactivity (default 0)
repeat_delay_max	`<seconds>`	Upper bound on emitter inactivity (default 0)

Standard Particle Affectors

Particle affector parameters are all specific to each affector type. The following types of particle affectors are specified with the `affector` block.

LinearForce

This applies a force to alter particle trajectories.

Attribute Name	Value Format	Description
force_vector	`<x> <y> <z>`	Force vector to apply to every particle (default 0 -100 0)
force_application	`<average> <add>`	How force is applied to particle momentum (default add)

ColourFader

This alters particle color over time.

Attribute Name	Value Format	Description
red	<delta_value>	Color component adjustment per second (default 0)
green	<delta_value>	Color component adjustment per second (default 0)
blue	<delta_value>	Color component adjustment per second (default 0)
alpha	<delta_value>	Color component adjustment per second (default 0)

ColourFader2

This alters particle color over time with a state change.

Attribute Name	Value Format	Description
red1	<delta_value>	Color component adjustment per second for the first state (default 0)
green1	<delta_value>	Color component adjustment per second for the first state (default 0)
blue1	<delta_value>	Color component adjustment per second for the first state (default 0)
alpha1	<delta_value>	Color component adjustment per second for the first state (default 0)
red2	<delta_value>	Color component adjustment per second for the second state (default 0)
green2	<delta_value>	Color component adjustment per second for the second state (default 0)
blue2	<delta_value>	Color component adjustment per second for the second state (default 0)
alpha2	<delta_value>	Color component adjustment per second for the second state (default 0)
state_change	<seconds>	Switch to second state with this much time to live (default 1)

Scaler

This scales particles in flight.

Attribute Name	Value Format	Description
rate	<units_per_second>	Amount to scale particles in x and y directions per second

Rotator

This rotates particles in flight.

Attribute Name	Value Format	Description
rotation_speed_range_start	<degrees_per_second>	Lower bound on random particle rotation speed (default 0)
rotation_speed_range_end	<degrees_per_second>	Upper bound on random particle rotation speed (default 0)
rotation_range_start	<degrees>	Lower bound on random particle rotation range (default 0)
rotation_range_end	<degrees>	Upper bound on random particle rotation range (default 0)

ColourInterpolator

This is similar to `ColourAffector2`, for up to six states.

Attribute Name	Value Format	Description
time0	<seconds>	Normalized (range [0.0-1.0]) lifetime interval (default 1.0)
colour0	<r> <g> <b> [<a>]	Color at time0 (default 0.5 0.5 0.5 0.0)
time1	<seconds>	Normalized (range [0.0-1.0]) lifetime interval (default 1.0)
colour1	<r> <g> <b> [<a>]	Color at time1 (default 0.5 0.5 0.5 0.0). . .
time*n*	<seconds>	Normalized (range [0.0-1.0]) lifetime interval (default 1.0)
colour*n*	<r> <g> <b> [<a>]	Color at time*n* (default 0.5 0.5 0.5 0.0)

ColourImage

This changes particle color over its lifetime based on colors in the horizontal range of the specified image.

Attribute Name	Value Format	Description
image	<name>	Name of image file containing image data (default none)

Overlay Script Attributes

The following script attributes and parameters are available in Overlay scripts.

Overlay Attribute

This attribute is available at the top-level overlay block. The top-level overlay block can contain `element` and `container` subblocks.

Attribute Name	Value Format	Description
zorder	<depth>	Stacking order of this overlay, range 0–650

Element and Container Attributes

These attributes are available in both the `element` and `container` blocks.

Attribute Name	Value Format	Description
metrics_mode	<mode>	One of pixels or relative (default relative)
horz_align	<alignment>	One of left, center, or right (default left)
vert_align	<alignment>	One of top, center, or bottom (default top)
left	<position>	Position of left edge (default 0)
top	<position>	Position of top edge (default 0)
width	<size>	Width (default 1)
height	<size>	Height (default 1)
material	<name>	Name of material to use (default none)
caption	<text>	Text caption for element (default blank)
rotation	<angle> <x> <y> <z>	Angle of rotation in degrees around (x,y,z) axis (default no rotation)

Element- and Container-Specific Attributes

These attributes are available only in specific types of `element` and `container` blocks.

Panel (Container)

Attribute Name	Value Format	Description
transparent	<true> | <false>	Whether to render the panel (default false)
tiling	<layer> <x> <y>	Tiling rate for layer texture in material (default no tiling)
uv_coords	<topleft_u> <topleft_v> <bottomright_u> <bottomright_v>	Custom UV coordinates

BorderPanel (Container)

BorderPanel has all attributes of Panel, plus the following.

Attribute Name	Value Format	Description
border_size	<left> <right> <top> <bottom>	Sizes in relative metrics
border_material	<name>	Material to use for border
border_left_uv	<u1> <v1> <u2> <v2>	Custom UV coordinates
border_right_uv	<u1> <v1> <u2> <v2>	Custom UV coordinates
border_top_uv	<u1> <v1> <u2> <v2>	Custom UV coordinates
border_bottom_uv	<u1> <v1> <u2> <v2>	Custom UV coordinates
border_topleft_uv	<u1> <v1> <u2> <v2>	Custom UV coordinates
border_topright_uv	<u1> <v1> <u2> <v2>	Custom UV coordinates
border_bottomleft_uv	<u1> <v1> <u2> <v2>	Custom UV coordinates
border_bottomright_uv	<u1> <v1> <u2> <v2>	Custom UV coordinates

TextArea (Element)

Attribute Name	Value Format	Description
font_name	<name>	Name of font to use for text
char_height	<height>	Height of text in relative metrics
colour	<red> <green> <blue>	Text color, component values [0..1]
colour_top	<red> <green> <blue>	Top color of color gradient
colour_bottom	<red> <green> <blue>	Bottom color of gradient

Font Definition Script Attributes

The following script attributes and parameters are available in font definition scripts. Only a top-level block is supported for font definition scripts, containing the following attributes.

Attribute Name	Value Format	Description
type	<type>	One of truetype or image
source	<file>	File name of either TrueType font file or custom glyph image file
glyph	<character> <u1> <v1> <u2> <v2>	Text character and UV coordinates for the glyph (for source image fonts)
size	<points>	Size in points of characters to generate for truetype font type
resolution	<dpi>	Resolution in dots per inch for character generation for truetype font type
antialias_colour	<true> | <false>	Antialias-generated font characters using color channel instead of alpha channel (default false)

Index

FIND IT FAST

with the Apress *SuperIndex*™

You Need the Companion eBook

Your purchase of this book entitles you to buy the companion PDF-version eBook for only $10. Take the weightless companion with you anywhere.

We believe this Apress title will prove so indispensable that you'll want to carry it with you everywhere, which is why we are offering the companion eBook (in PDF format) for $10 to customers who purchase this book now. Convenient and fully searchable, the PDF version of any content-rich, page-heavy Apress book makes a valuable addition to your programming library. You can easily find and copy code—or perform examples by quickly toggling between instructions and the application. Even simultaneously tackling a donut, diet soda, and complex code becomes simplified with hands-free eBooks!

Once you purchase your book, getting the $10 companion eBook is simple:

❶ Visit **www.apress.com/promo/tendollars/**.

❷ Complete a basic registration form to receive a randomly generated question about this title.

❸ Answer the question correctly in 60 seconds, and you will receive a promotional code to redeem for the $10.00 eBook.

2560 Ninth Street • Suite 219 • Berkeley, CA 94710

eBookshop

ASP **Today**

Apress®
THE EXPERT'S VOICE™

Offer valid through 3/25/07.